PRAISE FOR
TASSAJARA STORIES

"I have great respect for David Chadwick. He is one of the pioneers spreading dharma in the West. All my students study his books. I know all readers will love this book and these stories." —**Natalie Goldberg**, author of *Writing Down the Bones*

"Two in three Americans today say they are 'spiritual,' while one in four identifies as 'spiritual but not religious.' For full immersion in one of the deepest well-springs of this widespread cultural revolution, dive into these stories of free spirits and seekers creating a uniquely western monastic community rooted in centuries of Zen Buddhist practice and led by a teacher true to the moment. No one tells it better than David Chadwick, with a firsthand feel for the high adventure and deep play of mind-changing history embodied in the making." —**Steven M. Tipton**, author of *In and Out of Church: The Moral Arc of Spiritual Change in America*

"For those who care about the genesis of Tassajara and Zen in America, this is a fun read. David serves up a rich well of details and memories and a window into a very creative time." —**Jack Kornfield**, author of *A Path With Heart*

"This book is as priceless as discovering a previously unknown time capsule. David Chadwick, widely known as one of Suzuki Roshi's favorites, captures the wacky spirit, the dedication, and the courage required to leap into the unknown that characterized the earliest Zen students surrounding Suzuki Roshi. (Full disclosure: David became one of my earliest friends when I began my practice in 1974.) Fifty-one years later, an ordained priest and transmitted teacher, I still look up to David as an original member of the A-team. This book, in his authentic and unduplicable voice, is an absolute treasure. Read it. Give a copy to a friend." —**Peter Coyote** (Hosho Jishi), actor, director, author

"I had a good time reading *Tassajara Stories* and hoped they would never end. Just as you can't learn Zen from a book, you can't really know the Tassajara experience even through this amazing memoir. But you can get caught up in it, especially when it is written with such immediacy and love as David Chadwick has done it. There are valuable lessons galore and more colorful personalities than you could ever hope to find in a faraway haven in the enchanting but haunted woods." —**Thomas Moore**, author of *Care of the Soul*

"An engrossing account of the people and antics that defined the Tassajara monastery in 1967." —*Kirkus Reviews*

TASSAJARA
STORIES

—ALSO BY—
DAVID CHADWICK

Thank You and OK! An American Zen Failure in Japan

*Crooked Cucumber: The Life and Zen
Teaching of Shunryu Suzuki*

*Zen Is Right Here: Teaching Stories and
Anecdotes of Shunryu Suzuki*

*Zen Is Right Now: More Teaching Stories and
Anecdotes of Shunryu Suzuki*

*A Brief History of Tassajara: from Native American
Sweat Lodges to Pioneering Zen Monastery (editor)*

To Find the Girl from Perth

Color Dreams for To Find the Girl from Perth

The the Book

TASSAJARA STORIES

*A Sort of Memoir/Oral History of the
First Zen Buddhist Monastery in the West—
The First Year, 1967*

DAVID CHADWICK

MONKFISH
BOOK PUBLISHING COMPANY
RHINEBECK, NEW YORK

Tassajara Stories: A Sort of Memoir/Oral History of the First Zen Buddhist Monastery in the West—The First Year, 1967 © Copyright 2025 by David Chadwick

All rights reserved. No part of this book may be used or reproduced in any manner, except in critical articles or reviews. Contact the publisher for information.

Hardcover ISBN 9781958972892
eBook ISBN 9781958972908
Audiobook ISBN 9781966608196

Library of Congress Cataloging-in-Publication Data

Names: Chadwick, David, 1945- author
Title: Tassajara stories : a sort of memoir/oral history of the first Zen Buddhist monastery in the West : the first year, 1967 / David Chadwick.
Description: Rhinebeck, New York : Monkfish Book Publishing Company, 2025.
Identifiers: LCCN 2025012089 (print) | LCCN 2025012090 (ebook) | ISBN 9781958972892 hardcover | ISBN 9781958972908 ebook | ISBN 9781966608196 audiobook
Subjects: LCSH: Tassajara Zen Mountain Center | Zen monasteries--California--Carmel Valley--History--20th century | Zen Buddhism--California--Carmel Valley--History--20th century | Chadwick, David, 1945- | Zen Buddhists--California--Carmel Valley
Classification: LCC BQ6377.C22 C47 2025 (print) | LCC BQ6377.C22 (ebook) | DDC 294.3/6570979476--dc23/eng/20250611
LC record available at https://lccn.loc.gov/2025012089
LC ebook record available at https://lccn.loc.gov/2025012090

Book and cover design by Colin Rolfe

Monkfish Book Publishing Company
22 East Market Street, Suite 304
Rhinebeck, New York 12572
(845) 876-4861
monkfishpublishing.com

Dedicated to those who cleared the way for us—notably.

Soyen Shaku
Nyogen Senzaki
D.T. Suzuki
Sokei-an Sasaki
Ruth Fuller Sasaki
Alan Watts
Gary Snyder

We both step and do not step in the same rivers.
We are and we are not.
–Heraclitus

CONTENTS

Preface xiii

Chapter 1: Approaching 3
Chapter 2: Preparing 57
Chapter 3: Opening 107
Chapter 4: Resuming 147
Chapter 5: Continuing 201

Notes 237
About the Cover Photo 239
Acknowledgments 241

PREFACE

Tassajara stories have been piling up in my memory banks since I first went there in February 1967. This was shortly after the San Francisco Zen Center bought the old hot springs resort that lay deep in the mountainous woods of Los Padres National Forest a few hours south of San Francisco. In the late 1980s, I began collecting Tassajara stories—not intentionally—but as a side effect of writing about my teachers and experiences Zenwise and otherwise. For decades these accounts have weaved their way into the books I've done, the interviews, and other posts on my cuke.com website. But there were still many I hadn't collected.

One day I told my wife Katrinka an anecdote set at Tassajara that I'd just remembered. She asked if I'd written it down. The next day I did write it down and read it to her when she came home. The day after that I wrote down another one and read it to her. That continued daily for some time. I decided to throw these stories together with a bunch of other tales and memories I could mine out of Cuke Archives and the Alaya Vijnana and make a little book called *Tassajara Stories*. I kept the focus on the first ten years of Tassajara as Zen Mountain Center, the period in which I lived there two-thirds of the time. One thing for sure. I wasn't going to let the process drag out for five or six years again.

Ten years later I'm just about finished with this project. I guess I got a little carried away. There's too much for a single book. This volume takes us through 1967, the opening year of Tassajara as a Zen monastery with Shunryu Suzuki as the founding abbot.

You may notice there's a lot in these pages that didn't happen at Tassajara. That's because my life, our life at Tassajara didn't exist in a vacuum. Just like each of us, it had no separate existence. *Shakkei* is a Japanese term referring to a garden's "borrowed scenery." It's the outlying mountains and trees and whatever else one can see from a garden. If we look at what happened at Tassajara as being the garden of the book, then the other content is the shakkei. This borrowed scenery sets Tassajara and our experience in that valley in a broad context that gives background and color to who we were and how we got there, and includes the mountains, the woods, the road, our neighbors, the city, the times, the war, the counterculture, what was happening all around us.

Also, if you were around back then, you may come upon something you think happened differently or at another time. If so, please let me know, and I'll add your account to the basket of conflicting memories. If you go to cuke.com/ts, you'll find extensive notes and background material that will deal with those sorts of issues—and much more.

Tassajara stories swim in my thoughts, linger a while, and slip away. They are among my favorite indulgences. I'm not alone in this nostalgia. Those of us who were there shared a kind of magic. We learned how not to dwell on the past, yet it is still unforgettable.

So here it is—what occurred—and what occurred to me.

David Chadwick
Sanur, February 9, 2025

TASSAJARA STORIES

– CHAPTER ONE –

APPROACHING

Capsized Boys   SUMMER, 1964

Alan Winter and Ed Brown were paddling across Lake of the Woods in Ontario, Canada, on a windy day. It was their final crossing to retrieve the last of their belongings from the otherwise uninhabited island where they'd been camping for six weeks. They were about halfway when a powerful wave broadsided them, capsized their canoe, and tossed them into the glacial water.

They started to swim to shore but stopped as it was obvious the distance was too great. Anyway, they couldn't swim very well in heavy boots with their paddles, which they didn't want to let go of. And they wore no life preservers. Alan struggled to swim to the upside-down canoe and held on. Ed was having a hard time. Stretching as far as he could, Alan stuck his paddle towards Ed, who managed in the choppy waves to get close enough to grab the end. Alan pulled him in like a big fish. The two of them clung to the canoe until the wind carried them to the island shore.

That delayed their planned departure, but happy to be dry and alive they drove onward toward the San Francisco Bay Area in the '55 Chevy coupe they'd bought when they left Antioch for good at the end of their freshman year.

At Antioch, Ed had attended a thought-provoking class with

a Japanese professor of social psychology. The professor asked the students to answer the question, "Who are you?" in a word or two. One by one the students responded with, "I'm a woman," "I'm a student," "I'm Canadian," "I'm a Negro," "I'm eighteen." The teacher said, that's not who you are—those are categories.

Ed though had not listed a category. He'd written, "I'm answering your question." The professor liked Ed's answer, but Ed wasn't satisfied. He did a paper on anxiety and alienation for that class. He got an A but still felt anxious and alienated.

Ed's brother Dwite had been sending him letters with Zen stories he'd hand-copied out of *Zen Flesh, Zen Bones*. One story was about a young man who told his mother how well he was doing in school. She responded she didn't raise him to be a walking dictionary and asked, "Why don't you go to the mountains and attain true realization?" When he read that, Ed thought, *That's for me.*

At Antioch they had him fill out a form that asked why they were leaving. Ed wrote: "To go to the mountains and attain true realization."

Alan was from Chicago. Ed grew up in San Rafael, California. Dwite lived over the Golden Gate Bridge from San Rafael in San Francisco across the street from Sokoji, a Japanese Zen temple. A Zen master lived in that temple. Dwite and his wife Judy meditated at Sokoji. Ed got a two-room apartment near his brother's place. Alan moved in.

When they were still up at the lake, they weren't just fishing and canoeing. They did yoga. Ed had brought Dwite's letters with the *Zen Flesh, Zen Bones* stories. Alan was reading Heinrich Zimmer's *Philosophies of India*. He was determined to find a religion that spoke to him. In San Francisco, there was Shlomo Carlebach's free form synagogue, *The House of Love and Prayer*. He hadn't rejected Judaism but was avoiding anything Jewish.

Alan was out carousing with some friends one night. They stayed up so late that he suggested they join the morning meditation at Sokoji. So they did. But it was so quiet. And they had to keep still. When it was over, Alan noticed his friends were all gone. It wasn't easy, but Alan liked it and kept going there.

There was more than just sitting to pick up on. At the beginning of the period, a Japanese priest walked around the room. People were expected to have their palms together before he passed behind them. Nobody had told Alan that. When Alan didn't bow, the priest sternly said "Gassho!" Alan didn't know what gassho meant, but he kept coming and figured it out. And he learned that the priest's name was Suzuki Sensei.

After the meditation there was bowing to the floor, chant cards handed out, chanting in Japanese, and then more bowing. When it was over, the straw mats on the floor were folded and stacked on the edge of the room. People didn't leave by the same double doors through which they'd entered, but one by one walked through the entrance to Suzuki's office. He would stand there bowing with each person.

It was difficult for Alan to get up so early in the morning. So Ed got him up and read the *San Francisco Chronicle* while Alan was away meditating. That went on for a while until one day Ed said, "You know, I'm waking up every morning for you to go to meditation. I think I'll go with you."

But first, Ed wanted to check out Suzuki Sensei. It was May of 1965 when Ed and Alan went to Sokoji and met with him. Ed had wondered, *Will he like me?* But in meeting Suzuki he experienced a face that was impassive with no sign of liking or disliking. Ed felt seen though, completely received, as if he could just disappear into Suzuki's face.

Suzuki told them to wait until another priest, Katagiri Sensei, arrived. He would give them zazen instruction. That's what Suzuki called Zen meditation—zazen. Katagiri showed them how to bow to the cushion which he called a zafu, turn around clockwise and bow, sit on the zafu, turn toward the wall, cross legs as well as one could, sit up straight with the chin in, and follow the breath. What struck Ed was Katagiri's conclusion: "And many things will happen."

Alan told Katagiri that being Jewish, he had a problem with bowing to a Buddha statue, a graven image, something that The Ten Commandments forbids. Katagiri said that Buddha is a mirror and when you bow to him, you're bowing to your Buddha nature.

Alan decided he needed a skill, so he enrolled in a carpentry class at John O'Connell Technical High School. He was also studying Spanish at Marin College. There he met a Canadian woman named Marjorie and they moved into an apartment together on Bush Street just down from Sokoji.

Richard Baker stood out among the students. He was twenty-nine years old and the president of the Zen Center, the name of the incorporated group that practiced zazen with Suzuki.

In February, Richard and his wife Ginny drove Alan and Marjorie to Nevada to join others for a weekend of skiing. Alan didn't ski, but Marjorie did. Richard stayed behind to catch up on some work for UC Berkeley where he was doing graduate studies in East Asian religion and organizing conferences for the school. When he learned Alan was studying carpentry, he told Alan he knew a place where they wanted to hire a carpenter. It was a hot springs resort down south in the middle of mountainous wilderness in Monterey County. Richard had been there and met the owner who was interested in considering selling it or, more likely, a piece of property near it. Richard said he planned to take Suzuki there. The owner had suggested they wait until the snow level was lower at the higher altitudes and the county had done its spring refurbishing of the lengthy unpaved road in.

"I think you'd like it," Richard said. "It's called Tassajara."

The Scouts SPRING 1966

Alan went to Tassajara, met the owners Robert and Anna Beck, and was hired. He'd get room and board and $150 a month. With pay that low and a place so isolated, Alan wasn't surprised there was no competition for the job. He'd be back in a few weeks after completing the carpentry course. Meanwhile Ed was attending school again, San Francisco State, and was already tired of it. He'd become interested in cooking, starting off with *Zen Macrobiotics* by George Ohsawa. Alan urged Ed to apply for a job in the kitchen at Tassajara.

Alan was shotgun as Ed drove south on US 101 from San Francisco. In Salinas, they took the last exit, CA 68, and drove past fields of lettuce to Laureles Grade. Then up to the top and down to Carmel Valley Road, through Carmel Valley Village, into countryside with Coast Live Oaks and meadows.

They turned off at Cachagua Road with a sign that read *Tassajara Sprs 20*, then made a left at the fork which, according to the map, led to Jamesburg. All they saw, though, were a few houses and some fencing. At the last house, the pavement ended and then it was dirt, gravel, and rocks for fourteen miles. Up and around, through woods to a meadow with a sign announcing Los Padres National Forest.

Then up more, winding through oak, madrone, and manzanita past White Oaks Camp to five thousand feet and a cattle guard at Chews Ridge. Onward through pine woods with an empty Forest Service cabin, past China Camp, to a ridge with a wide view of the Salinas Valley and other valleys.

On the other side of the road, they saw a panorama of steep mountains and narrow valleys capped by a thin blue ribbon of the Pacific under the lighter blue sky and low-hanging clouds. Then down, steeply down, around switchbacks. So rocky, so narrow, perilous drop-offs, sandstone and granite outcroppings on rugged mountainsides, down, down, to a more gradual pitch snaking along a creek with steep valley walls. Then a straight shot finale to a sign that read *Tassajara Hot Springs* and over a short wooden bridge. They passed an open-faced shop with a truck parked in front, a chain saw on a stump, to come to rest before a great oak tree at the end of the road. Dust disturbed by their tires swirled up around them and scattered. The smell of overheated brakes.

The Becks weren't at Tassajara. Ed got hold of Robert Beck using Tassajara's crank phone. Robert said, "Come on by and let's talk." Ed drove to their home in Carmel and Robert hired him to be a dishwasher starting in May when they'd have more guests.

Alan worked with Bill Parker who was serious, tall, and solid. The job entailed more than carpentry. There was general handyman and grunt work as well. What Alan didn't know, Bill would show him. This was a sprawling old resort with a seemingly endless amount of delayed maintenance to do. And there were the hot springs, when work was done, and days off to check out the surroundings starting with Tassajara Creek. It ran from one end to the other of the narrow valley.

Alan made friends with the other employees—Jim Holmes, another handyman and his wife Laurie, and especially one named Penny who cleaned cabins and waited tables with Laurie and Bill's wife Kathy. Alan wasn't lonely, but he was glad when Ed took that four-hour drive from San Francisco and arrived to stay.

Ed joined Alan for early morning zazen. Alan had a little brass Buddha from Thailand, a small bell, and a tiny mokugyo, a wooden drum shaped like a fat fish which kept the beat when they chanted.

The first three redwood cabins over the bridge creek-side had four rooms each. Alan's room was in the second cabin on the left side in back. At Sokoji, the room where they did zazen was called the zendo. Thus, the room where Alan and Ed sat and chanted became the first zendo at Tassajara.

The Becks

At Tassajara, the Becks lived in a good-sized building with stucco stone walls situated across a courtyard from the dining room, bar, and kitchen. It was one of the oldest structures at Tassajara.

In earlier years it was called the Clubhouse because from way back it had been Tassajara's bar and gathering place. It had hand-hewn beams on the ceiling that jutted out from the building on both sides to support the wider second-story dorm where staff lived in diminutive quarters. The Clubhouse was one large room with a wood-burning stove. The Becks added partitions. It opened to a good size deck overlooking Tassajara Creek and a brook that ran down by the road into Tassajara. It was a good location for the Becks as they needed to be close to the center.

A popular place at Tassajara for the guests was the bar, often manned by a lanky, talkative, humorous fellow named Jim Cook. But Jim wasn't there all the time, so often Bill would step in—or Robert. Anna didn't at first because it was illegal in California and much of the United States for a woman to be a bartender. After a while they realized nobody cared so she would work behind the bar as well.

Jim Cook also helped in the kitchen sometimes. That seemed appropriate, considering his name. He was mainly at Tassajara in the warm months when most of the guests came.

Tassajara was never closed though because the Becks always needed more money. But when the days got mild and the nights chilly, they'd have to cut back on staff, even be reduced to just a caretaker in the coldest, darkest months or when the road was out.

During that summer of '66 they had an uptick in guests attracted to the workshops they were hosting. Photographer Morley Baer helped them in the planning and had arranged for a series of seminars with well-known photographers, him for one, and Eliot Porter.

Ansel Adams was the biggest draw. Alan noticed that Adams, in his mid-sixties, was not above flirting with the adoring young women in his class. Anna organized cooking classes, weaving classes in a cabin, and pottery workshops outdoors down beyond the big barn. She kept the area around the kiln clear of anything combustible. Fire was a constant concern in those dry woods and a forest ranger wouldn't be happy to see a kiln there at all.

Robert was encouraged and thought they might save the place by expanding on the workshop programs. Anna, however, was eager to sell. They'd always just gotten by. Tassajara had been up for sale before. They'd put some ads out in worse times, including in the

Wall Street Journal. They were still making payments on the place and had a long way to go to pay it all off.

They had a toddler, Adam, who would turn two in August. Then Anna found out she was pregnant and due around New Year's. If they sold the place and lived in Carmel, their life would be simpler. Robert could go back to teaching math and they could expand their already active antique business. But he wasn't ready to let go.

The first time Richard Baker brought Suzuki in, there was a special lunch for them in the staff dining area behind the kitchen. Jim Cook prepared it. He placed a pile of hamburgers on the table. He'd spent hours preparing a special Zen macrobiotic type vegetarian meal for Suzuki and served it to him proudly. Suzuki thanked him. People started taking their hamburgers.

"I like hamburger," Suzuki said while reaching for one. Poor Jim was crestfallen. Robert smiled.

Richard's Fortune

On their way back to San Francisco, Richard and Suzuki stopped at the Buzz Inn diner in Gilroy. The mood was buoyant. After years of visiting a number of potential sites for a retreat, finally one was right—better than right—it was perfect. Suzuki had danced in delight on the road at the ridge.

Tassajara wasn't available but Richard thought it would be in time.

There was a fortune-telling vending machine near their table. Richard asked, "Should we buy Tassajara?" and inserted a nickel.

The machine dispensed a slip of paper. Printed on it was the word, *Yes*.

The Horse Pasture

Richard had asked Alan before he left the city to be prepared to lead a group from Zen Center on a trail to the nearby Horse Pasture which was being considered as a site for a retreat. A bunch of folks from Zen Center arrived the day before the hike. They explored the grounds, went to the baths where they soaked in the hot sulfur spring water, dined on a sumptuous meal, and retired early to rest up for the following day.

The morning of the hike, Suzuki and his students gathered before dawn in the room where Alan and Ed had been sitting. They'd come prepared, zafus in hand, sat and crossed their legs. The room got quiet. Alan hit the bell to begin the period. The reverberations of the bell faded away. Stillness but for breathing.

After a month of just the two of them, doing zazen, with eight experienced sitters in that small room, Ed felt like he was floating on air.

A line of hikers trekked along a footpath cut into a dry grassy slope while the Beck's little black dog danced around in front. Behind the dog was Alan, who, with help from the canine scout, was making sure the pack didn't stray from the path, which became somewhat unclear in places. Alan had prepared for this day, as Richard had suggested. Ed of course knew the way as well.

Now this group of Zennies could check out the Horse Pasture as a candidate site for a Zen Center retreat. Among those walking along was artist Willard Mike Dixon and his scholar wife Trudy, art teacher Norman Stiegelmeyer, and tall Tim Buckley—not the folk singer—with a camera. Suzuki was in his black monk's work outfit with a white bandana covering his shiny pate. He and his students were in a buoyant mood of incipient possibilities.

The Horse Pasture Trail was about a mile and a half up the road from Tassajara. It took forty minutes to get to the Horse Pasture, a 160-acre parcel same as Tassajara. Since all of it bordered on national forest, there wasn't much sense of the inholding's size, just of the usable land. Most of the horse pasture was on a gradual slope. It was beautiful and incredibly remote. There was a little creek at the bottom. Robert Beck said there was spring water to be tapped. Richard had checked it out and found two sources. But there was no road. There were no buildings. They'd have to make a monastery from scratch and haul the materials way in there. But the attitude was—whatever it takes, we can do it.

Leaving the Horse Pasture, they took a cut-off down past a trickling waterfall, yucca on the dry hillside, to Tassajara Creek and from there walked on a trail upstream crossing the stream several times on stones and one log. Entering Tassajara, they passed a large barn and a smaller one, a good-sized pool, whitewashed redwood cabins, then into the central area where they relaxed under a grape arbor.

In the V of the valley, with sycamore, oak, stonework, and funky old structures, hot, tired, and thirsty, they drank miraculously refreshing cold spring water and were caught by the charm of the place. Then to those blissful plunges soaking in the hot spring water followed by casseroles, salad, and hearty bread before returning to the Bay Area.

Because it was near Tassajara, the Horse Pasture seemed appealing, maybe as a steppingstone. Suzuki had his heart set on Tassajara. He said, "We should try to buy the Horse Pasture—if we can buy Tassajara later."

Richard had kept up with Robert Beck since the prior year when Richard first walked through the place. He and Ginny had camped out at China Camp. In the morning there were guys shooting guns off right in camp, so they got out of there and checked out where the road led and saw Tassajara for the first time. Now Richard and Robert were circling in on some sort of deal.

Others who would have more dependable financing had expressed an interest in buying Tassajara. There was Mel Lane, the publisher of *Sunset Magazine*. There was a vice-president of Pacific Gas and Electric. Then there were the Monterey County Roughriders. They would trailer their horses into Paraiso Springs over on the slope of the Salinas valley, ride up by the Arroyo Seco River, and in via the Horse Pasture Trail, taking that steep cut-off down to Tassajara Creek. Richard did not want someone else to buy it. Neither did Suzuki. Robert and Anna felt the same, liked these Zen people. They made the place brighter.

Ed and Bread

Ed had started off washing dishes and keeping the kitchen clean. He was right where he wanted to be—in the middle of the mealtime action. He received trays of plates and so forth from Kathy and Laurie, pots, and pans to scrub from the cooks, Ray Hurslander and Jimmy Vaughn. To Ed, the meals those two were turning out were inspired and inspiring. Ed asked them to teach him how to make wholesome, delicious bread like they did. Since he was ten years old, he'd harbored a desire to learn to make great bread like his aunt Alice did in Falls Church, Virginia. Now in a remote wilderness, there was an opportunity.

Ed learned that the bread was made in a traditional way, the sponge method, "with the dough sitting, rising with about half the flour which would develop the bloom of the dough, the depth of flavor, as well as the sour and natural yeasts taking time to work for the bread to rise." In the era of Wonder Bread, it hit the pallet like a glorious discovery. And it had a spiritual lineage. Ray and Jimmy's bread baking mentor was a jazz musician named Alan Hooker who'd been a baker at the Theosophical Society in Columbus, Ohio. He met the anti-guru guru J. Krishnamurti there and followed him to Ojai in southern California. Ray and Jimmy had learned from Hooker at Ojai and spread that baking gospel at the Big Sur Inn and the neighboring Nepenthe Restaurant before venturing on to Tassajara.

Ed said, "The chefs were talented and made good, hearty food- not vegetarian, but with lots of vegetables. Their casseroles were legendary." Working there, Ed got to watch the final stages of a cookbook in the making. By mid-summer one could buy *The Tassajara Springs Cookbook* with an introduction by Robert Beck that stated, "If Tassajara cooking has a national flavor, it is basically American with French thoroughness and seasoning, with a Chinese emphasis on kindness to vegetables."

The French influence was no accident, as the Becks had lived in France. Their French wedding certificate was mounted on the wall of their home in Carmel. They served quality wine from Peter

Scagliotti's Live Oaks Winery in Gilroy. The book credited Ray and Jimmy, Robert's mother Gladys, and Anna, as key contributors. And others, including guests such as photographer Morley Baer's wife Frances, and rancher neighbor Bill Lambert and his daughter-in-law Rose.

There was a recipe from an earlier owner, Gela Sappok, "from whom we inherited Tassajara's reputation for food." The Becks soon learned that the *Sunset Magazine Cookbook* was also a contributor. Ray and Jimmy had forgotten the source of a couple of recipes. The folks at Sunset were familiar with Tassajara and didn't care as long as *The Tassajara Springs Cookbook* was only sold at Tassajara.

There was even a nod to a new cook, Ed Brown, who was eager to continue to elaborate on this rich and wholesome tradition.

Monte Cristo

Robert told Ed that Ray planned to leave soon and asked Ed to take his place. Ed had already been enthusiastically helping with the cooking when they needed it, especially on the cooks' days off. He'd learned how they fried eggs, made pancakes, and grilled bacon. Lunches were heavy on leftovers. Tuesday's leftovers would show up in Thursday's lunch. That made a more interesting mix and would be less noticeable. Leftovers hid in the casseroles and the soups with stocks made hearty by what was left from a leg of lamb. Almost every day there was a Jell-O salad for lunch, and Ed began experimenting with different ways to make it. Adding fruit, creating different textures.

Ed would wash the pots and dishes, make the bread, and still have time to cut vegetables. It didn't seem like too much work to him. There was plenty of time off in the afternoons to soak in the hot baths and the creek. Now that he'd be cooking full time, the Becks replaced Ed on dishes and bread baking with two young guys, one who was Morley Baer's son Josh.

Robert and Anna were quite pleased with how industrious Ed was. But they were concerned about his temper. For within a day of beginning to cook, he'd started screaming. At some point, there was a meeting in which his emotional outbursts came up. *What do we do about this?* they wondered. But Ed did such a good job. And despite his emotional turmoil, he got along with people. And, most importantly, Robert and Anna were fond of their temperamental cook.

The staff at Tassajara would work for twelve days straight and then get two days off. Everyone else would leave for their two days, but Ed wanted to stay, hike, hang out. Robert and Anna told him they wanted him to leave or otherwise pay something for the food he ate on his days off.

Alan left in the middle of summer. He and the Becks, especially Robert, did not get along. Robert was too much of a taskmaster for Alan. And Alan didn't always cheerfully follow orders and wasn't politic and diplomatic, as Ed pointed out.

Penny, who'd arrived pregnant, needed to leave to get ready to have her baby. Everyone chipped in to give her a going-away gift of cash. She left with Alan who drove her to the city. After the baby was born, they returned to Jamesburg and rented a house from Jamesburg rancher and boar hunter Bill Lambert. Ed could visit Alan in Jamesburg on his days off. But mostly he'd stay at Tassajara—and not pay for any food he ate on his free days.

After Labor Day things slowed down. October was even slower. A few of the Becks' staff were in the office looking at the calendar to see what to expect, and someone pointed out that no one was scheduled to come in on the following day, Tuesday, October 18th.

A voice rang out. "Hey, let's all drop acid!" Ed declined, so he was the designated straight guy for the day.

After some hours of tripping, all was peaceful and going well when Bill Lambert came in like gangbusters shooting a six shooter bam! bam! out the window of his VW bug and driving around in tight circles in the open space where the road ends.

The trippers retreated with, "You talk to him!"

Ed walked up to greet their neighbor. "Hey Bill, how you doing? What's up?"

"What do you have to do to get a drink around here?" Lambert answered loudly.

"Oh, I can help with that. What would you like?"

"I'd like some whiskey."

Ed, like Alan, had the good fortune not to have a yearning for alcohol. Ray and Jimmy would order gin and tonics on the sweltering afternoons, and if something like that became a habit, there went the measly stipend.

Ed went into the bar, but he wasn't sure which bottle to choose. He picked one that had the word whiskey on it and poured a shot. Bill took a sip and said, "That's not whiskey! That's Scotch! Get me whiskey!"

On the next try, Bill took a sip and nodded. He drank shot after shot, told Ed some tall tales, and drove off shooting.

The trippers were getting hungry. "Let's eat Monte Cristo sandwiches for dinner!" Kathy called out. This was a staff favorite. Monte Cristo sandwiches, popular in the South, can be made a variety of ways. At Tassajara, in those days, they were double-decker grilled ham, turkey, and Swiss cheese on French toast with corn flakes added for texture and topped with orange marmalade. Cut diagonally in two directions. For staff only. Perfect for trippers.

"It's actually rather good," said Ed between bites.

Cosmic Consciousness

Tim Burkett was a Stanford student who, in 1964, took an abnormal psychology class and became fascinated, then obsessed, with accounts of altered states of consciousness from mystics in various religions and those not on any spiritual path. All the way to a ski trip in Utah he read material such as Richard Maurice Bucke's *Cosmic Consciousness: A Study in the Evolution of the Human Mind*, published in 1900. Then he himself had such an experience. His sense of being a separate being vanished, and he was filled with an overwhelming joy.

On his return to California, he looked up Zen in the San

Francisco phone book and met Suzuki, who said Tim's experience was good but not Zen. Tim thought Suzuki must have misunderstood him but said nothing more. Suzuki took Tim into the zendo, showed him the zazen posture, and told him that zazen was sitting still and doing nothing. Tim asked Suzuki what the most important thing for him to do. Suzuki said, "Just get up."

Tim lived a forty-five-minute drive from Sokoji but got up early to attend zazen a few days a week, sleeping overnight at Sokoji sometimes to be there for the next morning's sitting.

Cleaning First

Suzuki performed a wedding ceremony in Los Altos and was intrigued with the area. Stanford was nearby. He asked Tim Burkett if he could get a sitting group going in the area. Tim did it.

Suzuki arrived early on a Thursday morning at a Palo Alto home filled with sleeping grad students, except for a few who joined him, the student who drove him, and Tim sitting in the living room. After he gave a brief talk, Suzuki started cleaning. That became the routine, but after a few weeks, Tim told Suzuki they had little time for cleaning because there were studies and classes. Suzuki said then they'd have to start earlier. Tim's enthusiasm didn't wane. He told Suzuki that he wanted to be a priest. Suzuki said not if he favored zazen over cleaning. For monks, it's cleaning first.

On another occasion after Suzuki's talk, Tim asked Suzuki if he'd explain the Heart Sutra to him. Suzuki said he'd do so after the cleaning was done. When cleaning was done Suzuki said he needed to get back to Sokoji. A month later at Sokoji, Tim asked Suzuki to please explain the Heart Sutra. Suzuki said okay, after we've cleaned the kitchen. After the kitchen was clean, however, Suzuki went off without a word.

Haiku Zendo

Tim put an ad in a local paper and, instead of a few, there were a dozen people for zazen. Suzuki showed them how to sit with their legs crossed, back straight, the head up, chin in, hands forming an oval mudra held at the lower abdomen. Tim asked if Suzuki could tell them some technique to calm the mind while sitting and following the breath. Suzuki said no explanation or technique would work. Tim asked for more on following the breath. Suzuki said sharply, "Breath breathes." Tim knew not to ask more. That wasn't enough for most people, but some came back.

Margaret Hall offered her home as a place for the weekly zazen meeting. After half a year it moved to Marian Derby's more spacious living room in Los Altos. Marian was intensely devoted to practice like Tim, and they became close. Suzuki started coming for Wednesday evening and Thursday morning zazen and talks. The size of the group grew. Marian got permission from him to tape the lectures for a possible book. In the summer of '66 she and her group turned her garage into a zendo with seventeen seats. She named it Haiku Zendo after the seventeen-syllable haiku poem. With Suzuki, Marian, and others, Tim sat on one of the seventeen cushions for the first Haiku Zendo zazen. Time evaporated. To him this was but an extension of the same zazen period the first time he sat with Suzuki in the dorm house living room in nearby Palo Alto two years earlier.

Semi-Hippy

I arrived in San Francisco in the spring of 1966 and moved into an apartment with Ronnie and Ken, some friends I'd lived with in Mexico City. I don't remember how we paid the rent and bought food. Buying more pot was at the top of the shopping list. The Fat Furry Freak Brothers' motto applied to us: "Dope can get you through times of no money better than money can get you through times of no dope." We would get high and go tripping around the Bay Area, especially enjoying the evolving scene in the Haight-Ashbury district.

One late afternoon we went to the Marin Headlands overlooking the Golden Gate Bridge and walked around in the dusk.

We got so close to a Nike Missile site that we triggered flood lights and caused German Shepherd guard dogs to bark menacingly. We noticed that they were in cages with openings facing out toward us and tiptoed away, not wishing to see those gates open.

We checked out some concrete artillery batteries that had been built to defend San Francisco from Japanese invasion. We went running around in the grassy, sandy terrain. I slid down into a pit resembling a golf course sand trap and there I was indeed trapped— by two soldiers in uniform with helmets and rifles. They said they were taking me prisoner. Really?

Turned out they were from the Presidio army base in a war game and thought I was a spy from the other side in disguise. I finally convinced them I was an innocent civilian caught in crossfire by asking if any soldiers were allowed to grow hair as long as mine. My hair wasn't all that long, but too long for the army.

"I'm not really a hippy," I told them. "Maybe a semi-hippy."

They laughed at that.

I said, "You know how some hippies write Love on the sides of buildings? I like to draw a slash and write Hate next to it."

They liked that too but told me to find my buddies and go back the way we came unless we wanted more trouble.

The three of us made a special trip one day to admire the Marin County Civic Center, designed by Frank Lloyd Wright. It was a unique low lying building that seemed to blend in with the environment. Ronnie, an artist who'd studied at the Road Island School of Design, said he'd read it was influenced by Mayan architecture. Walking around we discovered that its blue roof was easily accessible. We climbed up on it and walked and crawled around. Settled down and smoked a joint. Suddenly from right below us, a siren blared out and a police car sped away on some urgent mission. Next we saw a police car driving in. Then we noticed two policemen walking away from there toward a parking lot. Good lord. We were perched above a police station. We made a hasty exit.

On another outing, we ventured south on State Highway 1 that runs along the coast. At Pfeiffer Falls in Big Sur we admired the sixty feet of cascading water from below. Ronnie and Ken took the trail around. I climbed up the rocky side ignoring a sign that forbade it. Almost to the top I got to a place where I couldn't go any further. There was nothing above that I could get a grip on. Nothing to the side. Couldn't go down. Was slipping, couldn't maintain much longer. Way down those big rocks. Fear like a bolt. Suddenly a voice from a few feet above. "How's it going there?"

It was Ronnie sticking his head down, looking at me. "Ronnie," I said gravely, "Hand me your jacket."

"No way. You might pull me down."

"Ronnie, do it now," came my firm voice from a rarely needed internal reservoir of compelling command.

Ronnie took off his jacket and dangled it down. I grabbed the sleeve, not depending on it, just needing a slight bit of help and that's all I needed to scramble up over the top. I sat there gasping, numb, head spinning, stars sprinkled and flashing everywhere around me.

"Wow," Ronnie said, looking down to the bottom, "That was serious."

Draft Dodging

I had to go to Texas. I got a drive-away car to be delivered to Dallas. In my shirt pocket was an opened pack of Camel non filters. I'd smoked my last cigarette from that pack a few days before, but the pack was still almost full. I'd quit a number of times, but this time didn't give away or throw away the cigarettes. I kept them on me, figuring that this way the temptation could not be increased. Anyway, cigarettes taste much better in the humid coastal air we'd left behind. They're harsh in the deserts we'd be going through so that would help. Also, I didn't want any booze, which likes tobacco as company. We had plenty of a much milder and more rewarding smoke.

My friend Ronnie came along and brought a kilo of primo pot to sell in Brooklyn where he was headed. When we entered Nevada, the officer at the border check asked if we had certain vegetables that they didn't want to enter their state without going through fumigation. I said no. He asked if he could look in the trunk. I opened the trunk. There were some bags and boxes. He looked under a blanket a bit and said okay. But we had to pay some fee because I had a drive-away car. We didn't have enough money. Ronnie and I had to walk into town a few miles in desert summer heat. I bought someone gas with a gas card. They gave us the cash we needed and a ride back to the border. As we drove away, I told Ronnie that we needed to hide that pot better, that if he'd pulled that blanket back a little bit more, the officer would have seen it.

I had to go to Fort Worth because the U.S. Government's Selective Service had sent me a letter. I'd been drafted. Immediately my mind had shifted to focusing on dealing with that situation. I brought it up with everyone I met.

Harold was an interesting character I'd visited on Haight Street in the heart of the scene there. He was fifteen years older, well-educated, an engaging conversationalist. He had an apartment with a front door that opened up to the sidewalk. He'd leave the door open and talk to people who passed by. That's how we met. Mainly he was interested in inviting young, innocent hippie guys into his lair and getting close to them.

Harold and I shared another passion. We were adamantly opposed to the horrific Vietnam War. I told him I just wouldn't go. I'd go to jail first. And I said it wasn't only because of this particular war. I'd always known I'd never go into the army. In high school I'd say I'd rather be killed than kill. I read Gandhi.

I wanted to go to Fort Worth with a letter from a doctor that said I was unfit to be in the army. There was a doctor in Berkeley who was giving any guy who asked such a letter. There were others more cautious but eager to help if they could. But Harold had another idea. Why go to a doctor who has helped lots of kids escape the draft, a doctor they may be wise to? He said there was an old family friend of his, a shrink who'd recently retired from the Air Force and set up shop in the Bay Area. He said the guy knew Harold was a homosexual. Harold said he'd call him up and say he had a very special friend who he was worried about. "Don't worry. He'll have a set picture of who you are before you get there."

Boy did that work. I think I helped the situation with my preparation. I took a bunch of speed, stayed up for a couple of days, and didn't change my clothes. But I arrived on time, ready to play my part. I didn't say I wanted a letter. I just said Harold sent me. I don't remember what else I said, but I left with a letter stating I was a homosexual, schizophrenic, drug addict with leadership qualities, and that if I were to be in the military, I'd form troublesome schizophrenic dens. He concluded with, "Under no circumstances should this disturbed and potentially troublesome person be allowed in the service."

In Texas, my mother wanted to see the letter. No way. "But Mr. McKenzie is head of the draft board here…" she started.

"Listen, Mother," I said. "You decide whether you want me to come home in a body bag or not."

She sighed and acquiesced. "No man in our family has been in the military," she said. "Or graduated from college."

On the designated day, I boarded a bus full of fellow draftees. At the induction center in Dallas, I made no attempt to appear undesirable. I was clean. I answered all the questions on the form as well as I could. In the physical, standing in a long row of young men bending over with pulled down underwear, I learned I had hemorrhoids. When they were through examining me, I said I had a letter for the psychiatrist. The psychiatrist read the letter and asked where I was currently receiving treatment. "I'm not being treated for anything," I said. "I like myself the way I am." "Oh you kids!" he said, forcefully pounding the letter with a stamp.

I sat in a room with others who'd been rejected. A Marine sergeant stood behind a desk with a stack of papers. He picked one up and said, "Thompson!" "Yes sir," came the response. "If you pass the test next time, which would you prefer, Army, Navy, or Marines?" "The Navy, sir." The sergeant marked that down and said, "Better luck next time son." He continued thus picking up a piece of paper, calling a name, asking for their preference, and saying "Better luck next time." Then he got to, "Chadwick! If you pass the test next time, would you prefer to be in…" He paused. "Forget it."

The last person I saw was a nice man who asked if I'd sign something that allowed them to use my data for statistical and research purposes. I said sure and signed it. He looked at a form that was passed on to him. "Wow," he said. "Your grandmother will be drafted before you are."

I walked out of the draft center and down the street away from the bus ready to take me back to Fort Worth. No thanks. An enormous weight had been lifted. I realized I'd been carrying that weight for a few years. The walking became floating. I guess I floated home.

Bush Street

Back in San Francisco. I walked down Haight Street and there was Harold with his door open. "How'd it go?" he asked.

"I will forever be indebted to you," I said bowing deeply. I told him I didn't think I was long for the Bay Area. The scene was losing its charm for me. "I'm ready for a new direction, Not sure what to do. Got any bright ideas?"

"You're bright enough by yourself," he said. "Just wait. We're living in magic times. Something will come up."

I went to score some weed at an apartment on Bush Street. I'd gotten the address from a girl at a free concert in Golden Gate Park. A dark-haired, sultry woman somewhat my senior answered the door. I went inside and sat in a circle of young longhairs passing a joint around.

Indian music. Incense. Everyone quiet. The doorbell rang. Two men with coats and ties came in. They were looking for a runaway. Had a photo. Nobody recognized her. They walked through the place looking for her. Good lord. They were plainclothes cops. One of them stuck his head back in the room on the way out, looked at a smoldering joint and said, "Hey—don't you know that's illegal?"

On the landing outside I asked the sultry woman about the exotic looking building across the street. "That's Sokoji," she said.

"It's a Zen temple and the home of the Zen Center." She said she went there to meditate. Hmm. I was intrigued.

I moved away from my tripping buds. We got along fine but I'd grown dissatisfied. Near-death experiences and a powerful LSD trip I'd had while in Texas convinced me to quit messing around and find a guru and a community to meditate with. I was on the brink of flying off to India, but I'd heard some about the Zen Center at the San Francisco Art Institute where I'd been a few times to eat lunch and meet interesting people—and smoke pot. Now I knew where the Zen Center was. The bus driver told me where to get off. "It's the next block over," he said.

Sokoji Days

"It all went downhill after welfare. Welfare was the worst thing for the Negro. It's the white man makin' the Negro dependent and weak." "That's right, that's right," "I hear ya," came responses.

I was sitting out front of the apartment building where I lived talking with some old fellows. I was the only white person living there. I paid $50 a month for a small apartment one flight up. No furniture. Slept on the floor in a sleeping bag. It was next door to the Fillmore Auditorium. I could hear the concerts from my room at a lower decibel, or over there inside for ear smashing levels. So many great bands.

One night I lay on the dance floor and grooved with Cream. It was a high time, and I lived in a high crime neighborhood but one with a lot of soul. And it was an invigorating eight blocks walk to Sokoji.

I worked at the Rincon Annex to the post office and enjoyed it once I got away from sitting in a chair and sticking letters and cards in the designated zip code slots. When that was my task, I read every card. Almost every single one of them said something like, "Having a nice time. Wish you were here." One picture postcard totally dominated the field. It featured breast enhancement pioneer Carol Doda of the Condor Club in North Beach.

Other employees walked by with trays and collected mail from each zip code. I requested that role and got it. Noting how industriously I did that task, a supervisor put me on the dock loading and unloading mail bags into and out of trucks. I did it so well he'd let me do a whole truck by myself. Great job. Sometimes I'd smoke a little pot with other employees outside during our breaks. But I had other callings and often would clock out early "sick." As long as I wasn't out three days in a row, I didn't need a doctor's note. That was enough to cover rent, food, most of what I needed. I sold a little pot to cover the rest.

One morning just out the door on the way to zazen, I was knocked down by some guys walking in the other direction. I flipped my wallet up to one of them as soon as I'd hit the sidewalk. There was no money in it. The guy threw it back down at me, kicked me hard in the head, and they walked on. My head hurt for a few days.

Then a young woman in a room next to mine was murdered. The old fellows downstairs made fun of me for moving away. Called me a scaredy-cat. "I'll miss you," I said in parting. I got a little two-room basement place with a side entrance on Octavia Street one door from Bush Street with a walk down the block and across to Sokoji. It was $75 a month, and the neighborhood was much safer.

Zazen at Sokoji was so peaceful. Suzuki was in Japan when I first started sitting there, but I didn't feel anything lacking with just Katagiri to officiate the zazen and services. On our way out of the zendo, we'd walk through the office door, stopping there to bow. Then one day Suzuki was back, and instead of bowing at an empty door, we bowed with him. I didn't understand why we did that till then. That's how I met him—bowing with him.

I wondered why we hadn't bowed with Katagiri. That drove home what Katagiri had told me when we first met. I'd said I was looking for a place to meditate with others. He said I should have a teacher too. I asked if he could be my teacher. He said Suzuki would have to be my teacher. So Suzuki was the teacher and Katagiri was his assistant. But Katagiri was still considered one of our teachers.

Suzuki was a man with many honorifics. Some of the oldest

students referred to him as Reverend Suzuki. Others called him Suzuki Sensei. I heard a member of the Japanese American congregation call him Suzuki San. His wife called him Hojo San which meant the abbot of a temple.

There was one more honorific that had been used some but which at that time became official—roshi. Alan Watts had written a letter saying Suzuki should be addressed that way, that it was the way Zen masters were addressed in Japan. Suzuki didn't ask for it, but he acquiesced—after a hard laugh. So that's what I called him—Suzuki Roshi or just Roshi.

Many people had trouble sitting in lotus, but I was one of the fortunate ones who didn't. It did hurt toward the end of a period but almost everyone else was still, so I was too.

When zazen was over there was service which started with us bowing to the floor nine times at the sound of the large deep bowl bell. Then we chanted the Heart Sutra three times. That was dynamic. At first, I was a little spooked by the bows to the floor, but soon I saw them as fitting exercise after sitting cross-legged for so long.

We didn't really sit for just forty minutes. That's how much time there was between the bells that began and ended zazen. It was good to be seated at least a few minutes before the bell for the first period and some people would be there ten or more minutes early. There was afternoon zazen at 5:30 followed by a briefer service, and Wednesday evening and Sunday morning lectures by Suzuki or Katagiri if Suzuki was away.

There was an extended schedule on Saturdays in which there were two zazen periods in the morning. We'd sit for forty minutes, then walk slowly for ten minutes. That was called *kinhin*. After the kinhin we'd sit for forty minutes again. Then there was service, a silent work period, and a silent meal.

We ate on trays with chopsticks while sitting on cushions on tatami on the sides and *goza* mats in the middle. A Chinese American student named Bill Kwong was cook for the Saturday breakfast and it was almost always the same—white rice porridge, miso soup, some pickled cabbage or cucumber, a raw egg to mix with the hot rice. Sometimes a new student would think it was a hard-boiled egg and break it all over themselves. Tea poured into the empty rice bowl finished it off.

Before we were served, Bill would bring a little offering tray of food and step up to place it on the altar. Then he'd bring out Suzuki's breakfast tray and offer it to him. Then he'd offer a tray to Katagiri.

Suzuki and Katagiri's seats were on the elevated platform where the altar and bells were. Bill had an impressive style. He would slowly exit the kitchen with a tray held with two hands just below eye level. Then he'd swivel his back to us and move sideways facing the altar. As he moved along, I would gaze at his toes, impressive long toes, toes that would creep sideways one by one, each stretching to its limit. His toes seemed to be independently propelling him sideways while his feet and the rest of his body passively followed along.

Everything we did was called a form of practice. Practice, I learned, was extending zazen into daily life. Zazen and kinhin were formal zazen practices. Chanting, bowing, lectures, work, meals, walking home were all zazen in action. From what I gathered, everything was zazen—or at least potentially so.

In a lecture Suzuki said that Zen was nothing special, just sitting, sipping a cup of tea. Indeed, the practice at Sokoji was a testament to this. Just arriving, doing what we did there quietly, and departing. I'd nod to others. Maybe we'd have a few words. Smooth as satin. It filtered into my time away, and my life became more settled.

Not many rules—arrive clean and on time or sit in the balcony, don't come high. No one asked me to join or hit me up for money. There was a donation box outside the zendo though—and a sign on a bulletin board that read, "We need money to buy more kapok. See Pat." I found Pat. She was older with white hair. I gave her five dollars for kapok. She bowed and said thank you. Then I asked what kapok was. She said it's what we stuff the zafus with.

"Oh, I see. And what are zafus?"

"The round cushions we sit on."

One benefit of practicing Zen was that it expanded my vocabulary.

Inescapable Eyes

As a new and impressionable student, I heard Suzuki give a lecture in which he said that once the eyes of Buddhism are on you, you can't escape them. That struck a strange chord in me since it so perfectly paralleled the school song of the University of Texas, *The Eyes of Texas*, sung to the tune of *I've Been Working on the Railroad*.

> The eyes of Texas are upon you—all the livelong day.
> The eyes of Texas are upon you—you cannot get away.
> Do not think you can escape them—from night till early in the morn.
> The eyes of Texas are upon you—till Gabriel blows his horn.

And then everybody whoops it up.

According to biblical lore, Gabriel blows his horn to announce judgment day.

I grew up in Texas being brainwashed by this song among other insidious messages such as "bigger is better." It is possible this is the last song President John Kennedy heard before he was assassinated, sung by a group of school children in my hometown of Fort Worth—just before he went to Dallas. Many Texans think *The Eyes of Texas* is the state song. Many more Texans can sing it than the less catchy state song, *Texas Our Texas*. *The Eyes of Texas* has been used in a long list of movies including Elvis Presley's *Viva Las Vegas*. In my case, it could effectively ramp up the paranoia of a horror movie.

I liked growing up in Texas, but I was eager to check out other places as soon as I could. And I did—at nineteen. I escaped the clutches of the eyes of Texas and, after a couple of years in other parts, found refuge in the San Francisco Zen Center. And then one of the first lectures that I heard the Zen master of this Zen temple give was about how once the eyes of Buddhism are on you, you cannot escape them. He laughed and laughed, repeated it, rephrased it, and went on, but would return to that theme.

I turned my head to look for an exit. But it was too late. It fit perfectly in the old mold. Something in me clicked. I sat up straighter. Doubts vanished, and I nodded smiling, awaiting this small oriental man's next command.

The Site

Katagiri had a desk downstairs in an office that was for the business of the Japanese American congregation. He was friendly, so once when I got to Sokoji too early for the 5:30 p.m. zazen and found him in his office, I went in and said hello. He said hello too and in a welcoming way. I asked him what the chart on the wall was about. He explained it showed how much money had been raised toward the construction of a new temple on a lot around the corner the Japanese congregation was purchasing. "What will happen to this building when they move to the new one?" I asked. "Maybe Zen Center will buy it," he said. "But that would be many years from now." The red in the thermometer had a long way yet to climb. "Little by little," Katagiri said smiling.

So I was coasting along enjoying this new scheduled and calm carefree lifestyle when one day people were talking in the hall instead of leaving. They said there was a place in the woods down south that Zen Center wanted to use as a retreat. The board had approved its purchase and $2500 had already been put down on it. The total price was a dizzying $150,000, with $25,000 due in mid-December.

Mid-December? That was two months away. People were excited. It was as if the building vibrated and echoed with the revving up of a dormant generator.

Robert Beck had given the Zen Center till October to decide on whether to buy the Horse Pasture or not. On September 14th the board authorized Richard Baker to negotiate and sign a contract. Silas Hoadley, the treasurer, would fill in the blanks and deal with the details. People trusted his judgment and felt he'd be a good check in case the optimism of the moment got the Zen Center into shaky financial territory.

Overnight this group was squeezing every cent out of any talent and contact they had—we had. I started getting to know more people. Ardis Jackson and Trudy Dixon were sitting at a desk downstairs making hand-written notes requesting donations. The notes were sent in hand-addressed envelopes to people, many of whom were on Richard's contact lists which included his own, and those he got from Zen popularizer Alan Watts, beat poet Allen Ginsberg, and other friends of Zen Center.

The Japanese congregation now had to share their sleepy office with our supercharged activity. There were boxes of brochures stacked against the wall. I took one out and unfolded it. It announced in bold letters, A SITE FOR A ZEN MEDITATION CENTER IN THE CALIFORNIA MOUNTAINS. There were black-and-white photos of mountains, rocks, woods, meadows, a trickling streamlet.

Spending the afternoon on a cushion at the low table in his office, at the request of his student, artist Willard Mike Dixon, Suzuki concentrated on creating an *enso*, a *sumi* circle, for a poster announcing a benefit art show. Dipping his brush in the black ink, he drew one incomplete circular stroke after another, going through sheet after sheet of rice paper, until he brushed a stroke that satisfied him.

I asked him if he'd sign one of the rejects. An older student standing nearby kicked me gently and said in a soft voice, "That's not done." But Suzuki did it and I took it back to my place to proudly tack on to the bare wall.

I had a little trust fund controlled by my mother. Not much. Not enough to live on. She agreed to a donation. I enjoyed the surprised look on Richard Baker's face when scruffy me walked in and handed him a check for $500.

There was a big chalkboard in the hall showing how far we had to go. I could see that we'd already raised over $6,000. Suzuki looked at it, pointed to the $25,000 goal and said, "If we can get this much, we can come up with it all."

A Conversation

Once a month there was a one-day sesshin at Sokoji. Richard said sesshin meant mind gathering. So I decided to gather my mind and attend it—with some apprehension. The usual period in the morning, and in the afternoon, seemed like plenty of zazen to me and I went to extremes not to miss any. I'd run for blocks sometimes to get there to be still.

In the second morning period, it was challenging not to move my legs the last ten minutes. Now there would be more sitting till 5 p.m. broken up by kinhin, services, breakfast, and a work period. For lecture we also sat on our zafus. In the lecture Suzuki said, "First your intellectual activity will calm down, and later, your emotional activity will follow."

During the afternoon, Suzuki gave *dokusan*, private interviews, in the office downstairs. I sat outside with three others. I'd been told I should ask him a question. As I sat there, I was thinking about what to ask.

Suzuki had only recently come back from a trip to Japan. Silas had introduced us. We had seen each other after each service when we bowed together at the door to his office as everyone did on their way out to get their sandals or shoes on. I felt like Suzuki was looking right into me every time we bowed, not as if he was sizing me up, more like he was saying hello to a vast part of me I wasn't in touch with. But I didn't know who he was except someone who seemed to be awfully accepting and accepted by those of us filing by to bow with him. Later I saw him standing in his office talking to someone and I realized he was awfully short. He hadn't come across as that small when he bowed with me after service. It was like he wore a different size for different occasions.

Now I had to ask him a question. I hadn't read much about Zen. Before coming to Zen Center, I'd heard it was about whacks and yelling and fantastic insights, but there didn't seem to be any of that going on. There was sitting on and scrubbing the floor. What we did was all stuff I could do. I'd heard him say in a lecture that this practice *is* enlightenment, not a means to attain it, so you don't have to seek enlightenment—just do the practice. That was a relief to hear.

Finally, it was just me sitting alone downstairs in the deserted dank hall with the fading paint and dusty smell. I thought we'd have to have a lot more work periods to get this whole place spiffy.

"Excuse me." I heard a soft voice and looked up. Suzuki was standing at the doorway, the brown sleeves of his robe dangling down to his hand which held a short curved polished stick. *He looks so harmless*, I thought. *Surely he doesn't hit people with that.* I sat there with my head turned looking at him.

"I rang the bell," he said, "You should answer by ringing yours."

"Bell? Oh!" I said and picked up the handbell next to me and hit it.

"Too loud," he said, wincing. He took a few steps toward me, squatted, picked up the bell, and rang it. It had a ring that took me away for a second. "Like that," he said. "Not too much."

In the office, there were two square flat black cushions, *zabutons*, on a goza mat with zafus on them. On a small square table there was a little Buddha figure, a lit candle, and smoking incense.

Someone had shown me the forms for dokusan already, but he went over it again. Bow on the floor toward the altar three times and then stand up and bow once on the floor to him. After that I positioned myself on the zafu with my legs crossed in full lotus facing him while he folded his legs and adjusted his robes around them. We were quite close to each other—close enough for him to reach over and whack me with that stick. But I didn't feel intimidated by him. He had a gentle manner.

I sat looking at him for a brief moment and then he said, "You sit very well."

Thanks Granny, I thought, remembering my mother's mother often telling me, "Sit up straight!"

"I like sitting like this," I said. "I don't know what it's all about, but I like it."

He seemed a soft brown pyramid. "You look like you were born sitting," I said and looked him in the eye.

He averted his. "Do you have some question?"

Oh oh. Too buddy-buddy, I thought. "Hmm. I don't really have a question. I'm pretty new and just seeing what this is all about. I decided to sit for a year here. And then… I don't know." I was looking at his hands. They were stroking his stick. "Is that okay?"

"That is pretty good," he said. "Better not to have too many questions."

"I could ask a question for my mother," I said.

He nodded.

"My mother believes in reincarnation. Do you believe in reincarnation?"

"Oh, your mother believes in reincarnation? That is very unusual."

His voice was quiet yet firm. It reminded me of Mr. Gardener, a ninety-year-old man at the tennis courts where I'd played as a kid. He'd tell us stories, and I'd get lost in the mesmerizing quality of his voice. As with Mr. Gardener, I wanted to hear Suzuki talk more.

"Actually, I believe in reincarnation too," I said. "I have since she told me about it when I was still in elementary school. So do you believe in reincarnation?"

"I sometimes think so. But it is not something I know for sure. Maybe, maybe there is." Good lord. He didn't seem very sure of it for a Zen master.

"Where does your mother live?"

Ah, great, he wants to talk more. "In Texas."

"Oh," he said as if he were very impressed, "Texas. It's very wide."

"Not as big as Alaska," I said, "but if you melt all the ice in Alaska, Texas will be bigger." This is something I'd hear in Texas now and then after Alaska became a state and we were no longer the biggest.

"What does your mother think of your being here at Zen Center?"

"She likes it that I'm here. She says she figured I'd do something like this. But she wanted me to move out of the Fillmore closer to here where it's safer and I did."

"Yes, you should live close. And you should be near the older students. They can give you some guidance. Your life shouldn't be all topsy-turvy," he said waving his stick back and forth in short arcs. "Just keep sitting here and we will get to know each other. Okay?"

"Okay."

He reached down, picked up his bell, and rang it. I got up, bowed to the floor toward him again, and walked out.

I went back upstairs to more zazen which entailed some leg pain and thinking about that dokusan. I didn't get a cosmic hit like some people talked about, but still I liked it. I liked him. I envisioned Sokoji as a ship sailing on unpredictable seas, Suzuki as the trustworthy captain. And I had no interest in doing anything other than being onboard and going wherever that ship sailed.

Rockwell's Performance   OCTOBER 22, 1966

A friend of mine from Fort Worth named Jerry Ray had ventured out to San Francisco with his friend Tammy. I took Jerry over to Sokoji and he was blown away by Suzuki who he said had a joyful gleam in his eye.

Jerry was living with a fellow named Rick. Rick was a mild-mannered guy, more of an atheist socialist than a Zen Buddhist. He'd sat at Sokoji one time and didn't see the point. I took him to Zen buddy Loring's with me for a macrobiotic dinner of which he did get the point and especially liked the smoked dessert. We went to the Fillmore auditorium together and spent time with Jerry listening to a new Beatles album and getting stoned.

They were living on the third floor of an apartment building. Rick suggested we all go up on the flat roof to see the stars. The way to the roof was up a short wooden ladder off the back staircase landing. The nails in it had rusted heads, the paint was peeling. Three stories down. I thought of Pfeiffer Falls. Wouldn't do it. Spoilsport.

Rick told me that he was going to go see George Lincoln Rockwell, head of the American Nazi Party, who was coming to town. I'd paid a little attention to the nutty right since my senior year in high school. I checked out a John Birch Society storefront in Fort Worth to see what their latest take on the dangerous commie threat was and had heard Bircher General Edwin A. Walker speak in Dallas. I was aware of Rockwell, had read his *Playboy* interview. He was the most extreme of them, glorifying Hitler, denying the Holocaust while hinting at his own plans to execute Jewish communist traitors once he took over. Rockwell had a Hate Bus that he took through the South with racist slogans plastered on the side. He was an in-your-face, articulate, fervent opponent of integration and miscegenation, as those opposed to mixed marriage called it. But he was no ignorant yokel. He not only had a good East Coast education and a distinguished military career, but he'd also started a record company, been a magazine publisher, and was a graphic artist. And he knew how to work the media.

Out of curiosity, I went with Rick who reminded me on the way that he was Jewish. Rockwell's appearance was to be in front of City Hall. We waited there till he and his dozen or so Stormtroopers in Nazi-looking uniforms walked out onto a flatbed stage and stood at erect attention. They each held posters bearing swastikas with *White Power* boldly printed. Rockwell was high up at a lectern.

I wondered what on earth he would say. Never got a chance to hear anything. The moment he and his Stormtroopers appeared, the crowd was screaming and throwing things at them. Rick was screaming and throwing things. Rockwell and his boys stood firm amidst the strongest onslaught of fury I'd ever witnessed. They seemed to be accustomed to such a response from a crowd.

I saw Rockwell then as a conceptual artist who had created an extreme event. His Hate Bus was a negative version of Ken Kesey's bus named Further which went through the South displaying the message, "We have come for your daughters." Kesey had his Merry Pranksters Rockwell his Stormtroopers. Kesey was a laughing clown, Rockwell a sinister one. His message appealed to a minuscule minority, but his performances had been well-attended and followed nationwide for almost a decade.

Ominous Thumbtacks

Gil and Karen Pomeroy and I left the Zen Center office with a stack of flyers and posters for the scheduled November 13th Zenefit concert featuring Big Brother, the Grateful Dead, and the Quicksilver Messenger Service. The information was printed over a bluish photo of the mountains around Tassajara.

We headed to the Haight-Ashbury to place and hand them out wherever we could. First stop, the Littleman's Supermarket at Haight and Stanyan at the edge of Golden Gate Park. It was a chilly and windy Saturday, and I had a trench coat on. We needed tacks and tape. Hands full in an aisle, I stuck the tacks in a pocket to walk to the cashier.

I remembered the thumbtacks while standing in line and had the devilish thought that, okay, I'll steal this one thing in my life. Really, I'd never stolen anything. Just ten cents worth of thumbtacks. As soon as I'd stepped outside the door, two men got hold of me and whisked me into an office where they sat me next to several longer hairs they'd just apprehended.

APPROACHING

[A Zenefit poster: Grateful Dead, Big Brother and the Holding Co., Quicksilver Messenger Service, Avalon Ballroom, Sutter & Van Ness, San Francisco, Nov. 13, Zen Mountain Center Benefit]

The Haight-Ashbury back then was mobbed with young people who spent whatever money they could get hold of on pot, LSD, or other psychedelics—or the wicked one—speed. Walking down the sidewalk, approaching youth would inquire "Spare change?" with such regularity that I'd say it to them first to keep them quiet. That ragged crowd kept security at Littleman's busy and the holding cells at the nearby Park Police Station populated.

I sat cross-legged on a bench in a cell at that very police station, practicing zazen with eyes half open, unconcerned about my fate. A portly policeman walked by and then stepped back and looked at me. In a friendly good-ole-boy manner, hands on hips, he asked, "Are you a Hindu or a Buddhist?"

"I'm a human being," I replied loftily.

"No, I'm serious," he said. "There's some what comes here are Hindus and some what comes here are Buddhists and I just wanted to know which you were."

"I'm a Buddhist."

"Any particular type?"

"Zen Buddhism, Soto Zen."

"Thank you," he said, "I hope everything works out for you," and he walked on.

I got to ride in a paddy wagon to the central police station. They booked me and then sat me in a room with a table and chairs. There was a phone on the table. I picked it up and made a call, not to ask for help but to share my experience with Ronnie and Kenny. I made a few other calls too. It seemed funny to me that I, who didn't particularly want to make a phone call, could accidentally have the opportunity to make unlimited calls while I imagined others behind bars desperate to contact relatives, friends, lawyers. I wondered if there actually was a one call rule like in the movies.

Next they took me to an office with a social worker who asked me questions and said my case would come up Monday morning, that if I didn't have an attorney one would represent me, and that since I had no record, I'd get a fine and be able to walk out, and it would disappear from the records in a year.

Then to a cell with four other men, older than me and blacker. We chatted. I confessed my crime. They laughed. None of them were there for anything very serious. We compared backgrounds and jail experiences. They'd all been in jail before. All their male friends had been busted for pot or loitering or drunkenness or petty theft. Almost none of mine had. But I'd been in jails a number of times. They were surprised at that—till I told them why. I'd used jails to sleep in while in Latin America and small towns in the U.S. when hitchhiking. Doesn't count. OK.

I was also thrown in jail when I was sixteen after being chased down by a gaggle of cops that I didn't even know were chasing me. They found an almost empty fifth of scotch under my date Carol's skirt. The cop told me he'd never seen anyone drive so recklessly and not get into an accident—weaving in and out of cars on a freeway and exiting like a rocket, sliding sideways around corners on a country road. I noticed a flashing red light behind me at the time and pulled over. A half dozen police vehicles followed. Mother was not pleased bailing me out. Got a ticket for going seventy in a sixty—no other charge.

My cellmates just shook their heads amazed at white justice. Then I said I'd been a prisoner of war. No! Yes. They assumed it was in Vietnam, but I said I'd never been and would never become a soldier—by mutual agreement with Selective Service. But I'd been a POW. How the hell? I told them about the encounter with the Presidio soldiers in the Marin Headlands. They got a kick out of that.

"Oh yeah, I almost forgot," I said. "I was a political prisoner."

"What? You're makin' all this up!"

"No no. Really. Where do you think it was?"

"Russia?"

"Nope. Mississippi."

That got a reaction. I told them about getting thrown in jail the spring before Freedom Summer in Jackson, Mississippi, charged with drunk driving though I'd not been drinking or driving. "I had just gotten into a car and hadn't even started it yet and there were flashing lights behind me. Did three days for that. And why? Because I'd just walked out of the headquarters for a civil rights organization. They called us troublemakers. And you know what trouble we were causing? The whole thing was about registering people to vote. They didn't want some people to vote—and you know which people that was."

"They let us vote here," one guy said. "But it don't do nothin'. They still lock us up anytime they want."

Nods all round.

"How about a song?" I asked. "Maybe you know it. It's number one on the hit parade of freedom songs."

Oh freedom, oh freedom, oh freedom over me
And before I'd be a slave, I'd be buried in my grave.
And go home to my Lord and be free.

I sang the whole song and sang it again and they joined in, and others joined in. Moved on to some other freedom songs then some '50s rhythm and blues. We were swingin.'

"Chadwick!" a policeman called out interrupting.

"Yes," I said, startled.

"You've been bailed out."

"What?"

"Someone paid your bail. Time to go," and he opened the cell.

"I refuse," I said. "I want to stay."

"You can't. Come on."

After he threatened to come in and forcibly eject me, I said goodbye to my cellmates who called out farewells as I walked off to freedom.

Jerry's friend Tammy was there to pick me up. She'd heard about my arrest, had become concerned, and borrowed twenty-five bucks from Silas Hoadley for my bail. I knew her from Austin College in Texas where I'd gone briefly three years earlier. She had been married to the band leader there but now was single and living in San Francisco. She helped me develop muscles as I helped her move her harpsichord when she'd move from one third floor apartment to another. And she moved a lot.

That evening Silas dropped by my place. I opened a ceramic jar that was sitting on the kitchen counter, pulled out a twenty and a five and handed them to Silas with a "Thanks a lot for the bail money. That was stupid of me. Next time I won't get caught. Just kidding!"

Silas smiled.

He was a respected older student. And he was an entrepreneur, an importer. He went to Asia to set up deals. He'd been to Okinawa earlier that year. He had an air of wisdom and kindness. I asked him how old he was. Twenty-seven. I thought he was older than that. He said he would be twenty-eight on Christmas day. That increased his stature in my mind. I had him there, so I took advantage of his presence.

"Silas, I always thought reincarnation was part of Buddhism. But so far, I haven't heard or read anything about it Zen-wise. I asked Suzuki Roshi, and he was non-committal. Richard said he, Richard, doesn't even believe in life-after-death."

"I think Richard means that Richard won't continue, Silas and David won't continue," he said. "But what's fundamental continues. Maybe the essence is the same as our life here now."

"Hmm. OK. Something else. I was looking at all the old original going back to Buddha's day sutra books they have at Fields Bookstore. How on earth did monks preserve all those ancient Buddhist teachings before they had writing? I read there wasn't any for the first few hundred years."

Silas said he thought that reading and writing have shrunk our memory power.

Zazen is what it all seemed to be about at Zen Center, so I asked what I should do with wandering mind in zazen. He said when you're doing zazen and have some idea, just put it in a box marked ideas and let it go.

I liked talking with him about Zen and Buddhism because he gave short answers that were easy to understand. Not that I thought I understood anything.

There was a knock on the door. A visitor. I reached into the fridge. Sold a guy a few tabs of acid for two dollars each. LSD wasn't illegal, but that made Silas's eyebrows rise. He didn't say anything, but I got the message that it's best if we leave that stuff behind. I think the story of our lives can be seen as the story of our habits, the changes and the tenacity. Those dollars went into the jar. "This is for future bail money," I said.

"Just kidding," he added.

Kathy Cook

Kathy Cook was around when Zen Center was smaller and there was time for her to get to know Suzuki and his wife who was called Okusan. Okusan, I learned, meant wife in Japanese. Her given name was Mitsu, but no one used that.

Kathy asked Mitsu about the role of women in temples and in Japanese society. Mitsu told her it's not like America where women are equal to men. Kathy said maybe more equal but not equal.

Kathy talked with Suzuki about women and children and psychology. She'd been working at the Jung Institute. He told her Jungian psychology seemed much closer to the spirit of Zen than Freudian.

At one meal in the temple kitchen, Suzuki tried to teach Kathy how to noisily slurp when she ate the noodles Mitsu was serving. Kathy felt too self-conscious to suck them in the way they did. He kidded her about that. He had time in those days for that kind of intimate contact with students. They could go to Sokoji and just hang out. He asked Kathy to quit smoking, saying, "You can do it." She couldn't. At least not then.

When the drive to buy the Horse Pasture got going, Richard asked Kathy to deal with fundraising correspondence. She was the first paid employee of Zen Center, a decision that caused some resentment. She was in the eye of the whirlwind of what she saw as the birth of Zen Center as a real institution.

Lost in the Wilderness

In October 1966, another group went down to Tassajara from the city with Suzuki to see the land we were going to buy. This time there was more room for them to do zazen, and they could chant as loud as they wished.

A woman whose room was next to Alan's had asked him if they could meditate somewhere else because their chanting woke her up too early. So they started sitting beyond the pool in the small barn.

After Alan was gone Ed had been sitting and chanting alone there. He was happy to sit together with his fellow students again on the morning of their hike.

After breakfast they got rides up the road to the Horse Pasture trailhead. Richard trekked along as did poet Gary Snyder and bare chested and hairy Silas Hoadley. A friend of Ginny Baker's named Yvonne Rand ambled along with a naturalist and psychoanalyst named Sterling Bunnell.

Snyder was the senior Buddhist in the group. He'd recently returned from a decade living in Japan where he practiced Rinzai Zen at Daitokuji in Kyoto while part of Ruth Fuller Sasaki's translation team. In the '50s, before Suzuki had come to America, Snyder did zazen in a cabin he named Marin-an which he translated as Horse Grove Hermitage. It was on the edge of Mt. Tamalpais north of San Francisco. He lived there for a while in the mid-'50s with Jack Kerouac and again in the late '50s when others joined him practicing zazen regularly.

Silas enjoyed the hike but was not enamored with the logistics of bringing supplies in that far and sleeping in tents. It was Tassajara that impressed him. It would be perfect for their monastery.

Silas met Robert Beck on that trip and, after the hikers returned to camp, they spent some time off to the side in conversation. Robert asked him if he was related to Silas Hoadley, the early nineteenth-century clockmaker from Connecticut. Silas said that was his great, great, great, great uncle and that the family was still in Connecticut where they both were born. He said the first Hoadley arrived in the 1600s. Robert said he and Anna bought and sold antiques and that coming across a Silas Hoadley clock was a real find, that they still run good as new if they haven't been abused. Silas seemed dependable to Robert as well.

On the way to shower and soak in the hot spring plunges, someone asked, "Hey! Where's Yvonne?"

Most hikers walk along taking in the scenery as a whole while keeping an eye on the path in front where they're stepping. Yvonne and her friend Sterling had been admiring particular plants and geological formations, spotting birds, and naming and discussing the particulars. They'd lagged behind and then she lagged behind Sterling who saw the little Tassajara marker where a trail branches off.

Yvonne was paying attention to other details at that spot and continued on—and on and on—all the way for a few miles to Willow Creek just past where it meets Tassajara Creek. The creek widened there which made it easy to cross. She was hot and tired, happy to get wet and drink from the gentle flow. On the other side she came to the Willow Creek trail and a sign that indicated Tassajara was four miles away taking the trail in the up-creek direction. A couple of hours later she could barely see another trail branching off to the right. There was a sign. It was getting so dark she couldn't read it, but she took it. It went up and up and up. Guided by faint moonlight on her way down, exhausted and thirsty, she met a search party on its way up. She was on the rugged and steep Tony Trail which feeds right onto Tassajara property.

Thus, Yvonne became the first lost hiker during the Zen Center era which was beginning to materialize.

Loring Palmer

Suzuki and Katagiri shaved their heads as was traditional for Buddhist monks. A student named Loring Palmer had a shaved head too. Nobody else. Loring was quiet and considerate. He said a room had opened up in his apartment on Buchanan Street in the heart of Japantown a few blocks from Sokoji. He invited me to live there. Back to $50 a month. Tim Buckley lived in a room there too. He was serious yet congenial and had a deep voice.

Loring's was like our little sub-temple. There was structure. We walked to morning zazen together in the dark. Weekday mornings we came back, cleaned and swept, made breakfast, ate, then sipped Japanese green tea during which we'd break the silence. It was unlike anything I'd experienced before, another blessed answer to my quest.

Loring followed the macrobiotic diet, heavy on grains. We'd have oatmeal or another grain porridge for breakfast and not with milk, with gomashio, sesame salt. For dinner we had brown rice, miso soup, and vegetables cooked in a wok. We made unyeasted bread and ate it with a spread called muso, miso mixed with unhulled sesame butter.

Loring dealt high-end cannabis to a select clientele, including people in the local rock scene. I'd help him sometimes. Just enough to get by and have a little saved. We sold thirteen kilos of primo Acapulco Gold and donated the proceeds toward the purchase of Tassajara. Katagiri heard about that, said nothing to us, but expressed his disapproval unequivocally in a lecture.

Loring took Tim and me to a party at Gavin Arthur's just a few doors down. Gavin was a celebrity astrologer. At his apartment I was honored to meet Gary Snyder, Murshid Sufi Sam, Alan Watts, and his wife Jano. I told Watts I'd read *The Way of Zen* and asked him how many copies of it had sold. He said he'd lost count but that the penny he made on each one did help him survive to write the next book. Jano said, "I read a book called *Nature, Man, and Woman*, and I thought, *I'd sure like to make love with the guy who wrote that book.*"

The Deal

December came and there was the good news that the payment on the Horse Pasture had been raised ahead of time. The hall after zazen was all smiles. There'd been a number of benefits, and the checks had poured in.

Then, a few days before New Year's, we heard that the funds would be used as a down payment not on that wilderness property but on a doubly expensive Tassajara Springs owned by the same couple. What? I'd heard a little about Tassajara being a hot springs resort near the property we were raising money for, but nothing about buying it. Apparently though, the board had just authorized it.

The payments from selling the Horse Pasture would have made life much easier and less stressful for the Becks, but Robert, at

Anna's urging, realized that it was time to sell Tassajara. It was too much to think about with a toddler, a baby on the way, and continuing to manage the place. It was hard to let go but letting it go to the Zen Center felt right.

Robert loved wrestling with Richard Baker over which piece to sell, the price, how it would play out, and about life, love, and so forth. It seemed he liked dragging it out so they could meet more. Richard evidently enjoyed wrangling with him too. Robert was observant. He didn't assume what Richard was saying was what he was thinking. But there was a cautious mutual trust and respect as they moved closer and closer to an agreement. With the success of meeting the deadline of the first payment, the prospects of coming up with more for Tassajara itself looked good.

Christmas had passed and New Year's was imminent. Robert and Anna met with Suzuki and Richard for hours in Suzuki's office to finalize the agreement. Richard and Robert did almost all the talking. Anna sat and listened. It looked to Robert as if Suzuki were sleeping, but Richard would turn to him and ask if something was acceptable, and Suzuki would nod, and Richard and Robert would keep talking. They were getting hungry. Richard suggested a Japanese restaurant. Suzuki stayed behind.

"The deal to change from the Horse Pasture to Tassajara was made at a Japanese restaurant on Broadway Street," Anna told me later. "I was nine months pregnant. Robert and Richard did the talking. The lights were being turned off by the time we left. We did think we could have sold it for more but we both really wanted the Zen Center to have it. We were impressed with Suzuki and Richard. It was originally listed for $450,000, then we came to 375 for Zen Center, then 350—and finally 300. I felt like we were handmaidens of Buddha."

Team Work

I caught Silas on his way out of Sokoji and asked him how had this all come down? As treasurer, he was always in on the information stream. He said that after the dinner at the Japanese restaurant where the Becks had agreed to apply the payment to Tassajara, Richard had called a meeting of the board and older students. "It was a group process. Richard told them they had this opportunity."

"Richard did it," Silas went on, "but he included everybody. There was discussion of whether we could pull it off or not. I was for it. There was the certainty of income at Tassajara which seemed like a wonderful opportunity for the practice of serving. It gave us a commune and a community right off the bat. It was very exciting—plus the hot springs and the beauty were incredible."

Richard's far-reaching approach was in tune with Suzuki's vision and each in his own way, conveyed that perspective to the Becks. Silas saw that. But he wasn't on the sidelines. He had an essential role. He was soft-spoken, and practical. He gave the Becks confidence at a ground level.

"After Richard had done it with a broad brush," Robert said, "Silas would come and say this is how it will actually be done. Silas was the one who prepared the schedule of payments, who drew up the papers from the Zen Center, and worked with a lawyer to get it done. Silas was always reassuring. He invariably convinced us that we would get our money. He was the ace in the hole."

Finally, signatures went down on paper and the deal was done.

El Camino   FEBRUARY 1967

Silas had a Chevy El Camino which looked like a graceful cross between a car and a pickup. I rode in the back wrapped in a blanket and surrounded by tools. Four of us were eagerly on the way to Tassajara for a work weekend.

South of San Jose the freeway poured into one of those undivided blood alleys with a big sign announcing how many people had died on that asphalt so far in the year. Through Morgan Hill and San Martin gazing at the road behind was semi-hypnotic. It made me a bit queasy, and when we stopped, the view appeared to come racing in toward me. Glad to step down at the classic roadside diner,

Buzz Inn in Gilroy, garlic capital of the world. Walked around and got my bearings. Then it was weak coffee and victuals I had recently come to avoid but was eager to make an exception of in the name of going-with-the-flow pancakes, eggs, and bacon.

Before entering that old Monterey County resort, we were to spend the day working on the Tassajara phone line. Silas said it went a long way through the woods and had a break in the line we needed to find. A seasoned fire lookout named Fred Tuttle met us at a snack stand near a few homes and trailers, a place that was also named Fred, Fred's Camp. That's where the Tassajara phone line connected with Pacific Bell. First Fred tested the line at the Pac Bell connection to make sure the problem wasn't on its end. It wasn't. It lay somewhere between there and Tassajara.

We drove along the Arroyo Seco River flowing in a gorge through rocky pools. We parked where the line crossed the river running on top of a bridge too small for a car but wide enough for its namesake, the Horse Bridge. The phone line was regular old uninsulated metal wire—like galvanized fence wire but thinner. From the Horse Bridge it ran five miles in each direction through wilderness. Fred went to a spot where there were two porcelain insulators that held the line. He disconnected the wire between the two. Then, using what he called a field phone, he hand-cranked it on the Tassajara side of the line. Someone answered in the office. He tried the other direction. Nothing happened. He noticed it had a slight buzz on it though. So the problem lay between the Horse Bridge and the Pac Bell connection at Fred's Camp.

The line ran above the road and through an insulator on a tree up on top of an embankment. We climbed up there and followed it, going through some rough brush at one point, removing any obstruction we could reach, mainly branches it came in contact with. He said they weren't enough to kill the line. It had to be broken or on the ground. We followed the line to a dirt road which it followed until passing into fenced-in private property. Fred had a key to one of the locks on the chained gate and we entered a hibernating Girl Scout camp. We were lucky. Found the line unbroken but down on a metal roof where a live electrical wire also rested.

A tall tree that had held both lines had fallen. Most of us were concerned about the electric line and wanted the juice shut off before proceeding, but Fred picked it up with his gloved hand saying, "A little one-twenty never hurt anyone," and swung it off the roof. I could tell there was a lot to learn from Fred but thought back on my prematurely late neighbor who in 1957 took a first soak in the bathtub of his brand-new ranch house. The copper soap holder in the wall had been secured with copper screws, one of which unfortunately had pierced into a little 120.

The line back up, we drove out on the Arroyo Seco-Greenfield Road the way we came, but this time instead of following it to Highway 101, turned onto the tail end of the Carmel Valley Road. Onward through hilly, wooded countryside. Turned left at the sign that read *Cachagua*, that I would come to learn was pronounced *kashawa*.

Some miles later and higher there was snow on the ground. It got thicker as we ascended, especially at Chews Ridge, the zenith. But it wasn't deep enough to hold us back. I shivered in my blanket, but it was so beautiful and the cold air so clean with the scent of pine needles that I was happy to be shivering in such surroundings. Silas stopped and picked up a huge pinecone from the road. It was larger than a football. "Coulter Pine," he said. Wow. I'd never seen a pinecone that large—or anything growing on a tree that large.

We drove past a turnoff to a campground called China Camp with picnic tables at a lower level barely visible through the trees. Silas said it was called China Camp because the second half of the road was built by Chinese laborers and that's where they camped. There, we left the woods for chaparral and drove along a ridge.

Silas stopped again, and we silently watched the sun setting into the Pacific. Then down in the dusk around hairpin curves and past perilous drop-offs on a bumpy road often not wide enough for an approaching vehicle of which we thank goodness met none. Seemed to me there were places not wide enough for our one vehicle.

At one spot Silas had us get out and watch apprehensively as he drove past a spot where the right-side tires rolled over a wide plank where too much of the road had washed down a steep ravine. We proceeded with a frosty wind chill and spectacular dimming views of steep mountainsides, forested and rocky. Bumped along beside a small running creek that was on one side of us and then the other back and forth a few times to a twilight stop before a welcoming big old oak tree.

Silas opened the tailgate and I slid out. I was so disoriented from riding in back that I lost my balance and fell down, my first encounter with the ground of Tassajara. Silas helped me up, smiling, unconcerned. I brushed off, looked around. Rustic buildings and sycamore trees in a narrow, shaded valley amidst steep slopes with clinging oaks. Looked back toward the road we came in on. Then to the narrower road to the left and right. "Does the road keep going?"

"Nope," he said, "That's Tassajara Lane. It's for maintenance. This is the end of Tassajara Road."

A hot vegetarian meal awaited. But first a footbridge took us over the rolling rocky creek to the baths to clean up then to step into a spacious, gracious hot springs plunge in the crisp air. Sighs.

Zazen at eight around a glowing cast-iron stove. Crawled into my sleeping bag in a cabin as cold as the night to a lullaby from Tassajara Creek. Exhausted, refreshed, I fell into deep sleep.

Demolition Days

I awakened in nippy darkness to the ringing of an approaching then departing bell accompanied by running footsteps. Heard a rustling. The flash of a lighter illuminated enough to remind me I was in a cabin at Tassajara. How fresh the air smelled.

Ah yes, Tim Buckley got out of his sleeping bag. We'd come down together for another weekend of work. He lit a kerosene lamp. We brushed our teeth and splashed water on our faces in the shadows. Stood with others quietly drinking coffee on a deck. Chilly morning zazen and chanting in the former bar and lounge. A day of going through a mountain of dark old boards, knocking and pulling out the nails, rusted with square shafts making me feel tied to an earlier time. Loading the boards in a pickup. Getting more boards ready for the truck's return. Lunch at a picnic table. Cheese sandwiches and vegetable soup.

Four o'clock bath time. Silas led me naked and dripping from the plunges to a steam room. Sitting on hot slimy boards in the total darkness. Then screaming into the creek that surely would have been ice if it hadn't been moving. Held on tightly to a cable not to be carried downstream. Up sandstone steps to return to the plunge. As I descended into the steaming water, I could not tell whether it felt cold or hot where it first met skin, as if the drastic temperature changes had confused my body. Standing in the plunge against the back wall, submerged to my shoulders. A floating thermometer read 108 degrees. Gazed out the wide opening of the thick stucco enclosure at the steep hillside beyond the creek.

After the evening sitting, silent and still with my comrades, I carried my sleeping bag from the cabin and laid it out on a deck by the courtyard. Silas said goodnight to me as he walked by.

"Hey Silas," I said, "what is this that I'm sleeping on?"

"What was it?" he said, "It was the dining room. You were working with what's left of it today. It was taken down with the kitchen."

"The kitchen must have been a lot bigger than the one we're using now."

"Yes," he said. "Unfortunately."

I gathered from Silas that the facilities needed to get the place fully functioning were in usable though somewhat dilapidated condition the way the Becks passed it on to us. The kitchen had been condemned by the county, so the first major construction would be for a new kitchen. It could be built where the dining room was. The condemned kitchen we inherited would serve until the new one was ready. That was the plan.

A caretaker named Howard Campbell went to Tassajara as soon as the contract was signed. He and his wife Jeanne lived in Berkeley. I'd spent the night and sat morning zazen there with them and a few other Suzuki East Bay students who went over the Bay Bridge to Sokoji for lectures, the Saturday program, and sesshins.

Jeanne was involved with the fundraising for the next huge payment of $45,000 due in March, so Howard went to Tassajara alone. He joined a few people from Beck's staff who were told they could stay on if they wanted. With Howard's arrival, once again there was daily zazen at Tassajara.

Suzuki and Richard visited a few weeks after Howard had arrived and were shocked as heck to find the kitchen was gone! Only the floor remained. The dining room was gone too, but that had been planned. Neither had stone walls. They were easy to tear down. But like Humpty Dumpty, the kitchen couldn't be put back together again.

"You said it was condemned," Howard said to the dismayed Richard, "and that we were going to build a new one. So I thought the most important work to do was to get going on that."

Howard had only gone to Tassajara for six weeks. He left before I arrived and moved with Jeanne into an apartment across the street from Sokoji. His enthusiasm did result in expedited planning on a new kitchen. Meanwhile, a little shack in back that had served as a staff kitchen and dining area would, of necessity, become Tassajara's temporary kitchen. It already had a four-burner propane stove, a propane refrigerator, and a table. Now the larger four-burner from the demolished kitchen was in there. There was another refrigerator outside next to the coffee and tea area. The large walk-in refrigerating reefers on the creek side of the deck were big enough to keep a good deal of perishables. They were powered by electricity from generators up in the shop.

That was my bedtime story. Silas went off with a flashlight. I zipped my sleeping bag up and wiggled a little with delight to be right where I was. I turned my attention straight up and was overwhelmed with the clarity, the magnificence of the vast expanse of stars and planets, unimpeded by our earthlight. A shooting star streaked across the heavens.

Acid Trip Anfänger

I had my last acid trip with Tammy at Muir Woods. Loring gave me two tabs of Owsley's famed LSD that he'd acquired at the February 12th Watts Acid Test. It was my eighth trip and her first.

I turned lots of people on to psychedelics before coming to Zen Center and a few afterwards, but that petered out. Never had any problems. Had rules. I'd only do it if the person agreed to take it in a natural, non-social setting. No talking—that's where almost all the problems came from—and an empty stomach except for water. And we'd meditate beforehand.

Late in the afternoon, Tamara and I drove to Muir Woods in Marin County and climbed with sleeping bags in hand to the top of a meadow above the redwoods. We had a view overlooking a forest and the Pacific Ocean. Nobody else was there. Tamara took LSD first, and I sat with her. She had a stretch of discomfort but settled into it. She didn't have a lot to say later. Psychedelics open up mountains and rivers in us—more than we can imagine or report.

I took mine at sunrise. After some incalculable eons had passed, I watched Tammy going down the meadow to speak to a park ranger who then walked on.

At some point there was an opening in the sky and what looked like people from another realm in a semi-circle rather close, looking down at me. I had a vision of Suzuki and Katagiri standing in their brown robes, bathed in halos, waiting for me. I wondered why I couldn't join them. Then realized it was because I saw that union of form and emptiness as an event happening in the future, that I was headed toward step by step, whereas I was, all was, complete already and it could only be found in this immediate shining present. It wasn't something that actions and thoughts led up to.

I wanted to tell Tammy that I realized I was living with an idea of enlightenment being something to move toward but only got out the words "I was living" when in a powerful bright flash I was blasted physically backwards onto the grass. Up to that point, I'd sat full lotus without moving for eight hours. I sat for a couple more hours slowly re-entering normal consciousness. For a time, the word *anfanger* represented in sound and glorious color enveloped me, repeated over and over.

That night back in the city at Loring's we wondered about the word anfanger that had been so prominent in my visions. Tim had studied German in college. So had I—for a few months—and remembered nothing. He said that the vision had not gotten the spelling quite right. It's anfänger with an umlaut or could be written anfaenger and it meant "beginner." Beginner. Hmm. How appropriate. Suzuki had mentioned beginner's mind in lectures as something essential to practice, something not to lose. Indeed, I was a beginner which my opened mind had celebrated on that trip.

I marveled at the insights that had come to me on acid but could see how, even though it opened me up to possibilities greater and clearly more real than normal waking consciousness, it wasn't sustainable. That's it, I decided. No more tripping. I'll forsake seeking mind blowing epiphanies. I vowed not to aim my practice at the future. But wait a minute. Isn't the point of a vow to continue doing something into the future? Hmm. *I'll continue doing practice in the present*, I thought to myself. It seemed the future couldn't be avoided, at least intellectually. Suzuki said that truth was paradoxical and practice about uniting opposites. OK. I nestled into a practice of contradictions.

Ready or Not

Early March. I'd been back to Tassajara for another work trip. Tim and I rode down together in his Volvo. Good people there. Good zazen and sutra chanting together. The land was good. The waters, the food, the fresh air, the stars, the trees—all good.

I talked to Suzuki about going for a longer stay. He said I hadn't been around long enough, there weren't any senior students there, that I should stay in the city to get more familiar with Zen practice. Not long after that, Silas said they badly needed people now. There was a lot to do in the few months before the first guest season and then first practice period was scheduled to begin. I was a little crazy but was available and had good work energy. Suzuki agreed with Silas that I could go.

In no way was I tired of living with Loring and sitting at Sokoji. We had a good thing going. Tim felt the same. He said living with Loring had saved his life. He'd had some bad habits, been in dark places. He was wondering when to settle at Tassajara too. Going there would be moving from one good thing to another. But was I ready for that?

Suzuki was in the city, not down at Tassajara, though he would surely visit sometimes. Katagiri was in the city as well. I'd hate to miss their talks and their presence. But Tassajara was the future. People did zazen and practiced there. There were the hot springs, the wilderness, and the work that had to get done. And there was snow on the road we'd have to go through to get there. I could smell it.

Nighttime after dinner and cleanup. Loring and I sat facing each other. To the side was an altar with a small Buddha statue, a slender vase with a single flower, and a smoking stick of green Japanese incense. A candle provided the only light which reflected off Loring's shaved head and would be sufficient to read a few lines from a book which rested on the tatami. We sipped genmaicha in silence. We were there to decide whether or not I'd move to Tassajara. Silas said I could go down with him in two days if I wanted.

I was leaning but unsure. Loring was neutral. I knew nothing about the book, the *I Ching, the Book of Changes*, except that it had been used as a guide for a few thousand years in China and was popular in our counterculture circles. Loring lit a joint of Panama Red. We took one hit each, sat in silence for a while, then I threw the coins as Loring had instructed.

Loring opened the book. One line from the reading struck me: *The south furthers.*

— CHAPTER TWO —

PREPARING

The Vanguard MARCH 1967

There were about a dozen of us at Tassajara, including two couples who stayed on from before—Bill and Kathy Parker and Jim and Laurie Holmes. Good they did. They knew the place. And they were sitting with us, blended right in. Jim was the work leader. Silas came weekends and went over priorities with him.

We sat one period in the morning and one in the evening in the lounge. After morning zazen, we chanted the Heart Sutra one time. We had zafus and zabutons, a small bell, and a small mokugyo. A railroad bell on a pipe stand was rung to call us to zazen, meals, and work meetings. Getting up every morning in the same place as others, sitting together, chanting together, eating breakfast together and so forth all day was invigorating, motivating—added fuel to my engine.

All the cabins were made entirely of redwood except for the fir floors. We called them wooden tents. They were for guests in the warmer parts of the year, had no insulation. Air came through the cracks. The windows were just screened openings. There was a roll of clear plastic and a heavy stapler to deal with that when it got cooler. Cabins had toilets and sinks but no electricity—with a couple of jerry-rigged exceptions that would soon be disconnected. The warmest rooms were the small ones in the dorm with thick walls and sliding windows. The toilet for the dorm, though, was down the dorm steps and across Tassajara Lane or the path as we usually thought of it. At the dorm, the path diverged and descended to a stone-walled lower level by the courtyard, continuing past the kitchen-dining-lounge-office area rejoining Tassajara Lane just past the Pine and Stone Rooms.

I couldn't sleep on the demolished dining room's deck anymore because it was gone—down to bare earth and rock. I sought another spot to join the stars at night. Took a path to a flat spot on the hillside across from the best guest quarters, the Stone and Pine Rooms. I brought my sleeping bag up there, sat on it, and gazed at the stars so clear in the mountain air. Crawled in and fell asleep with stars in my eyes.

Woke up in daylight. I hadn't heard the wake-up bell. A visitor approached the opening to my sleeping bag, a scorpion. Quickly as I could, I unzipped the bag enough to get my arms out and deal with the impending invasion. As soon as an arm was free, I grabbed a nearby stick and shoved the critter away. It kept coming, but there was time to exit the bag and walk down the hill scorpion-free. I knew I wouldn't sleep under the stars there again. Darn.

There were large propane tanks beyond the shop. A gas pipeline ran underground from there to the kitchen to feed the stoves, refrigerators, and what we called the coffee machine—the type with large crocks like they have in restaurants. One day after the road crew had repaired and graded the road, the gas man came in driving a propane tank truck. I watched him filling up our ten-foot-long propane tanks and asked if they could explode in a forest fire. He said yes, they can but not ours because there was nothing combustible within thirty feet. "Actually," he said, "they have to be under extreme heat for an extended period which I don't think could happen here at all."

I asked what could happen if that truck was in an accident. He said that a large tanker truck had gone off a 400-foot cliff in Utah. The driver died, but the tank didn't lose a drop of gas.

I told him one of our refrigerators was losing its cool this morning. He came to the kitchen and showed me how to fix that problem. The flame had gone out. The flame in a refrigerator? Yep. It heats the propane liquid and turns it into gas. Obviously, the others there knew this because there were wooden matches and a clip that held them by the fridge. "Just stick the burning match through the opening at the bottom and push this button," he said doing just that. He told me some other tidbits about how to keep the fridge happy and I gave him a loaf of bread.

People were taking turns cooking meals. I offered to do lunch after a few days there. I was eager to apply what I'd learned from Loring. The reviews were encouraging, so I kept doing it. People made suggestions that added to the mix. Out of that came some adventurous casseroles. I hardly knew what the word meant before arriving.

I didn't stick strictly to Loring's macrobiotic regime—included eggs, cheese, milk, tomatoes, potatoes, eggplant, and peanut butter—none of which were in his kitchen. Mainly simple fare—lots of brown rice, miso soup, other soups, sauteed vegetables, beans, and whatever lettuce, spinach, tomatoes, and cucumbers we hadn't run out of for a salad. We didn't have the option of running out to the corner store if we were short on perishables. The milk we had for coffee, tea, or cooking was powdered or canned.

Bread—always bread. I made unyeasted bread I'd learned from Loring, Tibetan Barley Bread being the favorite. Laurie taught me how to make yeasted bread as she'd learned it from Jimmy and Ray. We had plenty of whole wheat and other flour—rice, corn, barley, millet, buckwheat. The yeasted bread was the best for sandwiches—cheddar with lettuce, tomatoes and mayo and/or mustard, peanut butter and jam, cream cheese and pickles. Others made those sandwiches which to me were food from a bygone era. Same for the yummy cookies that Kathy baked. I put my preferences on hold though and made sure that nothing went to waste.

Breakfast was open to volunteers who would miss morning zazen to get it ready on time. I was fanatic about getting to zazen so I'd get oatmeal ready to cook the night before and come in early, turn the burner on, throw together whatever else for that morning—cottage cheese and warm applesauce was a favorite—and it would be ready to eat when we were ready to eat it. Others would make pancakes or French toast with scrambled or fried eggs.

For dinner I'd gather all the leftovers and heat them up. People called the conglomeration gruel. It was the Wild West kitchen. People were working long, hard hours, were young and hungry at mealtime, and weren't picky. We'd crowd around the kitchen table and gobble it all up.

Bob and Sandy Watkins

The most enthusiastic diners on my amateurish creations were a couple who'd driven into Tassajara in February, Bob and Sandy Watkins. Bob was tall with a long red beard. Sandy was well over a foot shorter. They'd arrived unannounced and immediately made themselves useful as he knew construction and she knew gardening.

Bob was a decade older than Sandy and most of us. He was a Korean War veteran. He'd been involved in the movie business on the logistics end, sets and so forth, had a longtime association with Dennis Hopper. He said one task he had for a while was to bring Frank Sinatra a fifth of vodka every morning.

With earnings from a clandestine importing trip from Mexico via sailboat, he had bought a truck and fitted it with a camper that became his and Sandy's snug home. There were lots of little drawers and boxes with essentials perfectly packed, including grains, nuts, and dried fruit. They were strict vegetarians. The Tassajara diet included dairy and eggs. They ate neither.

They'd arrived in their old '51 Chevy during a snowstorm. In the lower parts it was raining, and the road was slippery and in terrible condition. Bob said he kept deliberately hugging into the side of the mountain to avoid sliding off the road down the drop-offs.

We shared our stories—where we came from, why were we interested in meditation, how we got to Tassajara. His answer was a lot shorter than mine.

"I spent my first nine years with my father's mother who was in her seventies, way back in the woods. There were boarding schools, military, Catholic. Then a few years on the streets in L.A. with my aunt, then the Airborne at sixteen, out a few years, then in prison three years where I read everything I could get on Buddhism."

Bob was lucky it was only three years. He was in prison for armed robbery, the getaway driver. He said they never hurt anyone, but one accomplice had a gun and that stuck with them all.

"In prison, I took a pencil and made a dot the size of a dime on the wall of my cell, then sat in front of it until things went away. Tried corpse asana lying down, but it was too much like a trance. Finally, I got hold of a D.T. Suzuki book and saw there was a school of sitting. Lost the sailboat when my buddy who owned half of it decided to make another run and got caught. Then I heard of a place near Big Sur named Tassajara. That's it."

Sandy was shy and quiet. When I asked her about herself, she said there was nothing to tell.

"She's the real Zen one," said Bob. "I'm just a wannabe."

Peter Schneider

In 1961 Peter Schneider got his master's in English literature from the University of Connecticut, headed west, and was soon living a footloose life in San Francisco's Haight-Ashbury with his older brother Jig and a few of Jig's friends he knew from their college days. Peter felt unsatisfied and unmotivated. He didn't have a job, was itching for more in life. He met an older guy who gave psychic readings and told Peter to quit smoking. Peter didn't see how that would help but he was open to anything. He quit and the guy was right—Peter felt like he got his will back. A little later the psychic told Peter, "Okay, now start meditating." Peter liked that idea and started doing so in his room.

A fellow named David McCain lived in the same house for a while. He and Richard Baker worked together in a warehouse as shipping clerks. Richard would drop by their place and became part of the scene. He told Peter that since he was interested in meditation, he ought to drop by the Zen Center and meditate there, go to a lecture by the Zen master, Suzuki Sensei. Peter wasn't interested in Buddhism though. Just in meditation. However, Richard kept mentioning it, so Peter finally gave up and tried it out. He liked it. And he liked Suzuki.

Peter got a new job and moved south of San Francisco where interesting high-tech electronic stuff was happening. People were calling it Transistor Valley. He'd hitchhike up to San Francisco for the weekend to do the Saturday practice at Sokoji and hear Suzuki's lecture. He'd stay at Richard's place. By then Richard had a job at UC Berkeley Extension. It involved writing and putting out a newsletter. Peter helped him with editing.

Peter finally got a job offer he liked, a two-year stint teaching English at a college in Michigan. He was to show up for it after a seven-day sesshin at Sokoji ended. He left his apartment and got permission from Suzuki to sleep at Sokoji during the sesshin. He shared the one bathroom in the basement with the Suzukis. No other students slept there.

Peter's seat in the zendo during sesshin was between Richard's and a stalwart Englishman named Grahame Petchey. Peter'd been sitting at Sokoji for only nine months and those two had been sitting for a whole year and a half. They sat upright without moving, so Peter did too.

On the third day in the afternoon, Peter started to cry. He didn't want to bother others, so he went and sat on the stairs. He didn't know why he was crying, hadn't cried since he was thirteen, and now he was bawling. Suzuki came out of the zendo and walked down the stairs, pausing briefly to put his hand on Peter's shoulder. This simple act on Suzuki's part had a profound effect on Peter. His sobbing subsided, and he returned to his seat, comforted. More than that. He felt an indescribable change in who he was.

While teaching English at the college in Kalamazoo, Peter learned of a program that would take students to India for the summer. It was a trip paid for by the government of India in exchange for rice shipped there by the U.S. government at a time of food scarcity. Peter was interested in this program because it concluded with two weeks in Japan. He signed up for a class as he had to be a student to be accepted into the program.

Once in Japan, Peter figured out where Suzuki's home temple was and how to get there. He took the train to Yaizu and a taxi to the temple, Rinsoin, showing up unannounced. That's not advisable, but it was no problem because, to his surprise, his visit coincided with Suzuki's first return to Japan since leaving for America four years previously in 1959.

At Rinsoin, Peter met one of Suzuki's first students, Jean Ross, a woman in her forties who'd been in Japan for over a year practicing at the mother temple, Eiheiji. He had a wonderful time getting to know Jean who was folksy and friendly. He hadn't been in an intimate situation with Suzuki before and felt completely comfortable with him. Suzuki was to him the most natural person he'd ever met, yet so ordinary.

Peter finished up his two years teaching in Michigan, then traveled around living in Spain, England, Florida, and upstate New York. In 1966 he was in New York City working as a tech writer. Richard let Peter know he and Suzuki were going to the East Coast to generate support for a retreat in the mountains near Big Sur. He asked if Peter could set up a speaking engagement for Suzuki and him in early 1967.

Peter quit his job and got on it. He had a friend who knew the city well and had just filled a job vacancy at the *Village Voice* covering the emerging hip and hippie scene. They'd go out together to happenings and clubs, coffee shops, and events, especially in Greenwich Village.

Peter arranged for Suzuki and Richard to speak at the Village Community Church which was Unitarian. The talk was sponsored by the Young Adults of the Village Community Church.

Richard sent Peter the poster used to advertise the Zenefit concert back in November. Peter modified it for the upcoming event, printed up a bunch of them, and he and his friend blanketed the

Village with them. The entrance fee was one dollar. The topic of the talk was "The Practice of Zen." Six hundred people showed up.

The next day Peter met with Suzuki and Richard over breakfast. They talked about Tassajara and the fundraising. He was happy to see his old pal Richard and to be with Suzuki who to Peter exuded confidence yet was so unassuming. Suzuki said to him, "Come to Tassajara and be the office manager."

Peter said, "I don't have the money to fly there."

Suzuki said, "You have $600."

Peter thought about it. He could go for a few months.

"Sure," he said.

Spring Arrivals

In early April, Richard Baker arrived at Tassajara with Ginny and their daughter Sally. They would stay in a large creekside cabin with a small kitchen. The March payment of $45,000 had been made and he deserved a rest—but of course he wouldn't be resting.

The fifth anniversary issue of the *Wind Bell*, which had come out earlier in the year, had a brief article announcing his resignation as *Wind Bell* editor so he could concentrate on fundraising for Tassajara—and be president of Zen Center and director of Tassajara whether he was there or not. He'd finally also resigned from his job of developing national conferences for UC Berkeley.

He had no time anymore to be chairman of the editorial committee of the Four Seasons Foundation, which published books of poetry, or to work on his doctorate in Japanese history and oriental studies. Once it was clear Tassajara was going to happen, he'd let the Center for Japanese and Korean Studies know that he had to back out of accepting their grant and going to Japan for a year in May with his wife and daughter. He'd already spent weeks that year on the East Coast drubbing up support for our burgeoning monastery.

I had an image of Richard being an engineer driving a bunch of trains, most of which had to come to a stop at Tassajara where their tracks abruptly terminated. Except the *Wind Bell* train seemed like it would keep running as he was now kicked upstairs to the position of publishing editor with top billing in the credits above the new editor, Trudy Dixon, who'd been assistant editor. They'd been doing it together for years. It now had 2000 subscribers, more than the number of Zen Center members.

I went to greet the Bakers, and Richard immediately turned to me and said he'd like me to run the dining room for the guest season coming up in May. He said Ginny had ideas about the look of the room and that I should work with her. Oh wow. Really? OK Sure. I'd been working mainly in the kitchen, but Ed Brown had just arrived to be the head cook. Perfect timing. The dining room was now my priority.

The first thing that Ed did in the kitchen was to create a space for an altar. He'd brought a small Buddha with him to sit on it. One morning he asked me to skip zazen and help him get breakfast ready. When I arrived, he said, "Let's bow in first." He lit a candle then lit a stick of incense on the candle flame and placed it in a small bowl of ashes. We bowed toward the altar and then to each other. When we finished work that morning, he said, "Let's bow out." We bowed to each other and departed. It was like turning the kitchen practice switch on when we arrived and off when we left. But of course, since our practice was seamless, the off switch simultaneously turned on the switch for the practice of walking away from the kitchen.

Peter Schneider arrived to run the office. Hardly anyone had ever heard of him and now he was to be one of the guys running the place. We learned he was an early student of Suzuki's, so that gave him status. He was sincere and friendly, so the hoi polloi were comfortable with him.

Phillip Wilson had been practicing with Suzuki since 1961. He was one of many who'd heard about Suzuki at the San Francisco Art Institute. Suzuki had ordained him as a monk back in '64 before Phillip went off to practice at Eiheiji in Japan. He'd returned to the U.S. in the fall of '66.

Suzuki had planned on Phillip going to Vermont to help with

a small Zen group there. Suzuki had been to the northeast several times and met and sat with them. But now he let them know Phillip was needed at Tassajara. As soon as Phillip arrived, he and Suzuki were working together on a stone garden in the courtyard. And now there was an American with monk's robes joining us for zazen and chatting with us in the breaks.

Paul Discoe came in on a motorcycle with his vivacious wife Ruthie. He'd been there before and wanted to see what it was like under the new Zen management. Phillip greeted them, and since the guest season hadn't started yet, said, "I love you folks, but you can't stay." Before long though, Paul was standing with Richard and architect Joe Droshin looking over plans for a new kitchen.

While so many of us had been going to college or dropping out, Paul had been working. He was an experienced carpenter. More than that, he was familiar with all aspects of construction. He'd worked on commercial structures and with back-to-the-land do-it-yourselfers. He and Ruthie stayed. She got right into gardening. Paul knew plants as well. He'd nurtured a substantial bonsai collection since he was a boy.

Dan Welch and Louise Pryor came in on a motorcycle with a sidecar. Dan had been involved with Zen since he was in high school. After high school, he lived in a Japanese Rinzai Zen temple for a year and a half. When he came back, he pursued art and played harmonica in a rock band. He showed me a photo of a huge chair he'd built that appeared to be intended for giants who wouldn't need a ladder to sit on it. His sister was Jeanne Campbell. While Dan was visiting with Jeanne and Howard, Richard had asked him to please come help us at Tassajara.

From the moment he arrived, Dan seemed to me to be an example of how it's done. He was industrious, focused on whatever he was doing with no hint of judgement or heavy pressure on us fledglings. His presence at zazen was immediately felt. He arrived early, sat up straight without moving, yet came across as relaxed and comfortable. "You don't get that," Bob Watkins said, "without experience." Dan got going doing any type of work that was called for and seemed to be good at anything he did. Louise was industrious too but more laid back and was at times humorous.

Kathy Cook came in from the city where she'd been in the office. Now she was working on a design for student robes. The Japanese priests wore three layers of robes: kimono on the inside, over it the Chinese koromo with the long sleeves, and the rectangular kesa worn on top in formal situations. Kathy was thinking of a simple single robe for us lay folk. Suzuki liked what she'd come up with.

Clarke Mason had heard about Zen Center and Suzuki through his friend Tim Buckley. He gave zazen a try and took to it right away. A few days later, there was a one-day sesshin. Meeting Suzuki for dokusan, Clarke easily slipped into full lotus. "Where did you learn to do that?" Suzuki asked. "It's what you said to do," Clarke replied.

From what Tim told Clarke about Tassajara, being there seemed like the next step. He wanted to take it right away. He'd only been sitting for two months, but he gathered Richard was the gatekeeper and made his case. Richard was non-committal. Clarke had been reading Zen stories and said if he wasn't accepted, he'd camp out at the gate. Richard didn't budge. Tim was back in the city moving out of his room at Loring's before returning to Tassajara for the long haul and Clarke was helping him load his car. Tim gave Clarke some advice about what to say to Richard. The next time Clarke saw Richard, he said, "I hear you have vehicles and generators at Tassajara. Maybe my misspent youth as a hotrodder can be useful down there. I've got tools."

Clarke arrived a few days later and got right to work on the two Willeys Jeep engines that generated the electricity consumed by the shop and the walk-in coolers. There was a line leading to a few old-fashioned streetlights near the entrance steps by the old oak tree. Other than that, the place was entirely lit by kerosene lamps and lanterns.

Many Changes

Tassajara was going through so many changes, and as more people arrived the rate of change increased. The shop, grounds, baths, cabins, and central buildings were getting spruced up. A rickety structure at the pool was torn down. The bridge that crossed the small creek and led to the cabins had to be fortified so heavier trucks could go over it. A couple of Paul Discoe's buddies brought in a chainsaw-mill and slabbed up some oak and a large sycamore that had fallen that winter. The sycamore slabs were long and installed as benches on that bridge. The largest one Paul marked for the future kitchen's long worktable.

Six-inch aluminum piping from the baths to the swimming pool was being re-installed since the creek had come down enough not to threaten to take it away. Through those pipes flowed hot spring water to take the chill off the cold spring water in the pool. Plumbing all over was being fixed and redone.

I was better acquainted with the plans for the guest dining rooms and zendos—dining rooms and zendos plural because we were going to be shuffling them around. There would be guests in May and June, then practice period July and August, then guests again in September and half of October.

The Beck's bar and lounge would be the guest dining room in May and June. By the practice period of July and August, that space plus the office behind the bar would be gutted and turned into our zendo. The Club House below the dorm would be the guest dining room in September and October. Until the practice period, we'd use the Club House and its deck for our zendo and meals. So the partitions the Becks had installed in that room were removed and new fir flooring was going in—but not until the subfloor had been made level. That old building had sunk some through the years on the creek sides. Meanwhile the dorm upstairs was being replastered and painted.

Before all this activity could happen, vehicles were needed to bring people and things in and out. An old chopped up VW Bus inherited from the Becks was used as a truck to haul stuff within the grounds. But we needed something heftier for inside camp and got a Dodge Power Wagon for $250. A pickup truck with a camper back was bought from a student to use for shopping and laundry runs.

Back in San Francisco, Richard drove a brand-new Toyota Land Cruiser out of the dealer showroom loaded with students. They were on the way to Tassajara, but they didn't get far before it broke down. It had no oil. An hour later they were cruising on the way to Tassajara in another new Toyota Land Cruiser.

The Essence of the Grain

There was a tug of war going on about what we ate, but it was more complex than just between two opposing factions on either end of a rope. There was a hodge-podge of beliefs and desires about diet decisions—raw food-cooked food, brown rice-white rice, dairy-no dairy, Japanese-Western.

Richard said with all the grains, sesame, sunflower and other seeds, that we were eating like birds. He thought we should eat more potatoes which he said were close to being a complete food. And he wanted more salads instead of all the cooked vegetables.

Everyone agreed we should eat healthy and nutritious food but there was not always accord on which foods were healthy and nutritious. Someone would quote Suzuki saying we should eat what we're served with no discrimination. Then someone else would say that doesn't mean we don't decide what to eat. As Paul Discoe said, "Everything about food is socially and emotionally charged."

I started making gomashio, sesame salt, at Tassajara soon after I arrived. I'd learned how from Loring back at our Buchanan Street apartment. Sixteen parts roasted unhulled brown sesame seeds to one part roasted sea salt ground up together—twice the sesame the macrobiotic cookbooks suggested. Not at all the normal Japanese gomashio I'd seen in Japantown with some black sesame seeds in the salt. Since the salt ratio was so low in the gomashio I made, we used vast volumes on the brown rice and other grains and veggies served. At Loring's, we ground it in a ceramic suribachi with pestle, but the amount we were going through at Tassajara called for the hand-cranked Portland Mill.

Our numbers had more than doubled since March when we'd all eat at the table in the kitchen. Pancakes and fried eggs were a rarity now. For breakfast we were mainly serving hot cereal like oatmeal or our kitchen-ground brown rice cream with an array of condiments to cover everyone's preferences. Thus, there was milk, white sugar, brown sugar, honey, yeast, and gomashio.

One morning I was in charge of breakfast and had a thought. When Ed told Suzuki about all the conflicting complaints he was bombarded with regarding the food—Suzuki had told him he's the cook and it's up to him. I thought, well, this morning I'm the cook and therefore how I serve breakfast is up to me. I made oatmeal, cottage cheese, and sliced apples. I served the oatmeal with only sesame salt on the side. None of the other condiments. A number of people were clearly not pleased to have their preferred choices removed, but it was a silent meal so they could only express themselves with eye daggers. I wondered if I'd gone too far. I was definitely pushing my trip on others.

At the conclusion of the meal, Suzuki spoke. He said, "You notice that there is only gomashio with the oatmeal this morning. That's so we can experience the essence of the grain. From now on, this is how we'll be serving it."

Because Suzuki, who did not like food fanaticism, and who did not weigh in on every issue, had thus spoken, I got no feedback. It looked like I'd just been following orders. After that, only gomashio was served with the meals as a condiment.

Bob Halpern

There was a new fellow on the back porch by the kitchen at the coffee and tea area. At first, he seemed somewhat arrogant, with a serious, determined look on his face like a samurai in a Kurosawa film. Then he morphed into a persona more like a used car salesman. He dropped that after a while and was outgoing and friendly. His name was Bob Halpern.

We talked until dinner then talked until zazen. After zazen he suggested we do more zazen, so we sat on two boulders in the creek. After a while, he said he was hungry. I seconded, and we went to the kitchen and made verboten cheese sandwiches. Soon we knew abridged versions of each other's lives.

Bob had been sitting with Taizan Maezumi down in L.A. since 1965. Back then he had a bookstore on the Sunset Strip called the Satori Shop and was one of the first people to sell psychedelic concert posters. He lived in back. He not only got an education from the books with ancient wisdom, but he also learned from customers well-versed in such matters.

There were other benefits for Bob in that time of discovery and new horizons. Young starry-eyed hippie lasses would come into the store and he'd woo them with Zen riddles and then, if there were no other customers, invite them to see his oriental cookware. When they said yes, he'd put up a closed sign, escort them through a curtain to his quarters, and show them a wok.

Ear Ache

After zazen on a moonlit night, I was sitting solo on a massive stone down in the small creek by the bridge to the cabins. The fire watch had gone round hitting the clackers for all lights out. I sat with the smell of the woods and the surrounding sound of flowing water, saw a vision of an Indian dancing on the stones down in Tassajara Creek. I kept sitting.

Suddenly there was a great intrusion, a painful attack that knocked me back. It was a shrill sound that penetrated and unsettled me so that I involuntarily screamed out, "No! No! No!" I lay sideways on the rock clutching my ears and wondering what had just happened and then I was looking up at Bob who kneeled there with the bowl-shaped brass bell and striker from the zendo. He had snuck up behind me and struck the bell hard a few inches from my ear. Now women's heads were sticking out of dorm windows up above. I sat up, holding my ear. Bob grimaced and shook his head with hands holding bell and striker up in the air showing he had no idea the result would be that calamitous. I shook my head in disapproval and muttered, "Please don't play Zen master with me like that."

"No talking after evening zazen," he whispered with an index finger on his lips.

Deadly Roofs

I was preparing the dining room for the coming guest season and was surprised to see Loring standing in front of me. He was in a serious mood and asked if we could meet that evening after zazen.

He came to my room. True to Loring style, we sat facing each other with a candle and incense lit between us. No sacramental marijuana was smoked as it and alcohol were against the rules. After a while, he spoke.

"Rick," he said, "has gone to the other shore."

"What? You mean Jerry Ray's friend Rick got enlightened? He doesn't even believe in it."

"No. Rick has passed on to the next bardo."

"Rick died?"

"Yes."

"How?"

"He fell off his roof."

We didn't speak further, just continued sitting silently till the incense burned out.

Jerry came to Tassajara and filled me in on the details. Rick had rolled a couple of joints that he and Jerry planned to smoke on the roof of their apartment building. Rick went first. The short ladder off the back landing to the flat roof, the ladder with the rusty nail heads and peeling paint that I'd not trusted months before—had not held. Rick had fallen with the ladder in his grip three floors onto the concrete below. Jerry ran down the steps and kneeled by him.

Rick was obviously dead. Jerry thought he'd better get the joints out of Rick's shirt pocket before the police arrived. He reached inside Rick's blue jean jacket and felt around, heard voices, looked up, saw people on back landings looking down at him. He realized he must appear to be someone robbing a dead person.

Later that summer, George Lincoln Rockwell, founder of the American Nazi Party, who Rick and others had screamed and thrown things at, was assassinated outside a laundromat at a shopping center parking lot in Arlington, Virginia. He was shot by a disgruntled Stormtrooper perched on the roof. I thought maybe Rick's spirit had guided the assassin's trigger finger and hoped that what passed on of Rockwell and Rick might meet in the afterlife and make up.

The Haramaki

Silas drove Suzuki in to stay for a few days. During the day Suzuki worked with Bobs Watkins and Halpern on the stone retaining wall that ran along the small creek below the deck to the Clubhouse. At bath time, he joined us. We were all hyper-aware of Suzuki's presence. He was quiet so we were too.

We had continued the Beck's practice of keeping the women's side of the baths for women and the men's side for either. Suzuki seemed comfortable with the mixed bathing.

We had to clean up in one of the rectangular tiled tubs or take a shower before entering the big plunge. Bob Halpern made sure that he went at the same time as Suzuki so he could offer to scrub Suzuki's back in the small tub which, though small compared to the plunges, was large enough for two to sit in. Bob was well-versed in Zen lore and knew that scrubbing the master's back was a traditional role for a disciple to play.

Bob noticed Suzuki wore a sweater which only covered his abdomen, a *haramaki*. Bob ordered one for each of us from SK

Uyeda in L.A., a department store that catered to the Japanese American community. It seemed to me Bob ascribed a degree of magical power to Suzuki and thus to the haramaki.

Cool Lemonade

The temperature was in the high nineties. The railroad bell rang. People came walking toward camp central from their various tasks. Some strong young sweaty fellows climbed out of the large pit they were digging in the rocky ground. It was to be the leach field for a new septic tank, and it was going in right across the pathway from the former lounge and planned zendo. The good folks of the kitchen crew had put a five-gallon crock full of lemonade with ladles hanging off the side, ladles which busily filled glasses for parched throats.

The lemonade was unsweetened. There was white sugar, brown sugar, and honey on the side. Many students regarded sweetening as something to be minimized and white sugar as toxic. There were students who didn't pay attention to all that and took whatever they wanted. Some added just a smidgeon of brown sugar or honey after serious consideration. A few of us, including Bob Halpern and me, boldly drank ours straight and sour.

Suzuki came sauntering down the path from the baths. When he was noticed, everyone got quiet, gasshoed, and stepped back so he could approach.

"Oh, lemonade!" he said, as if it were some great treasure.

Bob got to the ladle first and filled a glass for him. We stood around awkwardly watching and waiting. Suzuki took a tiny sip to test, puckered his lips in displeasure, picked up a spoon and said, "Oh, sugar! I love sugar!" He slowly added teaspoon after teaspoon of white sugar to his lemonade—until the bottom quarter of the glass turned white. He stirred it, admired it, and then drank it down.

"Ummmmmm. Good lemonade," he said after wiping his mouth with his hand. Then he gasshoed and walked down the path, leaving the lot of us rather flummoxed.

The Bishop

A priest from L.A. came to Tassajara. He was the bishop of the North American Soto Zen temples that ministered almost entirely to Japanese Americans. He wasn't new to the older students, as he'd visited Sokoji several times a year for sesshin and ceremonies. His nephew came with him, and they stayed in the first stone room. The Bishop was nobody special to us. We saw that old-fashioned Soto Zen temple stuff as being like an American church trip, but Suzuki treated him with respect, had him lead services, asked him to give a talk, and introduced him to us as if his visit were a great honor.

The Bishop had been in America for a couple of years and his English was pretty good. His lecture was about how Hui Neng became the sixth patriarch. In this famous Zen story, the fifth patriarch asked disciples to submit poems to help him choose a successor. Shen Hsiu, the heir apparent, posted a poem about wiping the mirror mind clean of dust. Illiterate rice washer Hui Neng had that poem read to him and dictated another one in which he said there was no mirror and no dust which had no place to alight anyway. So he got the robe and bowl and is the hero of the story. The point of the Bishop's lecture was that Shen Hsiu's understanding was also good, that the practice of wiping the mind clean is important, that purification and transcendence are not mutually exclusive.

I took the Bishop for a walk up the Hogback Trail and showed him the waterfall across the ravine. He taught me one of my first Japanese words: *taki*, waterfall. He was nice, but he was also sort of smarmy with a big toothy smile. I kept thinking he looked like Dracula. He invited me to his room, but I said I had to get back to work. The thought of being alone with him gave me a little tingling fear that soon he'd have his fangs in my neck.

His nephew was a somewhat effeminate artist who complained to me about what a tyrant the Bishop was over him, making him practice zazen while they were there. He also told me he wasn't really the Bishop's nephew.

Back in L.A., the Bishop sent me a letter with a sheet of stamps, some of which I could use to write him back. He asked me to visit him when I went to L.A.

Food Tripping

I did some research on food and materials sources for the Tassajara kitchen and dining room. In the Bay Area I went to two places I'd shopped at with Loring. One was the Oakland Food Mill, which was the best place I knew of to get whole grains, nut butters, and other wholesome, nutritious dry foodstuffs. I dropped by Fred Rohe's small yet prototypical New Age Natural Foods in the Sunset section of San Francisco. It was the only such store I knew of. Fred advised us to grow as much as we could, and for what we buy, try to focus on locally grown produce. Use as few packages and cans as we could. He suggested Koda Brothers organic brown rice in Dos Palos. And he mentioned a few places down south. One was Organicville in L.A.

I went there. Sought advice from the owner. He had a lot to say, mainly about how the health food world was full of crooks and junk. From the second story deck outside his office overlooking the store below, with a sweeping gesture, he made disparaging comments about what people were buying. "It's 80% crap down there—supplements, vitamins, packaged snake oil." His large store had little more produce than Rohe's small one.

I told him I'd been to Hain, the company that made "cold pressed" oils that health food stores were buying. Mr. Organicville said, "Cold pressed doesn't mean what people think. It still gets up to 120 degrees." I told him the stocky man I met in the office there smoked a cigar and wouldn't let me look around. The Organicville owner said that's because he didn't want me to see the pigs they were slaughtering in back to make their margarine. "Actually," he said, "that would be better than the partially hydrogenated oils they use and that all margarines use. They're also called trans-fats. Better to eat butter."

We were torn between wanting to make healthy food choices at Tassajara and not wanting to succumb to food fanaticism. We kept serving margarine with bread, which was usually served with lunch. Hain margarine, which we thought must be at least a little healthier. But muso, the mix of sesame butter with miso, was more popular.

Taizan Maezumi

While in L.A., I stayed with Taizan Maezumi at his home, which doubled as the L.A. Zen Center. He'd invited me when he came down to check out Tassajara. He was a gracious host, friendly.

He had recently married a woman named Charlene. I was surprised to learn she was a Nichiren priest. She said we should buy organic soap for Tassajara and showed me what she used. I wrote down Dr. Bronner's for personal use and Basic H for cleaning.

After dinner, Maezumi treated me to hot sake. His English was awfully good. He came to L.A. in 1956 to assist at Zenshuji, the Soto Zen temple in L.A.'s Japantown. There wasn't any zazen group there, so Maezumi sat with Nyogen Senzaki, who'd been in America since 1905. I said I loved Senzaki's and Paul Reps's book, *Zen Flesh, Zen Bones*. Maezumi said that Senzaki was a Rinzai monk but that he had left behind monastic practice and priestcraft.

"He wore robes, but over his western clothes, and a rakusu like what I'm wearing now." I asked what the significance of the rakusu was. They're like bibs that hang around the neck. All the priests wear them—but not to the zendo. "Why is that?" I asked. He said priests wear okesa to the zendo, the robe of ordination that wraps around them. The rakusu was just a miniature kesa for less formal occasions. He showed me the backside of his. It had white cloth with calligraphy that his master wrote. "My father was also my master," he said.

He said in 1959 he went to summer school at San Francisco State, studying English, and met Suzuki at Sokoji not long after Suzuki had arrived from Japan. "What was your impression of him?" I asked.

"Gentle, quiet. There were Caucasians around, so he already had students. Later I met his wife when she came. She and I would go out drinking. He didn't like to drink so much."

After zazen and breakfast, Maezumi sat me down opposite him at a low table and ranted at me for the longest time about the fact that not only would Richard Baker not allow the L.A. Zen Center to be associated with the San Francisco Zen Center, but that there was not even a mention of his center in the *Wind Bell*, the Zen Center's publication. He had worked hard to get a zazen group going in L.A. but had gotten no support for starting one at Zenshuji. He implored me to get "just one sentence" in the *Wind Bell* about his center. I said I had little weight at the Zen Center, but I'd do what I could.

The Bishop's Disciples

I called the Bishop from Maezumi's because I'd promised him I would. He invited me to lunch. We met at a Japanese restaurant. He brought two young American students whom he introduced as his disciples. We ate and talked and had a charming time. He asked me if I'd like to stay at Zenshuji and, when I said I had a place to stay, invited me over for the evening, but I said my schedule was full.

When he went to the restroom, his students begged me to ask if they could go shopping with me. I did so, and the Bishop said okay. He went off and they joined me driving here and there. The first thing we did was to get some ice cream which they gobbled with glee. Both these guys were in their early twenties and had come to Zenshuji independently just because it was a Zen temple, and they'd read about Zen and enlightenment and wanted to get enlightened.

John had studied in Stockton with a man named MacDonough, whom he called MacDonough Roshi. MacDonough had robes and said the abbot of Eiheiji had given him transmission. He drank beer a lot. John said MacDonough had a catalogue that he ordered the robes from. He said he'd stayed with MacDonough for far too long and had found it to be a bizarre and unrewarding experience.

I asked why he stayed so long if his experience was so bad. He said that he thought the problem must be his and kept at it till he finally got physically ill and had to leave. He went to L.A. and discovered there was a Zen temple there. He'd been at Zenshuji a while when the other fellow came to the door. He said the Bishop normally shooed away enlightenment-seeking Westerners but, since they were both insistent, he had accepted them. This seemed in accordance with the Zen tradition of telling prospective monks to go away until they'd sat steadily outside the temple gate for some days or weeks.

They said that the Bishop made them get up early in the dark to do zazen and that after a few hours he'd have them join him for a morning service. They ate almost entirely white rice, miso soup, and pickles. He told them not to talk with each other and had them clean the temple. For study, he had them copy Chinese characters for hours in a small dark room. They had no idea what the characters meant or how to write them. I dropped them off at Zenshuji in the late afternoon. They were not happy we were parting.

Joshu Sasaki

Tim let me drive his Volvo down to L.A. again. I pretended I had business there, but I had other things in mind. First—to visit Warren Lynn, a friend from my brief stint at Austin College. I'd met Jerry Ray through Warren. Warren was selling pharmaceuticals and had uncomplimentary things to say about that business. One complaint was they had him pushing pills with known side effects to get rid of that stock before pushing the new type without those side effects.

We attended zazen with the Rinzai teacher, Joshu Sasaki, on a Saturday morning in a gymnasium. There were twenty or so people in two facing rows of zafus. While I was sitting, a monitor tapped me on the shoulder and said, "Roshi will see you now for sanzen." *Sanzen*, I gathered, was the Rinzai word for dokusan, private interview. Oh. I hadn't counted on that. I was shown how to bow and sit before him. He was tough looking, gruff, exuding a vibe worthy of the reputation of the temple where he trained, Myoshinji, which I'd heard called the Marine boot camp of Rinzai Zen monasteries in Japan.

He looked at me, shook his head muttering, "Very poor, very poor," then told me he would give me a koan: "Who am I when I'm driving my car?" I had nothing against that or any koan but didn't take it to heart. I was just visiting.

After zazen and the Heart Sutra, Warren and I were invited to join Sasaki and his students at a home for refreshments. Two older guys, maybe in their forties, inquired about us. I said I was practicing with Suzuki Roshi in San Francisco and now was at our new monastery, Tassajara. One of them, standing next to the door, said, "Oh you've got that Baker guy there. He's quite a businessman."

Now everyone was listening. "He's more of a university guy," I said, noting Richard had been organizing conferences for UC Berkeley and had never been in business.

"Well, he sure knows how to raise money and buy real estate. But does he know anything about Zen?"

"Gosh, I don't know."

"Sasaki Roshi knows," he answered. "He's told us about your Suzuki. That guy has got you all fooled."

"Oh?"

"Yeah," the other older guy said, "Roshi has told us how your Suzuki isn't even a priest. He just bought robes in Japan and came over here to masquerade as a Zen master."

I stood there feeling like I'd stumbled into a hostile party at a rival high school. I turned to Sasaki who was paying attention though he didn't seem to know much English. I gave him a look that expressed, are you really going to let your students treat a guest like this? I got an answer.

"Tassajara Zen, play Zen!" he said strongly. "You want real Zen, come Sasaki! Until then, go!" and he dramatically gestured to the door.

Warren and I walked out past a group of silent students.

The Koan

I spent the night with Maezumi again and brought him some reading material. It was the January-February issue of the Zen Center's *Wind Bell* publication. I showed him there was a notice about him and his group with schedule, address, and phone number, and it mentioned that he'd helped Suzuki early on. It even said his group was affiliated with the Zen Center in San Francisco. He said Charlene must have taken that copy of *the Wind Bell*. He was embarrassed he'd gone on so about his problem with Richard and asked me to forget it, said that it wasn't appropriate for him to badmouth Richard to me or to anyone.

I told him about the reception I'd received at Sasaki's place. Maezumi said he'd received the same treatment and so had Eido Shimano from New York Zen Studies, and Eido was a Rinzai priest like Sasaki.

The next day, the Bishop treated me to lunch again with his minion John. There was only one student now. After lunch he allowed John to go with me and once again John was like a crazed hermit come down from the mountain, ravenous for sweets and conversation. He said he hadn't been out on his own, that I was the only person the Bishop would let him be with or talk to.

His fellow student had walked out one day. Just couldn't take it anymore. Before that, they'd been put through a grueling seven-day sesshin with zazen morning to night, and the Bishop didn't join them except to come hit them with his *nyoi*, or priest's short staff.

John said that the Bishop had given him a koan. Koans are not normally given by Soto Zen teachers but there is a long tradition in Soto Zen of studying them. Dogen, Soto Zen's founder, had completed koan study when he was a Rinzai monk (after he'd been a Tendai monk) and he wrote tons about koans. Suzuki frequently gave lectures on koans, mainly from the *Blue Cliff Record*. But I hadn't heard of anyone at Zen Center being given one.

John said he had accompanied the Bishop to the home of a wealthy lay family to assist in a memorial service. The home was an hour's drive from Zenshuji, so the Bishop suggested they stay in a motel for the evening. John thought that was good because it would give him more time to be with his teacher and maybe he could glean some insight that had, up to then, eluded him.

That night, the Bishop said that it was good for master and disciple to be close. John was a little taken aback when the Bishop added, as he pulled back the covers of one of the queen beds, this meant they should sleep in the same bed. John said he slept better by himself, but the Bishop insisted on leaving no sheet unturned in pursuing the course of being mind to mind and body to body. *Maybe this makes sense*, John thought. The Bishop then said that they should have no clothing between them. He disrobed and told John to do the same. John felt resistance arising but labeled that as a barrier between him and the enlightenment he sought. *Don't resist*, he thought. *Say yes to the master. If you don't obey, you'll never break through to a realization of buddha mind.*

"What a dedicated student you are," I said. "Please go on."

Alone and naked they stood in the motel room facing each other. The Bishop told John that he would now give him a koan.

"A koan?" John asked with eager anticipation.

"Yes, a koan. And this is the greatest of all koans. This koan is called the diamond koan." He told John that if he penetrated this great koan, he would know the mind of the buddhas and patriarchs. "Are you ready," he asked?

"Yes, I am ready," John answered, trembling with excitement and awe that his long months of punishing Zen practice had brought him to this moment with the promise of breaking through his ego to the infinite.

With that, the Bishop reached forward and grabbed John's private parts. John sloughed off an instinctive quiver of revulsion and took it as a classic example of an unexpected act from an enlightened master. He called out bravely, "It's Buddha!" *No*, he thought, as the Bishop fondled him, *not good enough*. "It's no-mind! Mu! The oak tree in the garden!" He kept trying to give incisive, non-conceptual, intuitive Zen answers to the koan, but nothing seemed to work. Finally, he realized that he'd failed. He didn't want the Bishop to be touching him any more like that, so he pulled back.

"Don't give up," said the Bishop.

"I give up," said John, and he went to the other bed, crawled in, and pulled the covers over his head.

I asked John what his take was on it all now. "I mean," I said, "Don't you think that maybe he was just horny?"

"Yes, sure. I guess so."

He said that wasn't the first sign he'd had of the Bishop's predilections. A young fellow had come to the temple and told the Bishop he was plagued by fears that he had homosexual tendencies. The Bishop had taken him in and seduced him. The guy had gone berserk and had to be taken to a psyche ward. John's fellow student left after that without saying goodbye to the Bishop.

I suggested to John that maybe he could find some other teacher that he'd have a more fulfilling experience with. I encouraged him to meet Maezumi or Sasaki—right there in L.A. Or come to the Zen Center in San Francisco and Tassajara. "It's like you're torturing yourself, man."

John nodded and said yes, he should go somewhere else, do something different. But not yet.

A Reading

Before coming to California, a family friend named Bob Howe told me I should look up a psychic in L.A. named Fred Kimball. Howe told me Kimball was regarded as one of the best psychics in the country and was famous for reading animals. He'd go on the radio and people would call in to have their pets read. Howe had years of experience around the paranormal realm. He'd worked at the Edgar Cayce Foundation in Virginia Beach, Virginia, and had helped bring psychics and law enforcement together in Texas.

He told me about a case in Austin where two girls had been murdered. The psychic was taken to the scene of the crime and gave a reading that was helpful to the police. But when they returned with the press, the psychic was thrown off by all the attention and gave a different and useless reading.

My mother became interested in Edgar Cayce and his readings on past lives after my father died. She said it helped her to understand why things happened to her she felt she didn't deserve. She took me to a meeting with Cayce's son, Hugh Lynn. A few times Mother sent me to psychics to check them out. I was not impressed with two of them. Bob Howe sent my mother to an old black female psychic in Fort Worth who mother liked a lot. She told mother I would move to California where she saw me surrounded by many people. Mother asked me to call her up and make an appointment. I did, and the psychic said to me, "Honey, I ain't gonna meet with you. I'm old and weak and your vibrations are too strong for me."

I met Fred Kimball at his home in Glendale. We sat in his living room. He was a large tough-looking guy. But he came across as gentle when he spoke. He didn't ask me anything. I said nothing except, "Hello. I'm David. Bob Howe told me to come see you."

Fred just told me to sit down. He looked at me and said, "The first thing I like to do is see if you're planning your own death." That made me sit up straight. After about thirty seconds, he said, "Nope. I see a lot of rooms, buildings, houses, trailers. That's positive. You're on a good path, but you've got a block there." He pointed to the air on my right side. "A black spot." He paused. "When you were about, umm, seventeen and a half, you told yourself you weren't gonna let anyone or anything push you around anymore. You were setting yourself free. The problem is you didn't make it clear enough and so you cut off your psyche and subconscious somewhat. You don't want to do that. You want them to have full access. Just make clear that it's outside forces you don't want to push you around. Your psyche and subconscious will both do what you ask if you make it clear. Always say please and thank you. Thank you for all the good things you've brought me and please bring me more of whatever it is you want. You don't have to be polite to your subconscious. I call mine 'you stupid idiot' because it blindly follows orders."

"You mean you see us as divided up into parts?" I asked. "The conscious, the subconscious, the psyche?"

"No," he said. "It's not divided. Just make clear what you want. When you wake up and your mind is more open, say, I want to be happy, I want to be healthy, I want to have plenty of money, I want a good sex life, whatever you want, make it clear."

I said, "I'm studying Zen with a teacher named Suzuki now. Do you have anything to say about him?"

"If you're talking about D.T. Suzuki, he died last summer."

"No. Not him. Shunryu Suzuki."

"Zen," Fred said scoffing. "What's the sound of one hand clapping and all that crap. I used to go to Nyogen Senzaki's meetings. I can get you further. They take too long. Just go to the top of a mountain and face east and have an invocation. Stay there all night. Or sit for hours on end staring at a candle flame.

"Now, let me see what you really think about this Suzuki you're with and this Zen stuff." He cast his gaze in my direction. "Hmm. You say you like it, that it's working for you." And then, "There—you scratched your right cheek. That confirms it."

"Scratched my right cheek?"

"I've been all over the world as a merchant marine and I've noticed that scratching has the same meanings everywhere. I've got a chart on it. Hmm. Let me look at this Suzuki. Umm. He's not having sex. That's not good. I'm fifty-five years old and have sex every day with my wife. But he says he's found what he was looking for, he's satisfied. People come to him and say why am I unhappy? He says because you want too much."

That was quite an introduction to Fred. He certainly was the most impressive psychic I'd ever met. He made the one comment of something he saw in my aura I guess—that blocking he said I'd created in my teens. I could match it with a pivotal experience and that age seemed about right. I could see how I shut off my higher mind. I had no big problem at home, but I was tired of the restrictions society and high school imposed. I wasn't overly rebellious. Sneaky maybe.

But I thought it wasn't mainly people and society I felt pushed around by. I was experiencing ecstatic highs for days and then depressed lows. We didn't get high back then—except with booze on the weekends. This was just my mind. It was so overwhelming. Then one day I drilled a command into myself and slammed that door shut. And it stopped happening. I felt fine but didn't get those extreme highs and lows anymore. Things were relatively steady after that.

On the road back north, I thought about what Fred said. He'd given me a way to open myself up more. Whatever it was I was reprogramming, I kept it nameless. Didn't try to figure it out. I could do that without believing anything. I grew up around stuff like this and had a distaste for how people would glom onto believing all sorts of stuff without any direct experience. Fred pointed out what he saw and left the rest up to me. He was also the cheapest psychic I'd ever met. The reading went on for over an hour and cost $25.

I gazed at the road ahead and thought, "Who am I when I'm driving my car?"

The Pinwheel

Driving back into Tassajara on a moonless night, I stopped at Chews Ridge just beyond the cattle guard where the road veers left and there's a fork to the further left that leads to where the fire lookout tower is. I pulled over because of a tall contraption silhouetted against the night sky. I walked up and saw it was a big wide cylinder with a ladder leading to the top. A young man and woman greeted me. It was a telescope. I didn't know they came in that shape.

"How'd you get that thing up here?" I asked.

They said they brought it in the back of their pickup, that it wasn't as heavy as it looked. I turned the vehicle lights off and talked with them in the dark under an amazingly beautiful array of stars in a crystal clear sky. The Milky Way, in such fine focus, like a vast blanket. They said that the Santa Lucia mountains, and specifically right where we stood, was one of the best places in the world to observe the night sky. Bill Lambert had told me he'd always heard about stars twinkling, but to him the stars in those parts didn't twinkle.

The couple explained twinkling was from differentials in the atmosphere. The pure clean airflow coming in from the Pacific made the stars twinkle less. They told me there were plans to build an observatory just beyond the lookout tower. They invited me to climb up and look at the galaxy they were viewing at the time, the Pinwheel Galaxy with spiral arms. Oh my gosh. I could see the arms. So amazing. They said it has an estimated trillion stars. I went to sleep that night marveling at it all. Beyond comprehension.

Mysterious Darkness

If there's a good size moon up at Tassajara, one can see without lanterns. But if there's no moonlight and the lanterns are blown out, you can't see your hand in front of your face.

Sometimes I'd be out after the firewatch when everyone else was asleep. If there was no moonlight, I'd be in total darkness. I'd go slowly because I'd naturally veer some and bump into a tree or stone and then correct course. Over the bridge to the baths. Into the plunge's hot water in the pitch dark. Alone.

The windowless steam room was a challenge. Imagination would conjure up fantasies. Stories I'd heard would come back to me. The hot spring area is where the Indians had come for thousands of years. Occasionally, a guest would report seeing one or seeing something they couldn't explain.

Robert Beck told me Marie Williams from Monterey had been coming for years to go to the steam rooms to commune with the Indians. The surface of the interior walls was always crumbling, so he painted both steam rooms with an expensive epoxy. Next time Williams was there, she stormed into the office furiously complaining they'd killed the Indians. By the next guest season, the paint had peeled off and she reported the Indians were back.

In the old days, mules did the heavy hauling to and from the mines over at Willow Creek. There were miners who followed the custom of attaching bells to the mules' tails. Robert and Anna said that some old-timers insisted they still heard the bells coming down the Tony Trail on mules that never arrived. Sometimes the Becks thought they heard them as well.

While on the trail coming down from the Horse Pasture toward Tassajara Creek one day, Robert said he saw two figures in black robes cutting a tree in the distance. This was before any contact with the Zen Center. When he got below, there was a tree down, but no one was there. Back at Tassajara they said they hadn't seen anyone. It didn't make sense to him.

An experience that made even less sense happened on a cold winter night when Robert and Anna were snowed in with their caretaker, Ralph Burdett. It rarely snows at Tassajara but there was snow on the ground that night. And if there's snow at Tassajara, there's monstrous snow up top. The three of them sat around the fireplace. There were partitions around them to keep the heat in and they were bundled up reading near the fire.

A knock on the door. They didn't respond because there couldn't be anyone who'd come in over the road—the snow would be too deep. Another knock.

Robert went to the door. There was a man with a peg leg and a reddish white beard wearing a Mackinaw. He wanted to know the way out. Robert said there's only one way out and that's the way you came in. There was a car with its lights on above the stone steps. The man said thanks and returned to his car. Back inside Robert had a strange feeling. He, Anna, and Ralph went out, couldn't hear any car sounds, nor were there any tracks of a car having been there.

The next morning at breakfast Robert asked if someone had come the night before. Ralph and Anna slowly agreed. Yes, someone had come. But they couldn't remember anything beyond that for a while. Then Robert remembered the man at the door. Slowly it all came back to them. But they couldn't believe it.

Tresidder Lecture

In 1966 Bill Shurtleff was living in Joan Baez's Struggle Mountain Commune in Los Altos while attending Stanford University. He and Bob McKim, a professor of engineering, started a program named "Esalen at Stanford" to bring people who had led workshops at the Esalen Institute in Big Sur to Stanford. Many of the workshops took place in the homes of participants. Tickets went on sale at the start of each quarter. On a typical weekend there were three workshops. Each ran from Friday evening to Sunday noon. The cost of a workshop was $5.00. Most were limited to thirty attendees.

Bill went to the Haiku Zendo in Los Altos for a weekend of practice with sensory awareness teacher Charlotte Selver, joined by her husband Charles Brooks. Bill met Richard Baker there and heard Suzuki give a lecture. He was so impressed he invited Suzuki to give a talk as part of the Esalen at Stanford program. Richard liked the idea. Suzuki agreed. His talk became part of a weeklong program in February on Zen Buddhism sponsored by the Tresidder Memorial Union Board. Alan Watts also gave a talk that week. A flyer stated that Suzuki's talk would be on "Zen Beyond Consciousness." Over 500 people showed up.

Tim Burkett from the Haiku Zendo drove Suzuki to give the talk and sat next to him. This was before the talk he gave in New York that Peter Schneider arranged. He'd never spoken to a group this large before.

Suzuki squeezed Tim's hand and said, "I'm scared." Once he started speaking though, he looked as comfortable as if he were giving a talk at Sokoji. By the time the program was over, Bill Shurtleff had firmly decided that he wanted to live and practice at Tassajara.

In the spring of '67, Bill visited Tassajara and practiced zazen on a zafu for the first time, a painful experience for him. He determined to get his body used to sitting like that and receive his master's in education before returning. "Suzuki Roshi seemed to me to be a simple, almost ordinary man and his disciples were superb," Bill wrote. "I think that the best way to judge a real teacher is by the kind of disciples he attracts."

Car Talk

Driving Suzuki from Tassajara to the city. We stopped at the Thunderbird Bookstore in Carmel Valley, browsed a bit. I felt obligated to buy something if I went into a store, so I got a copy of *The Prophet* by Kahlil Gibran, which had influenced me when I was in high school. Back then it was the best-known non-Western wisdom book and had been a bestseller for decades. I wondered what I'd think of it this time around.

We dallied in the Thunderbird a while, me drinking two cups of coffee and Suzuki, an impressive three. Back on the road, cruising in silence, I was revved up by the caffeine and felt compelled to express myself. "Suzuki Roshi?" I said, "May I ask you a question?"

He said yes.

And then, using an abundance of verbiage, I earnestly expressed how totally devoted I was to following his teaching. I told him I'd do whatever it was I had to do, went on and on making sure that he was thoroughly aware of my sincerity and dedication. "Just tell me what to do and I'll do it," I said.

I turned to him for an answer. He was sound asleep.

L to R—Phillip Wilson, Shunryu Suzuki, Mitsu Suzuki, unknown, David Chadwick, Richard Baker

The Chicken   MAY 1, 1967

The kitchen was orderly and focused with Ed at the helm. When the kitchen crew arrived, they would gather at a little altar Ed put together. He'd offer incense and everyone would bow to the Buddha statue and then to each other. Ed would give instructions in a quiet voice and people would go about their tasks.

Dogen said to treat vegetables as if they were your own eyes, and Ed had picked up on that spirit. Then one day he came in from a walk-in cooler with a dead featherless chicken, put it on a cutting board, and chopped down on it with a meat cleaver—shocking the other students there doing meal prep. Our first guest dinner was coming up that evening.

"I thought we were vegetarian," came a whimpering voice. Ed kept cutting.

"We are," I said to him. "But the guests aren't. And anyway, we're not pure vegetarian. The student diet here is lacto-ovo vegetarian."

"What's that?"

"We eat dairy and eggs but not meat or fish."

"But cows and chickens will die because of that. We're still making them suffer."

"Buddha wasn't a vegetarian," I said. "He'd eat what was given."

"But Tassajara went out and bought this poor chicken."

"Take it up with Suzuki Roshi."

Ed kept cutting up the chicken.

Exploding Streetlights

I was walking in the pleasant night air below the steps by the big old oak tree once called Gossip Oak. It was our first week with guests. Dinner cleanup was over. It would be a while before zazen. People were walking by chatting on the road above the steps. There was the muffled sound of guests laughing, others playing bocce ball from down in front of the Pine Rooms.

The area was illuminated by the few funky streetlights powered by electricity from one or the other of the old Willys Jeep engines with their clunky rumbling up in the shop. Moths gathered around the light sources. Outside of the main area, Coleman kerosene lanterns had been placed at intervals. Suddenly the engine was revving up higher and higher, the lamps of the streetlights rapidly grew brighter and brighter and then, with blinding light exploded like fireworks one after another.

In the daze I saw Clarke Mason running up to the shop. I heard the accelerating pitch of the whirring engine straining at the bolts holding it tight to its concrete slab until suddenly—silence in the remaining dim natural light of dusk and nearby Coleman lanterns. People were wondering what the heck had just happened. The fan belt had broken. After that, we took out those few streetlights.

Sharing Tassajara

Robert and Anna Beck came in for the first day of guest season. They'd made a point they wanted us to continue with the guest season. Anna said it was in the contract. They didn't feel they were just passing on a piece of property, but a century-old tradition of stewardship over a unique sacred spot, a place of healing and rejuvenating, a place that should be available to the public.

Silas made a good case for continuing the guest season in the early discussions with Richard and Suzuki and the board. We needed the money and the grounding of interacting with the public. The Zen Center had sent out a letter announcing the Tassajara guest season to the Becks' mailing list and a selection from our own. Guest rates of $9.00 – $18.00 a day per person were slightly lower than what the Becks had been charging. The idea was that the cost could be increased once we were confident that we knew what we were doing.

There weren't many guests the first week. There could have been, but we were starting slow on purpose to get a feel for it. The only experience I had working in a restaurant was some substitute shifts busing at the Coffee Cantata on Union Street in San Francisco. But this wasn't like a restaurant. There was no menu. People would sit down, and the food would be on the table in serving dishes. That's how the Becks did it—and that and buffet were how it was always done.

The guest dining room was the former Becks' bar and lounge in the central stone building. Some guests asked where the bar was. Sorry. They'd been told they were welcome to bring their own wine, but we didn't have any booze to serve or sell. We could have had a healthier cash flow if we had. We used the bar counter to keep the beverages and its backside as a way station for the dishes coming in from the kitchen and going out to the dishwashing area. Another student would be assigned to help me. Often Bob Halpern would volunteer to work with me at dinner. And the Becks were there to guide us. Anna pulled me away from talking to Bob and told me not to do that, to keep my eye on the guests.

At first, the guests who had been coming for years were apprehensive about the new owners, wondering how cultish and weird we'd be, but after a couple of days, I could see they were getting comfortable. Students were occupied working and doing those things we did in robes. And we weren't proselytizers. Quite the opposite. Some guests asked why the students were so serious and unfriendly. I'd reply they were busy and tired from getting up so early for zazen.

It all went fairly smoothly even though Bob and I were nuts. We could get like that generator without a fan belt. Running back and forth from the kitchen with food, pouring coffee, tea and water, crouching behind the old bar gobbling from the leftovers on the serving dishes, especially the baked chicken. Downing the remains of the half-and-half, looking sideways to make sure Peter didn't walk out of his office and catch us being naughty.

Ed Brown was under tremendous pressure, and we'd be running circles around that small room often confused about what to do next. Nothing we did fazed him. Unperturbable. Everyone else was figuring out what to do as well. We got the job done, and there were no complaints. I guess we conducted ourselves with enough civility while interacting with guests and probably gave them a sense of relief not to be met with the serene loftiness generally assumed as a by-product of Zen practice.

Nixed Nudity

The baths were open to guests from early morning till 4 p.m., Suzuki's bath time. The student bath time was from 4:45 till 5:45 p.m., when the bell for evening service started. They opened to guests again from 6 p.m.

The hot baths were my first experience of extended casual nudity with both genders. I'd been in hippie communes where there was some nudity, but this was total nudity. Mixed bathing was only on the left, the men's side. The right side remained just for women. Bathing suits were not permitted in the baths, a rule passed down through the decades.

I found it didn't take long for mixed nude bathing to be no big deal. I understood why people go to nudist camps. It's liberating. Not that I was totally without discrimination. I admired some female bodies, especially Kathy Cook's, but I didn't ogle or fantasize.

Then one evening Suzuki said he appreciated how free we were with each other at the baths, but for students the baths were a place of practice second only to the zendo. He said that from then on, males and females would bathe separately. There was a mix of disappointment and acceptance. A few were upset, especially the two couples we'd inherited from the Becks who left soon after that.

I was glad we'd had those few months of mixed bathing. It was educational. I was grateful that Suzuki had allowed us to have that experience. For the guests, the men's side remained officially open for both sexes after 6 p.m. Not every student could get to the baths during student bath time, so there were exceptions. I'd go down in the evening after zazen sometimes. There weren't any police. And for those who missed our mixed nudity—there was always the Narrows downstream with its cascade into a deep pool and room to sunbathe and picnic on smooth granite.

The Legend

Before entering the men's side of the baths, there was a mural on the wall which depicted two American Indians with a story inscribed in the mural, the oldest Tassajara Story we knew of. It read:

> *The Tassajara Hot Springs Legend*
>
> *There once was an Indian chief, who was all powerful. He was the favorite of the Sun God that ruled the universe and from this deity received his powers. So supernatural was he that he could hear the grass grow and see his enemies and game a day's travel away. The chief had a young sister who was very dear to his heart and when she became stricken with a strange malady, the hills and dales were ransacked for herbs by the medicine man for a cure. Everything failing, the brother started her on a trip to the big water, hoping that the ocean would help her. By the time Tassajara Creek was reached the sister had failed so much that she could not go further. All powers of the chief had failed and her life was ebbing slowly. Finally in desperation he prayed to his Sun God, offering his own body as a sacrifice. He fell prone on the ground. Although it was mid-day the sun was soon obscured and the earth became dark. The body of the chief stiffened and he grew ridged and was turned to stone. As he dissolved into a mass of rock, hot tears poured forth. The sister fell prostrate over the sacrifice, and was soon covered with hot tears of her sorrowing brother. When she rose she was completely cured. The news of the miracle spread among the Indian tribes of California, and every year the lame, the halt and the blind wend their weary way to bathe in the hot waters which poured from the rock where the chief had died.*

I asked Robert Beck about the mural and gathered it was done just a couple of years before they bought Tassajara. A waitress named Annemarie Brunken had been painting watercolors of different scenes around Tassajara and the Sappoks, who owned the place then, asked her to do a mural on a wall at the baths. She discovered the legend at the Monterey Public Library. He said I should ask Fred Nason, an Esselen elder about it. He lived on the way to Jamesburg. Tassajara was in Esselen territory.

Old-Timers

Robert Beck and I were walking past the baths. Robert noted the dilapidated second floor above the plunges. "We never used those rooms," he said. "They were too far gone when we got the place."

"They're gonna be gone before long," I said.

They still had some use. I'd happened to catch a glimpse of a couple of students coming out of the door at the end and I don't think they were on official business.

Robert was looking for a site to build a home. Part of the deal with Zen Center was that he and Anna had a lifetime estate at Tassajara. He looked at the area where the creek bends before the baths. He liked that spot but said the water would flow over that area with heavy rains. "We built a little dam down there," he said. "Now there are only the cement pillars on the side. We'd slide 2 x 12s down between them and create a wall. It held enough water during the summer to expand the pool behind it to a good size. We'd take the boards away before the rains came in winter. We could build our place here, fix the dam up, and have a pool in our backyard. But maybe up on Grasshopper Flats at a higher elevation would be smarter."

He stopped at a spot in the Flats. "Bill Parker was the handyman. Tall, strong, serious guy. Quiet. He was here until recently, right?"

I nodded.

"A few years back there were shots coming from this direction. Bill and I walked out to see what was up. There were a couple of guys standing right where we're standing now, one with a bottle of Jack Daniels and the other with a rifle shooting at trees. Bill went up to them and said that they were on private property and that they had to go elsewhere to use the gun. The guy with the rifle pointed it at Bill and said, 'Yeah, and who's gonna stop me?' Bill said, 'I am,' stepped up to him and took the rifle away from him. He said it would be in the office waiting for them when they left."

We went up the Hogback Trail and looked across the valley at the waterfall.

"You can find arrowheads here sometimes," Robert said. "Indians came from all over to drink the water and make sweat lodges. More than just the Esselen. Indians from other tribes. Apparently they all got along. They'd build mud huts over the steam coming up from where the steam rooms are now, cook in there as long as they could stand it, then go into the creek and scrape their skin with the rib of a deer. They'd hunt, and dry meat here and that's what Tassajara means—a place where meat is hung to dry.

The Jesuits rounded up the Indians and made them live in the missions back in the eighteenth century. Not much to show that the Spanish were here back then, but they were. There's some writing at the caves over at Church Creek Ranch. Some say it was inscribed by Junipero Serra who founded the Carmel Mission. Other Europeans started coming a century ago or so. Bear hunters. Trappers. They killed all the grizzly and black bears. Then the word got out and people would walk or ride horses in for the healing waters of the springs. Camp out, fishing, hunting.

"A businessman named Quilty built the road and a big sandstone hotel in the 1890s, a lot with Chinese labor. He kept the cooks for his hotel. After he died, his widow Helen ran the place till World War II when it closed. She married the warden of San Quintin, and they used to say she was the warden of Tassajara. She was a very strict old lady. I'd hear stories about her.

"One story was from Pete Stolich, who was a Slovenian from Watsonville. He used to come here from the time he was a kid. He'd get very-very drunk. One time he had been uproariously drunk for one whole evening. He was in a cabin down by the swimming pool. In the morning he needed to get to the hot baths to soak himself out. He was going up the creek, hiding. Mrs. Quilty used to sit up at the old hotel when the stone hotel was there and she had a little kind of watch tower, like a warden would have. She saw Pete going up the creek. She called to him to come up. She got him into her little office and just gave him hell. Evidently, he'd created a lot of commotion the night before. So she upbraided him, and then she opened the drawer of a cabinet and pulled out a bottle of whiskey and said, 'You need a drink.' The Quiltys owned the place for fifty years.

"A guy named Ralph Myers bought it from Helen Quilty. He died when his private plane crashed. His widow was from the Church family."

"The Churches who own Church Creek Ranch?" I asked.

"Yes. Then she married an actor who'd been one of Joan Crawford's husbands. They were ruined when the big old sandstone hotel burned down in '49. They sold it to the Sappoks, who were hotel people in Watsonville. At Tassajara it was said they gave meals away and sold whiskey and made their money that way. They had a very active bar and Tassajara was known as a place to go to have a roaring drunk.

"A lot of the old-timers from around Watsonville came, mainly because the water here was very much like the water at hot springs in Yugoslavia where many of them were from.

"Frank Sappok died in a jeep accident on the road. It was found turned over.

"Mrs. Sappok sold it to the Hudsons, Admiral and Margaret Hudson. They were an older family from Monterey with money. They owned Point Lobos and eventually sold it at a loss to the State Parks. I hear she's the one who bought Tassajara and did so to preserve it for its historical importance and he wasn't so interested. I heard they didn't sleep here one night. They had it for a year and realized it was a mistake. We got it from them."

"When did you first meet Suzuki Roshi?" I asked.

"I'd met Richard before, but I first met Suzuki Roshi up on the road a year ago. I was there waiting for them to come in—at the first place on the road from which one can almost see Tassajara—where Tassajara is a few thousand feet down and miles away—where you start to come down after you pass the Church Creek Road on your way in. There's a place where you can pull out. That's where he looked from. He looked and he knew that this was the place. There was never any question in his mind, I think. He knew that it was going to happen. I think Richard knew it also. And I guess I knew it was going to happen too. It was a question of how we did it. When we sat there at the temple last December and negotiated, it was all kind of fore-ordained, and it was just a question of filling in the details. That's what we did. It happened."

Monterey Pop JUNE 13, 1967

While we were deep in the mountains and woods learning how to run a guest season and continue our practice, a momentous cultural event was taking place just outside—the Monterey International Pop Festival. It was the first big crowd venue for a number of soon to be famous musicians. Guests came into Tassajara raving about performances by, among others, Jimi Hendrix, Big Brother and the Holding Company with Janice Joplin, The Who, the Mamas and the Papas, Simon & Garfunkel, Otis Redding, the Grateful Dead, Eric Burdon and the Animals.

The day before the festival, Bill Thompson, Jefferson Airplane's manager, arranged for the whole band to go to Tassajara. They all dropped acid, walked around, and played some impromptu music for students. Suzuki was asked to join them for dinner. He did so. No one said a word the whole time including Bob and me who served them.

A few students did get to enjoy some of the festival thanks to the often playful nature of Richard Baker. Driving the Land Cruiser with seven students returning to the city, Richard said, "Let's go to the Monterey Pop Festival." When they arrived, Richard told them he only had two tickets but that when they got up to the gate, "just walk through and get lost in the crowd." Richard stood last, held his tickets high so that the ticket taker could see them. They all walked through as planned. Richard followed. The ticket taker was too busy trying to keep up to notice.

The gatecrashers were mesmerized listening to a good part of the four-hour concert by the Indian sitarist Ravi Shankar. Shankar urged his audiences not to get high before going to his concerts. He said that yoga and meditation were the best ways to cleanse the mind. Richard Baker's contingent guaranteed that there were at least eight people in the audience who were only getting stoned by the ragas.

Poets Visit

Poets galore came down the road to Tassajara. Most had sat at Sokoji or were familiar with the Zen Center or knew Richard from the poetry conference he'd organized for UC Berkeley two years before.

Poet Michael McClure did a couple of readings at Tassajara that summer—one from his *Love Lion Book*. He'd just come out with a book called *Freewheelin Frank* about Frank Reynolds, the secretary of the San Francisco Hells Angels. He said that Reynolds had a serious interest in Zen.

McClure and I went for a walk downstream to the Narrows and on the way, he introduced me to *yerba santa*, the holy herb. He told me the California Indians made a tea out of it if they had a cold or cough. He took a tiny top leaf and gave me one, told me to chew on it and keep it in my mouth. A little later when I took a sip of water from the creek, a delicate sweetness followed.

In 1954, McClure had come to California from Kansas with Dave Haselwood who sat at Sokoji with Suzuki in the early '60s and whose upscale Auerhahn Press published McClure's second book and was first to publish Philip Whalen and other notable Bay Area bards. McClure and Haselwood had teamed up with Sterling Bunnell and early Sokoji sitter, poet Joanne Kyger, for walks in the woods and wilds of the Bay Area.

I recognized poet Richard Brautigan with his handlebar mustache and wide brim hat walking on Tassajara Lane above the courtyard. His novella, *Trout Fishing in America*, had come out that year and circulated through the cabins. A Japanese guest said that Brautigan's work was popular in hip Japanese literary circles.

The biggest deal was when Allen Ginsberg, Lawrence Ferlinghetti, and Daniel Moore came in. They meditated in the zendo and in the evening read their poetry, sang, and chanted mantras with students joining in. Ginsberg played his harmonium with Ferlinghetti and Moore on Chinese horn and Hindu bells. Ginsberg sang the melodic rendition of the Heart Sutra in English he'd taken from a chant card at Sokoji with Suzuki's blessing. It was not English intended to be chanted, just the basic meaning of the sounds.

Daniel Moore had been a serious student of Suzuki's. The year before he'd founded the Floating Lotus Magic Opera Company. Loring had talked about Moore and admired his flamboyance. In his flowing, colorful robe, which smelled of marijuana, he and I took a stroll out to Grasshopper Flats, well illuminated by the moon.

Moore said that back in 1964 on his way to morning zazen at Sokoji, in the rubble of some street work he spotted an interesting piece of asphalt with tarpaper stuck to it that bore what looked like kanji, Japanese characters. After zazen he showed it to Suzuki. "He looked at it for a moment," Moore said. "Then his eyes crinkled. He waved his finger above it, forming the same looping characters in the air. 'Yes. It says: 60!' he said. 'And today is my sixtieth birthday!' 'Then happy birthday to you!'" Moore replied with a sweeping bow.

There had been a party in Oakland for Zen Center folks at a home with a pool. Suzuki was standing with his back to the pool talking with some people and Moore started tripping on "how easy it would be to push him in and what a moment it would be for future annals of Zen. I stood there with these powerful thoughts pounding through me, but made no moves, and after a short time failed to act on them, losing the utter spontaneity, and finally quelled them completely. At that moment I heard Suzuki remark with amusement, 'He was going to throw me into the swimming pool!'"

The Bauls

Two mystic minstrels from West Bengal arrived at Tassajara in traditional attire and serenaded us with Baul music. Their tradition emphasized cosmic love that transcends narrow sectarianism. We didn't understand a word, as it was all in Bengali, but they left a translation of a song—written under the curly Bengal script.

> Everyone asks: "Lalan, what's your religion in this world?"
> Lalan answers: "How does religion look?"

I've never laid eyes on it.
Some wear Hindu malas around their necks,
some Muslim tasbihs, and so people say
they've got different religions.
But do you bear the sign of your religion
when you come or when you go?

The Philosopher and the Gardener

Paul Lee was a close friend of Richard's, a professor of philosophy at UC Santa Cruz who'd studied with theologian Paul Tillich. Lee was cherubic, often smiling. He gave a talk at Tassajara about existential and mystical Christianity and how much the higher spheres of Christianity and Buddhism had in common. Lee had helped Richard organize the first major conference on LSD for UC Berkeley and had been the keynote speaker. He had lent his support to our fundraising in several ways, one being a quote for a fundraising brochure Zen Center sent out to thirty thousand recipients in which he called what we were doing "an important event in the history of religion in America" and urged support for "this oldest of ventures—the establishment of a community for the cultivation of the spirit."

Lee came another time and brought with him a master gardener, a Brit with the distinguished name of Alan Chadwick who made bio-dynamic gardens in the tradition of Rudolph Steiner. He'd also been a Shakespearean actor.

I walked up to Alan Chadwick sunning himself by the pool and said in greeting, "Mr. Chadwick?"

"Yes," he said in a drawn-out deep baritone turning slowly toward me.

"I'd like to introduce myself. My name is David Chadwick."

He brightened and stood up. "Well then certainly sir, we are related!"

Even though Chadwick was fully involved with an ambitious

and already flourishing garden project at UC Santa Cruz, Richard asked him if he might find time to help with the gardens at Tassajara. But he was too busy. Maybe later.

Banana Split

When the fundraising for Tassajara got going, Tim Burkett told Suzuki he didn't see how that would be possible, that his students didn't have enough money and there weren't enough of them to do it. Suzuki told him, "Maybe it's impossible. Maybe it's possible. Let's try it and see."

Tim and his wife Linda signed up for the first practice period. They were living across from Sokoji by then. Suzuki rode with them to Tassajara. Suzuki would be quiet while riding in a car, but he'd talk if someone else initiated it. Tim brought up the sad recent loss of the eminent scholar D.T. Suzuki and Shunryu said, "He'll be at Tassajara too."

"What?!"

Suzuki repeated, "He will be at Tassajara too."

Tim told Suzuki he'd been purifying himself for the practice period for weeks by eating only grains, fruit, and vegetables, and drinking water. Suzuki asked Tim to pull over at the Buzz Inn in Gilroy. He ordered coffee. Tim asked for a glass of water. Suzuki eyed what a customer at another booth was eating and asked what it was. Tim told him it was a banana split. "I want one," Suzuki said. When it arrived, he looked it over for a minute and said, "Just like America—everything mixed together." He took a tiny bite from the whipped cream and each scoop of ice cream—vanilla, chocolate, and strawberry, then pushed it over to Tim saying, "You're American. This is for you." Tim couldn't refuse his teacher's offer—and enjoyed it.

Our New Friend   JUNE 23, 1967

I first saw the new priest when he stepped out of the Land Cruiser, wide-eyed, eager, and in a new element. Bob Halpern and I happened to be at the bottom of the steps and greeted him with enthusiastic gasshos. He said his name was Kobun. Bob asked him what his full name was. Kobun Chino Otogawa. Bob asked if we should call him Otogawa Sensei and he said, "Just call me Kobun. I will be your Zen friend." Before anyone noticed, Bob and I took him off to the Hogback to look at the waterfall. A while later, Silas found us and whisked him off to talk about the upcoming ceremonies.

Bob and I pestered Kobun after zazen till late on his first night, asking him about everything we could think of. He had a yellow robe so we thought he must be completely enlightened. When? Where? What was it like? He told us of sitting alone reading poetry then walking in moonglow in his master's garden—and disappearing into a subtle light.

He had come to be a priest for the Los Altos Haiku Zendo, but we needed him more at Tassajara which hadn't been on the horizon when he was invited. He was close to the age of most of us, twenty-nine. He'd been at Eiheiji for years, longer than most monks. He helped take care of three Suzuki students there, Jean Ross, Grahame Petchey, and Phillip Wilson. Right away he was showing all of us how to do things the Eiheiji way. His English was adequate, though halting.

Kobun's and Suzuki's cabins had tatami mats which don't mix well with tables and chairs. I hardly knew how to use a saw, but with Paul Discoe as an advisor, in my spare time, I quickly made low tables for each of them using a discarded door and scrap redwood for trim.

Kobun was most grateful and offered a sumi painting in return. I expected him to create it on the table, but he did it on the tatami which he protected with newspaper. He'd brought handmade rice paper, sumi ink, and brushes from Japan. He quickly produced one—then another—and kept going till finally he approved of one, a sumi-e as he called it.

A year before I'd been a stoned semi-hippie in the Haight and now I was sitting in a Zen monk's cabin drinking the special green tea he'd brought from Japan as he hypnotized me with a brush.

— CHAPTER THREE —

OPENING

Zenshinji Prep JULY 3, 1967

A prominent sign had gone up outside the entrance gate on two posts with three horizontal slabs reading *Tassajara, Zen Mountain Center, Zenshinji*. Now it was time for the *Tassajara Closed* signs to go up at our gate and at Jamesburg where the dirt road begins. Closed for the practice period. But not closed to those who would attend the opening ceremony to inaugurate this new monastery.

I asked Silas how many were coming and he said he had no idea. I wondered if our closed signs would confuse or discourage any of them from continuing on in.

In a few days, Paul Discoe and crew had transformed what we'd been using as a dining room and office into a zendo. For over a month they'd been preparing the pieces in the shop to be assembled quickly. The night before the opening ceremony, they worked well past the firewatch when all other lights were blown out.

The new zendo had a simple altar on a raised platform that covered the old stone hearth. Now there were four rows of zafus on zabutons on tatamis where there'd been tables and chairs. What had been our zendo up to then, the old Club House with its deck, would be a room for study and meetings, and when guests returned in September, their dining room.

Some new, impressive, and large instruments to accompany the chanting and call us to the zendo had arrived by ship from Japan with Kobun Chino. There was a huge *taiko*, a round wooden drum with the head over two and a half feet wide. Kobun said it was made from a single piece of zelkova wood and that the drumhead was from a special brown cow whose leather stayed tight. It rested on a stand that placed the center of the drum at my eye level. Kobun picked up two batons and struck it. The sound was deep. There was a heavy brass bell he called a *densho* to hang just outside the zendo. There was a large new mokugyo to replace the one we'd been using, which seemed a toy in comparison. The striker for it was larger than a baseball bat with a soft cotton pad on the end. There was a wide brass bowl bell and a smaller one. These were gifts from Shumucho, Soto Zen Headquarters, which were engraved with "for Zenshinji, in the time of Shunryu."

We already had a *han,* han meaning wood. Paul Discoe had made one from a thick piece of oak. It was about a foot and a half high and about two feet wide. One side was for striking with a mallet. On the other, Kobun wrote a poem in elegant calligraphy. There was an arbor across the path from the zendo where the han hung next to the densho bell. Kobun said these instruments would be our orchestra and our clock.

Another Gift

Before the opening ceremony, a Japanese priest in robes arrived on foot over the road carrying a kyosaku, the long stick, with a rounded end to hold and a flat one to strike the shoulders of a sleeping sitter. He presented it to Suzuki. His name was Ejo Takata, a disciple of the great Rinzai master, Mumon Yamada. Takata had founded a zendo in Mexico City in 1961 with the help of psychologist and humanist philosopher Erich Fromm. He spent much of his time with peasants in Oaxaca, cultivating soybean crops and showing people how to use soybeans to make soy milk, tofu, and other products for their protein-deficient diet, and to help them become more self-sufficient. I'd heard about Takata from people who'd practiced with him in Mexico City. I wished I'd known about him when I lived there in 1965. When I heard he was at Tassajara, I looked for him, only to learn he'd already walked back out. Darn. Missed him again. I heard his own kyosaku down in Mexico bore the kanji for "Learn for yourself—I cannot teach you anything."

Planting a Seedling

The new zendo was crowded for the opening ceremony. Students sat close together and filled the aisles. A multitude of guests sat on chairs in back. We took our seats amidst the dramatic booms from the taiko, the cracks of the mallet on the wooden han, and mellow gongs from the densho. There were more priests than I'd seen at one time before.

During the ceremony, Suzuki and the Bishop installed a ten inch tall polished golden bronze Buddha statue on the altar. Kobun was on the brass bowl bells on the right side of the altar platform. Maezumi was there, as was another Soto priest from L.A. who'd also been in America since the mid-'50s, Kazemitsu Kato. Kato had been a great help in Suzuki's first years at Sokoji. He was amazed witnessing "this blooming of Suzuki's quiet, patient efforts over the past eight years." Three early Suzuki students ordained as priests were there—matronly Jean Ross, serious Claude Dalenberg, and burly Phillip Wilson who would attend the practice period.

And there was a new priest, Richard Baker, ordained in a ceremony the night before and given the name Zentatsu Myoyu, head shaved, not yet settled in his robes, junior to the other priests ordained by Suzuki, but bumped up to the head of the line by Suzuki as Tassajara's first *shuso*, head monk. Kobun said being head monk was like the second ordination and that usually there would be years of practice between the two. He said the shuso has no other role than being the head monk and found it quite unusual that Richard would continue to be Tassajara's director and president of Zen Center.

During Richard's ordination ceremony, Suzuki said, "I am

so grateful to Richard Baker for all he has done to help establish Buddhism in the West."

When I heard that, I remembered something Mitsu, Suzuki's wife, had told me. She said her husband ignored her, so one day she asked him what he was thinking about all the time. He answered, "How to establish Buddhism in the West."

No Big Deal

After the opening ceremony, there was the mingling of many, some who had not seen each other in years. Members of the Sokoji Japanese congregation greeted Kato. I paid my respects to the Bishop, who asked when I was coming down to L.A. next. Ed Brown and crew somehow fed everyone. A bunch of us helped to get the food out on tables. Ed was in his element. He excelled when under pressure.

Throughout the crowd there was the realization that miraculously, in such a short time, Zen Center now had its retreat center for real, and a traditional Buddhist practice period was about to begin.

"We just opened the first Buddhist monastery in the Western world," a student remarked.

"Nope," came from Claude Dalenberg. "There's a Tibetan monastic center in New Jersey that was founded in the late '50s. They're open to lay people too. They've been practicing there since then without all this hoopla."

"OK—the first Zen monastery."

"Japanese Rinzai monks lived together and farmed in Hayward in the East Bay sixty years ago," Claude said. He was no newcomer, had been into Zen since he first heard Alan Watts lecture in Chicago in 1949. He'd followed Watts to the Bay Area and was involved with Sokoji before Suzuki arrived.

When we were getting the place ready for the ceremony, we were sweeping and cleaning everything as spotlessly as we could. There was dusting, wiping, raking, and straightening. I said to Claude that more hours went into cleaning at Sokoji and here at Tassajara than I've ever experienced.

"There's a better way," he said.

"What's that?"

"The Chinese way."

"What's that?"

"Dirt."

Richard and Shunryu

"Well," Robert Beck said, "Baker actually pulled it off."

"With a lot of help," I said, "like from you and Anna, and Silas and all of us. But it's true, Baker was the general, and the rest of us were mere soldiers in his army."

"And where does Suzuki Roshi fit in?" Robert asked.

"He's the inspiration."

Richard had been in such a torrent of activity. But since the March payment was made, there was momentum and commitments from donors and the wide community that took much of the pressure off. Besides meeting the payments, there were enormous expenses in getting everything ready to open and just the day-to-day costs. Silas had a hard job estimating how much money we needed to keep Tassajara functioning and what to budget for various tasks. A fundraising mailer had pointed out that students working without pay had already saved an estimated $50,000 in labor costs. Another way that students not on scholarship helped out was to pay a tuition of between a dollar and two dollars a day depending on how long they were there for.

Richard and Suzuki had been to the East Coast twice early in the year, and the results were significant. It wasn't just Suzuki's quiet magic, as many assumed. Richard's dynamism and way with words conveyed an assurance that there was an organization behind Suzuki that could take care of the material end.

Richard said Suzuki was content to be, whatever was happening wherever they went. Suzuki's role was to just be himself. Richard said when he told Suzuki they should sit in the back section of the plane because those were the safest seats, Suzuki said, "Then we should leave those seats for others." At a hotel in New York City, Richard woke up in the middle of the night to find Suzuki sitting in the empty tub reading. When Richard asked him why he was reading there instead of in bed with good lamplight, Suzuki said, "I was worried the light would disturb your sleep." Richard said Suzuki left hotel rooms like a spy would, with no trace that he had been there.

Tangaryo Daze

A few who'd been at Tassajara for weeks or months left. There were too many rules for some. Others, including some who came for the practice period, found the thought of *tangaryo* too daunting. Tangaryo was the initiatory three days of sitting with no walking meditation and brief breaks only after meals. Suzuki had wanted five days of tangaryo, but Richard told him that was too much too soon, so Suzuki agreed on three.

There was a scene with a woman who wanted to stay as an artist in residence without having to follow any schedule. She was insistent but so was Richard. She held out in bushes by the railroad bell at night with a candle and a long kitchen knife. I worried she was going to hurt someone. She did—herself. Gouged her hand with the knife. After her hand was bandaged, Richard carried her to a car kicking and screaming, to be driven out.

One student left because of something I'd said. He was walking slowly in a Chinese robe on the road above the courtyard looking so miserable and I urged him to come on to the zendo. There was just a minute left to get there on time. "Suzuki Roshi gave me permission not to go," he said. I told him he should go sit anyway. That pained him so much he left. I didn't know till later that he was Ed Brown's big brother who'd been around Zen Center since 1964.

The night before the tangaryo, Richard spoke to the seventy students about to sit all day for three days. He said the term tangaryo meant "waiting room." We should not approach it as a sesshin but as a challenge to remain in our one spot on the tatami in the zendo all day long. We could move, we could sleep, but we should remain in those few square feet for three days from four in the morning to nine at night except for brief breaks after meals, during which he advised us to use the toilet. He turned to Suzuki who said, "Be prepared to sit."

Tangaryo was a novel experience for the group. Sitting that long with legs crossed was painful to varying degrees no matter how many positions one used. One person interpreted the stay in that spot rule by standing up for a while. Mostly we sat quietly but not in silence, for birds chirped and the creek flowed through our ears. The calm was punctuated by those changing position, coughing, sneezing, groaning, laughing, crying, and now and then someone walking out and the sound of their car driving past the gate.

Richard was in the zendo most of the time, but was out some, likely involved with planning details that weren't on the minds of those of us trying not to squirm. Suzuki and Maezumi would make extended appearances in the zendo with us. Kobun was there almost all the time. He'd fall asleep but, other than nodding, hardly ever moved.

After it was over, Maezumi told me that Suzuki had asked Kobun and him to be there to encourage the students. He said that's not the way it's ever been done. A teacher might go in and hit the initiates with their nyoi to encourage them and walk out. Senior monks would come in to yell how lazy and worthless they were but not sit with them. It's their trial. He added three days was an awfully short time, that at Eiheiji it was a week.

Dan Welch said at Ryutakuji, the Rinzai temple where he had been, one had to sit three days on the temple steps before being accepted for the tangaryo, and during those three days they were expected to keep their hands in gassho on the side of the head with the head tilted down on the shoulder, a painful ordeal. But tangaryo in a Japanese temple was for serious long-term commitment. Those doing tangaryo at Tassajara were required to commit to nothing more than the one or two months they'd signed up for. It was decided that after this experimental summer, tangaryo would be five days.

At about 4 p.m. on the third day, we learned it was over and there would be an entering ceremony for the fifty-five of us who remained. In that ceremony we all stood up in front of our cushions and, after some chanting and bells, walked in gassho in a snaking line around the two aisles of the zendo, stopping to do a standing bow before Suzuki.

Then, Suzuki, Maezumi, and Richard each had something to say. Suzuki went first, then Maezumi. Once we were out of the zendo, I could tell something was amiss. Richard was furious with Maezumi and demanded that Maezumi publicly apologize. When we returned for zazen, Maezumi did apologize. I didn't know what he was apologizing for. Mainly I noticed the bad vibes.

The next day, Mickey Stunkard explained what had happened. He'd been sitting closer than I had—and paying better attention. He said, "Suzuki was lecturing and Maezumi nudged him with his elbow. Suzuki looked over, and Maezumi pointed to his watch and frowned. Given Japanese culture, a monk talking to a Roshi like that, that's terrible. Suzuki gasshoed. 'Oh,' he said, 'I see, I've been talking too long. Thank you, Maezumi Sensei, I'll stop now.' Incredible that kind of egolessness, or whatever it was. He thanked Maezumi for what I thought was being terribly rude."

Stunkard was speaking of Maezumi being rude in Japanese terms, a subject he was qualified to comment on. He had lived in Japan and studied Zen and done sesshin with Soen Nakagawa, Hakuun Yasutani, and on the East Coast with a teacher I'd not heard of before, Isshu Miura. A medical doctor and psychiatrist, Stunkard went to Japan after the war to be a doctor for Japanese prisoners and war criminals in U.S. custody. Judging by Stunkard's interest in Japanese culture and Buddhism, one of the war criminals suggested he meet the Buddhist scholar D.T. Suzuki, who lived in Kamakura, not far from Tokyo. Stunkard then became D.T.

Suzuki's doctor and student, a relationship that had continued until D.T. Suzuki died.

When Stunkard had his first dokusan with Shunryu Suzuki, he burst out crying, "You're just like Daisetsu Suzuki!" Suzuki responded, "Big Suzuki," and pointing to himself, "Little Suzuki."

Shunryu Suzuki introduced Stunkard to us as a teacher and asked him to give a lecture. Stunkard feared the students wouldn't like it. But his twenty-two years of Buddhist study and practice came through. Afterwards, he returned to the comfort of just being a student among students and cleaning pots and pans.

The Schedule

The entering ceremony and tangaryo behind us, we slept soundly and woke at the ringing handbell, knowing there was no time for celebration. We quickly learned what practice meant: following the schedule. The schedule was the practice. Wake-up bell at 3:30 then just keeping up with all the zazen, kinhin, services, lectures, meals. Suzuki told us how to do it—without hesitation. "When the bell rings, get up" was like a mantra. He told us how he'd had a hard time getting up as a young monk until he learned to get up right away without thinking when he heard the bell. That same attitude had to be applied all day long.

The long-term plan for practice periods was to have two per year, one in the fall and one in the winter/spring. But there was an eagerness to get going with the first one in the summer to meet the enthusiasm of the moment and as a trial run to see what worked and what didn't. Traditionally, practice periods were for ninety days and just for monks. There would be few monks, and it would last less than sixty days. Participants had the option to attend the first or the second month. Most had come for both July and August.

There were parts of the schedule that weren't followed on zafus: kinhin, breaks after meals, lunch outdoors at picnic tables, morning and afternoon work periods, and bath time. We did it all and did it again and again because we supported each other. Hard to fall over when you're with others side by side.

After breakfast, there was a half-hour break and then we returned to the zendo for a study period, a study period seated on our zafus. Each of us got a flimsy copy of a book Suzuki would lecture on. He did so in the afternoon in a hot zendo. He had an authentic hard cover copy. After some introductory words, he turned to the book and read the title. "*Buddhist Wisdom Books: The Diamond Sutra and The Heart Sutra*. George Allen and Unwin Ltd." For Ltd., he just read the letters. Then he opened the book, and he read the name again and the author, Edward Conze, from the title page. He continued to the copyright page and read the name of the publisher and its address, and the date published and the ISBN number and whatever words and numbers were there. He continued thus until he got to the text. Suzuki read from the text for a while and then started commenting on it. After that, it was mainly him riffing on the Diamond Sutra. I hadn't seen Suzuki read during a lecture before.

Taking Care

In the few hours of work, Tassajara was going through a makeover. Hot and cold spring reservoir roofs and cabins were being shingled, cabins were being painted white, gray, and green. There was digging for a septic tank, stonework, gardening, kitchen work, dishwashing. Paul and Ruthie put me on planting a walnut tree down by the pool. I'd never planted anything before. They gave excellent guidance.

The students were going through a makeover as well. We were learning new ways to interact. Suzuki said that bowing was second only to zazen. Now we were to gassho in passing. This made getting from one place to another a practice in itself. Suzuki and Kobun seemed to flow through these interactions gracefully. Most of us did so awkwardly. Some students would do a quick gassho when they met you while hardly slowing down. Others would come to a full stop, carefully place their palms together, elbows extended, and do a slow, deep bow, then pause before continuing on. If I was headed to the baths toward the end of our bath time, and there was a whole line of people coming from the baths, I'd consider going up the creek or climbing along the hillside to avoid the path and the inevitable stop and go traffic.

Suzuki made a fist and placed it between his ankles to show how far apart the feet should be in kinhin. He taught us to stand equidistant between the person in front and behind. That way the gaps would even out. To maintain that sameness throughout kinhin, students would have to be walking at the same speed. But we weren't yet of one mind. There would be sincere practitioners who would walk slower than everyone else, thus creating a pile-up behind them and a long gap in the rear.

We were also learning how to be more mindful with the physical world, with objects. To Suzuki, there was no dividing line between objects and people. Everything was to be treated with care—the tools in the shop and the objects on the altars. Things should be carried with two hands. Thus, rather than bring two teapots at a time from the kitchen to the serving table in the back of the zendo, bring one with two hands. The wicks of the kerosene lamps had to be trimmed frequently, shaped in a gradual arc, set not too high or too low for the flame to burn cleanly and not smudge the glass chimney. To remove a hot chimney, one picked it up with two fingers from the cooler bottom—and even if it's not hot—from the bottom so that one's skin oil doesn't smudge the glass.

Back in the spring when there were fewer of us, after giving a brief talk, Suzuki asked if there were any questions. Bob Halpern pointed out how students were talking during work and at the baths and asked if we shouldn't have more rules as in Japanese monasteries. Suzuki said, "Rules, yes, we should have more rules." He pointed to a broom standing on its bristles and said that would bend the broom out of shape. To take proper care of the broom, it should stand on its handle. He concluded with, "There—that's a good rule."

Tea bowls are used in tea ceremony. Suzuki said if we didn't know the culture and history of a tea bowl, then we wouldn't know how to treat it properly, wouldn't understand it. It would just be a bowl. He said the same applies to people. We can't help them unless we know who they are.

Bob Halpern and I were visiting Kobun in his room. Bob brought up what Suzuki had said about knowing things more deeply. Oryoki was a wrapped set of nested bowls with utensils that were used for meals in the zendo. Bob asked Kobun if he knew what the large bowl from his oryoki was made of. "Mahogany wood," Kobun answered. "The lacquer is from Wajima on the Noto Peninsula."

"The bowls we use for student oryoki," I said, "were bought in a secondhand store in San Francisco. They were Navy surplus. So, to understand those bowls, I must study the history of the U.S. Navy. Right?" Kobun didn't get it. He made tea for us.

Ango Samu

Some called it a training period, and some called it practice period. There was resistance to the word training as sounding like military school. But others said that practice sounded like something we were doing to prepare for really doing it. Suzuki used both words, but practice seemed to be the official one. Bob asked Kobun if we should call it practice period or training period. Kobun said, "Call it *ango*." That's what they call it in Japan. We liked ango. It was devoid of the baggage of meaning for us. We tried to infuse that word into the local vocabulary along with the word *samu*, work practice, but our attempts fell flat, and we were accused of putting on airs.

Phillip Wilson did stonework with Suzuki during work period. Others did stone and garden work with Suzuki, but no one but Bob Halpern was craftily positioning themselves to maximize their chances. Bob would make sure to give Suzuki the idea that he was available when Suzuki stepped out of his cabin to work in his garden. The head of whatever crew he'd been assigned to wouldn't intervene if Bob told him he was "working with Roshi this morning."

Bob said Suzuki had a special relationship with stones, that he would move one, barely touching it with his hands, that the stones seemed to move however Suzuki wanted them to.

L to R—Bob Halpern, Shunryu Suzuki, Phillip Wilson

Forest rangers brought us a dozen fire extinguishers and fire-fighting tools, gifts from the U.S. Forest Service. There was now a row of these long-handled tools hanging in a special area—four each of pointed shovels, huge hoes with a hefty rake called a McLeod, and Pulaskis with a vertical axe backed by a curved horizontal chopper.

Putsy was a friendly ranger who worked the trails. He'd come in over the Tony Trail as much as down the road. At a work meeting with most of us present, Putsy showed us the principal use of these tools which was for creating fire breaks. For instance, the axe on the Pulaski can be used to cut away small trees and the wide side, which he called the adze, was for getting at roots and brush and digging to create a barrier. Next, we'd need hookups for fire hoses, but for the time being regular garden hoses could reach all the buildings.

We were to get rid of combustible materials within thirty feet of structures, though the rangers ignored ornamental plants that were watered.

Suzuki came to the shop to check things out. All our new firefighting tools had been used for other day to day work. That was okay as long as they were returned to the proper place. There were other long-handled tools in that area—axes, sledgehammers, pickaxes, rakes, hoes, flat blade shovels. Suzuki looked at the line of implements, sighed, and said, "At Eiheiji all the tools would be polished and neatly arranged." Hmm, I thought, it is all a little messy and they could be cleaner. But I knew we'd never be or try to be anywhere near up to Eiheiji standards. Sorry Roshi.

One day Silas brought in a whole truckload of new workers—ten hives of what he called Italian honeybees. I walked out to Grasshopper Flats the day they arrived. They were not hospitable. I didn't get stung, but they sure chased me away. Later I saw Silas working with them with his shirt off. I still didn't get close. After a while, the bees and I got used to each other. I needed to because at times I was working nearby. I made a couple of signs to alert others as the hives were near the trail up the Hogback. They read, *Do not disturb—100,000 working bees and possibly one curious rattlesnake.*

Oh yes—there was a rattlesnake hanging out at the base of a hive one morning. Sterling Bunnell happened to have just brought a king snake in from his Sonoma property and let it go by the bee hives. Sterling said king snakes are immune to rattlesnake venom and like to squeeze them to death and eat them.

Hard Practice

Tim Burkett threw himself into the practice at Tassajara. He was serious and intense. He didn't like all the Japanese influence on the forms though. He especially hated the complex oryoki eating ritual and chanting, which dragged the meal out to an hour with little time for the actual eating. But he went along with it because it was important to Suzuki that we eat that way. His wife Linda though excelled at oryoki and saw it as an art related to tea ceremony. She did it gracefully and was asked to help people struggling with it and teach it to newcomers.

We recited the meal chant in English at breakfast, the sole nod to our native tongue. At one point, when the bowls were unwrapped and ready to receive the food, we chanted, "Seventy-two labors brought us this food. We should know how it comes to us. Receiving this offering, we should consider whether our virtue and practice deserve it." The chant continues, but one day Tim stopped at that point and considered whether his virtue and practice deserved it. He rewrapped his bowls and practiced zazen for the rest of the meal.

I wondered how he was going to follow that up and visualized him gradually turning skeletal like statues of Buddha before he gave up asceticism. But that didn't happen. Tim must have figured out a less literal way to interpret the chant by the next meal.

Suzuki the Alchemist

"Did you see the kyosaku Ejo Takata gave Roshi?" I asked Bob.

"He didn't bring a kyosaku," Bob answered.

"Ejo Takata," I said, "the Zen priest who has a group in Mexico City. I heard he walked in before the opening ceremony, presented Roshi with a kyosaku and walked out."

"He didn't bring a kyosaku," Bob repeated.

"Kyosaku - the long stick to hit sleeping sitters on the shoulder," I said emphatically.

"I know what a kyosaku is," Bob, said.

"Ohhhh," I said, " I get it. He brought a nyoi, the short teacher's stick. That makes more sense."

"Nope,"

"Well, why did I hear he gave a kyosaku to Suzuki Roshi then?"

"Whoever said that," Bob said, "Doesn't know what really happened, doesn't know that Suzuki Roshi performed an act of alchemy."

"He turned lead into gold?"

"That's only one type of alchemy."

"What type of alchemy was this?" I asked.

"You see," Bob said, "Takata Sensei is a Rinzai priest. The stick that we Soto Zennists call a kyosaku, they call a keisaku. So Takata Sensei brought a keisaku and when he handed the keisaku to Suzuki Roshi, once in Suzuki's hands, it transmuted into a kyosaku."

"Now I get it," I said. "That is so amazing. From now on I'll think of him as *Suzuki the Alchemist*. And he's teaching *us* how to be alchemists. Really. He transformed himself and now he's trying to help us to transform ourselves from…hmm… from lead into gold."

Peanut Allergy

At dinner we were often served leftovers mixed in a gruel, a tradition we'd started back in the winter. The early experimental days had produced some questionable combinations—such as throwing leftover salad and salad dressing into the mix. The character of the gruels had become less controversial under Ed's more disciplined culinary reign. There were still some though, mainly of the female persuasion, who found the gruels to be unpalatable.

There was a student who was highly allergic to peanuts. Eating even a small amount of a dish with peanuts or peanut butter could send him into anaphylaxis, which would make it difficult or impossible for him to breathe. Everyone knew it and everyone needed to because we all had to make sure he didn't get the slightest smidgen of peanuts. I'd be in the kitchen and hear, "Are there any peanuts in this?" If there were, they'd serve him the same dish without peanuts or something else. It would only take one slipup to lead to an emergency.

One day when there was gruel for dinner. I took the first bite and instantly a subtle and almost hidden taste in it set off an interior alarm. Immediately I stood up and pointed to the peanut allergic fellow seated on the opposing side of the room facing me. He caught the signal and spat his first bite into his hand.

First Sesshin

There was a five-day sesshin for those who only came for the first month. Maezumi assisted Suzuki in leading it and remained there sitting with the others almost the entire time. It was held in the room where the zendo had been before, the old Club House. Suzuki was seeing people for dokusan during this sesshin. When it was over, Suzuki had a board inscribed with *First Tassajara Sesshin* and had all those who'd attended sign it.

Mickey Stunkard was one of those who attended that first Tassajara sesshin. When he went to say goodbye to Suzuki, Suzuki said he had to go to the city, too, so Stunkard drove him. For someone with the Zen and professional credentials Mickey had—he was head of the department of psychiatry at the University of Pennsylvania—I found it touching how excited he was to be driving Suzuki to the city. He said it seemed like such an honor.

I told Mickey that Richard had once suggested to Suzuki that he learn to drive and get a driver's license so he didn't have to depend on others. Suzuki told Richard, "I never want to be alone."

"But you know," I added, "he loves to be alone."

Axes and Saws

I had what was for me the most enjoyable job much of that practice period—cutting firewood for the winter. There was a mountain of wood scrap out at Grasshopper Flats from the demolition that had happened so far—one-by-twos, fours and sixes, two-bys, bigger than two-bys. The stuff that looked reusable we'd stack with the used lumber.

Bob Watkins, the work leader, put me out there with Nelda Foeste to cut the scrap into firewood. We had axes, saws, and stumps. She did not want to use an axe. So she picked up the boards, held them down on a stump, and I swung the axe. We got into a pleasant rhythm. There were tree branches too.

I'd tackle them first with a hatchet. Nelda would deal with the droppings. For the bigger stuff we had Swedish saws and for the biggest, a jumbo one-handled timber saw and what was called a two-man timber saw—even with a female on the other end. The timber saws came with the place. We learned how to keep them sharp and made a big dent in that mountain. With the bees and the trees—whacking away. I loved Zen.

A Scolding

Richard gave a brief impromptu talk in which he scolded us all for not taking the practice seriously enough. I thought that nervy of him because he didn't act like what we thought of as a serious student. He wasn't following the schedule like we were, was in his cabin, on the phone in the office, and off to the city for a meeting. He would strike up a conversation if he joined in on the *silent* work. Tim Aston, who'd been around longer than I had, said Richard wasn't in the zendo at Sokoji that much. "Just ask any of the older students who they remember coming every day," he said. "To me Silas and Dan are examples of good practice. Richard is just incapable of practicing." I realized Suzuki must have different criteria as to what practice and understanding were all about.

I asked Silas what he thought about what Tim said. "Richard was there," he said, "maybe not as much as some, but he was there. And as for his understanding, my perception of Richard and Roshi's call on him is that Richard's attainment is at a higher level than anyone else."

Higher attainment or not, Richard's blanket dissing seemed like such an insult to the other older students like Silas. But if Suzuki didn't chastise him, I sure wasn't going to. Richard had been carrying the massive responsibility of securing Tassajara and keeping it running. Fundraising and all sorts of decision making couldn't be put on hold. Richard said he had to sacrifice his practice to do what he'd had to do. Anyway, he said he'd already done the work with Suzuki.

It seemed to me that Richard was in another league from the

other older students. The front seat on the right side, the men's side of the zendo at Sokoji was Richard's. One day at Sokoji we were all sitting quietly as Suzuki entered the zendo. Before taking his seat, he walked over to a new sitter who was perched on the right front zafu and told him softly that was Richard Baker's seat and please sit somewhere else. That was the only seat I saw him treat as special to that extent. It was Richard's whether or not he was there.

Richard mildly berated me one day for spending too much time with some hikers who were passing through Tassajara on their way to the coast. I told him that sometimes he was like an uptight high school principal. He just smiled. Insults seemed to bounce off him—unless they were physically painful.

We had lunch outdoors. I was going around pouring hot tea into people's cups, when some of it splashed onto his hand. "I'm so sorry!" I exclaimed. He calmly said I seemed to have some hostility toward him. "No more than average," I replied. Laughter at the table. He sighed.

The inescapable fact of the matter was that Suzuki had crowned Richard the shuso of the practice period—and he didn't make Richard take a break from his other duties. Anyway, to me, it didn't matter how Richard expressed that role. Mine was clear—follow the schedule, do my duty, practice with Suzuki and with my fellow students. It was the greatest thing I'd ever been involved with—beyond anything I'd hoped for. Richard had made all that possible and was busting his posterior to continue to make it possible. The rest of us had the luxury of following the schedule and taking pot shots at him.

After Richard's comments in the zendo, Suzuki sat silently for a while and then in a soft voice said, "Don't forget why you came here."

Village Voice

Jack Goddard was a West Coast stringer for the *Village Voice*. He lived in Big Sur and in April had hiked in to do a story on what was going on at Tassajara. He met Peter Schneider. They soon discovered they had mutual friends who worked with that esteemed rag, especially the guy who'd taken Jack's place when he left New York, the guy who helped Peter publicize Suzuki's talk that led to Peter coming to Tassajara.

In mid-July, Ginny Baker brought in a few copies of the *Village Voice* with Goddard's article. In it, he first described people working. He was fascinated with how much work was going on in the creek—to divert it in spots, shore up walls, get gravel for cement.

Goddard noted women were in the kitchen. Maybe he passed through when there happened not to be any men. And he wrote that what we did in the zendo was "hard work of another kind."

He called Dan "Farmer Dan" commenting that he and Louise seemed to be walking right off the remotest of west Kansas farms in their rural roughness, Dan with shoulder-length hair in faded overalls and Louise in a long plain dress. They, like a lot of us, had evolved in terms of style since arriving.

The article concluded by stating "the start this spring has been auspicious" and with a quote from an unnamed older student who said, "Tassajara has all the right vibrations. Zen belongs here."

Liz Wolf

Paul Lee arranged for Suzuki to go to UC Santa Cruz to give a talk in May 1967. After the talk, he took questions. A student asked if he'd meditate with them. This was something he'd suggest when speaking to neophytes, but she beat him to it. He was pleased to do so.

Afterwards Richard went up to her and introduced himself. Her name was Liz Wolf. Richard complimented her on her suggestion. Did she have any prior experience? She said she'd read *The Three Pillars of Zen* and practiced zazen in Pasadena at the home of a woman named Martha Rose Bode. She'd spent three weeks in a Vedanta ashram, which didn't give her the grounding she felt she needed. She'd never met a real live Zen master before, and now, after feeling the peacefulness of meditating with him, she felt encouraged, drawn to him. Richard invited her to come to Tassajara. She arrived in June.

Tassajara was way harder than she expected. She'd thought it would be "people going outside to sit and mediate as the sun went down and things like that." Nope. It was rising while it was still dark, and the ordeal of tangaryo. Liz was in her late teens, short, weighed only 100 pounds. She liked working in the kitchen, but when they served the meals in the zendo, the pots of gruel or soup were so heavy she hurt her back, which then was painful in zazen. She fought depression and had trouble getting to sleep. But she stuck with it.

Liz was straightforward. She didn't talk about Zen or have a lot of ideas about enlightenment. She just tried to follow the schedule, get to the zendo, do the work. But she felt inadequate to the task. Before her fellow students, she told Suzuki she just couldn't do the practice. From his seat he said, "Just pick one thing to concentrate on and that will be enough. That will work." That left a powerful impression on Liz and her spirits were lifted.

Bulgarian Salt Loaf

Mike Daft was head cook for the day. He'd come in before morning zazen to get started with the bread for lunch, enough for eight loaves, whole wheat with twenty-five percent brown rice flour. I was working in the kitchen that day and was getting the serving implements ready to go out to the table at the back of the zendo. Mike cut some steaming slices straight out of the Wolf oven. It's so good that way. But as soon as it was in our mouths, it was out. Yuck! What's that? Salt! It's way too salty!

Oh—he realized he'd put in cups of salt instead of tablespoons.

The zazen period at eleven was just ending. The brief noon service would start in a minute. It was time to serve up and hit the *umpan*, a metal plate hanging outside the zendo, and bring the serving pots and baskets out to the back table as students sat on their zafus in the zendo to chant and receive lunch. Mike wondered if he should announce that lunch would be served without that course. But there were three bowls to fill. They were always filled. We searched for leftover bread. Just a few slices. Leftover rice. Nope—it went into last night's gruel. It seemed the bread in hand had to be served.

I made a suggestion. Mike thought about it, then nodded. In the zendo's silence, before the servers walked down the aisles, Mike bravely announced, "Today's lunch features Bulgarian Salt Loaf." Extra margarine and muso were served as condiments. The baskets came back with more uneaten slices than usual, but there were no complaints. Bulgarian Salt Loaf was, however, never served again.

Four and Nine

On days whose date had a four or nine in them, we'd have a relaxed schedule. Kobun called those days *shikunichi*. *Shi* is four, ku is *nine*, and *nichi* is day. We also called them four-and-nine days or days off.

They used to follow that practice at Sokoji. I heard people would forget or, in the case of new students, not know, show up for zazen, find the door locked, knock on it, and Suzuki would stick his head out of a window and tell them it's a day with a four or nine in it. Actually, I just assume that's what he usually did. All I heard about were times he'd just call down to them to go away without telling them why, leading to students walking off and wondering what was up.

For us at Tassajara, they weren't quite days off. Kobun explained to us that they were days to do laundry, clean one's room, and take care of any other personal matters. Shikunichi should not be considered a break in the practice, which is to continue in all activity.

On shikunichi there was only one morning zazen, so we woke up later, the service was shorter, and after breakfast in the zendo we were free all day till evening service. There was a sit-down lunch, or we could make bag lunches. Dinner was in the dining room, a special treat, and there was one zazen instead of two in the evening.

We weren't free to drive out without permission like for a doctor's appointment, but we could take hikes.

We could also go to the baths any time before evening service. The men's side of the baths would be crowded in the shikunichi morning with guys shaving their heads. There were two long sunken tubs we'd fill with hot spring water and sit in—two to a tub. Some shaved their own heads. Others teamed up and shaved each other. We had small aluminum buckets we'd clean the razors with then dump the soapy, hairy water into the creek where it would quickly disappear. If a student expressed concern for the health of the creek and the critters that reside there, I'd point out we used Dr. Bronner's organic Castile Liquid Soap for our bodies and Basic H organic soap for cleaning the place. The one soap at the baths that I assumed was not good news for the creek was the Fels Naptha, a laundry soap that came in a bar and was kept in containers marked *For poison oak only*. Fels Naptha aggressively cut the nasty oil poison oak would leave on skin.

Since we got up an hour later, Bob Halpern and I stayed up later the night before. We used this extra time in different ways—a visit to the kitchen or the baths or to the kitchen and the baths. One female student took advantage of this time to plan a trip over the mountain. She told a male student she'd become friends with that she had to go to Monterey overnight for some tests. She offered him the use of her cabin which she had all to herself due to the premature departure of her cabin mate. He took her up on it and hadn't fallen asleep yet when she came in, said that she'd decided to go to town on another day, disrobed, and joined him under the covers.

Kobun to the Narrows

On the first four-and-nine-day, Bob and I invited Kobun to come with us on the trail downstream to the Narrows. He said he'd come when his room was dusted and swept. We made bag lunches including one for him. He met us wearing the most uncomfortable and impractical looking footwear I'd ever seen. He called them *geta*.

They were a type of sandal made of a flat piece of wood elevated by two pieces of wood running horizontally on the bottom—like mini-stilts. Bob and I wore zoris which are also Japanese but obviously much more comfortable. Kobun had zoris too and after some insisting by us, he wore them instead.

It was going to be a hot summer day. Bob and I were in shorts and t-shirts. Kobun wore a black monastic work outfit he called *samue*. Samu was monastic work and "e" meant clothes. His samue were baggy pants with a drawstring to tighten them at the waist and elastic to hold the bottom of the pants to the calf just above the ankle. The top piece to this outfit was fairly baggy too with elastic at the wrists. It looked hot to me but that's as informal as he could get.

Kobun asked if there were any poisonous snakes. I told him, yes, there were rattlesnakes, but they're not aggressive. Just don't surprise them—watch where you're walking and don't put your hands somewhere you can't see. Doctors said bees were the greatest danger. We kept epinephrine in the office in case someone had an allergic reaction to a bee sting. Poison oak, however, was public enemy number one. It was all over. Don't touch it. Kobun said there was a plant in Japan like that, *urushi*, from which the finest lacquer was made.

We stopped at a place after the third creek crossing to take a tiny top bud of yerba santa and savor the sweetness released with a small sip of creek water. The rule with creek water was to drink from it after a stretch where it was running fast, a natural purifier. Kobun showed surprise at finding a tubular green grass he said they had in Japan. It had rough vertical ribs running down its shaft. He said it could be used like sandpaper. We pointed out a century plant with its rare bloom rising into the sky and together we climbed up to it and ate some of the crunchy flower buds. Kobun was so fascinated with everything he saw that Bob and I kept our mouths shut and let him enjoy this new realm.

We crossed the little stream that ran down from the Horse Pasture, went past the trail that led up there, and soon came to a spot where the dirt trail became granite. We had to skirt along a stone wall with huge boulders not far below and then the view opened up to the Narrows with its smooth marbleized walls sloping down friendly enough so we could scoot down to the creek which, through the millennia, had polished a winding route to a cascade that poured down six feet into a deep pool. Sitting on the edge of the pool, we ate our bag lunches. Then Bob and I stripped down to our birthday suits and rode the flow over the edge and into the pool.

We beckoned Kobun to come join us, but it seemed just getting there was enough adventure for him, so he sat and watched. We waded out the far side of the pool and came back via the natural stone path plenty wide which rose ten feet above the pool. Jumped back into the pool and again urged Kobun to join us, but he wouldn't budge. Then Bob whispered to me, "I bet he can't swim." Bob and I went back to our jumping spot and climbed the cliff wall a little higher and stood on a ledge. Kobun called out "No!" We smiled and waved to him. I looked down. I was sure I could clear the ledge below, but a misstep could be a disaster. The edge was uneven and sharp in places. Now Kobun was begging us not to jump from there. We ignored him as Bob and I leaped out. Splash! Splash!

He was relieved to see we'd cleared the ledge and, as we crawled out, asked if we could please not do that again. That was fine with me. It scared me too. The walk back was even quieter than the walk there.

It bothered Richard the way we fawned over Kobun who was two years younger than he was. Richard said that Suzuki's senior students had practiced just as long. Richard had been with Suzuki for six years and Kobun was the son of a priest, grew up in a temple, and was ordained as a monk at twelve. Regardless of the numbers, Kobun had earned our respect and affection by just being who he was.

A Late Call

On another shikunichi, Maezumi invited me to his cabin for tea. I learned he was thirty-six years old and had been ordained quite young as a monk by his father. Hmm. Kobun the same. Suzuki the same. I was beginning to see a pattern. I asked Maezumi how things were with Richard. He said it was all going along smoothly, that Richard was awfully busy and that they didn't have any problems. I mentioned the Bishop and how friendly he'd been with me and asked how their relationship was. He said it was fine. I could tell he wasn't going to descend into bad-mouthing. So I did. I told him about John's experience with the Bishop including the diamond koan. That didn't surprise Maezumi at all and he shifted gears into his own story.

He hadn't gotten along with the Bishop or the bishop who'd been there before. He'd wanted to offer daily zazen and neither of them were interested in that. They wanted him to stick with ceremonies and temple duties. Finally, he was allowed to start a *zazenkai*, a zazen group, but temple members complained about the Caucasians, and it was canceled. Maezumi got fed up with the situation. He'd been working for Zenshuji for ten years and finally left and started his own group.

He said that he helped the Bishop with important ceremonies and events and that they had to deal with each other about various issues but that they often disagreed. The most divisive issue, he said, was that he wanted his Zen group to be sanctioned as an official temple by the Soto sect. He and the Bishop would have screaming arguments with each other in which the Bishop would threaten him with expulsion from America and that he'd yell back his connections were more powerful in Japan than the Bishop's. He acknowledged it was all just petty threats. The main thing was that they had an unpleasant relationship. He couldn't get what he wanted from the Bishop or get the Bishop out of his way. Then one night he got a call.

It was very late. So late you'd call it early. The Bishop's voice was shaky. He asked Maezumi if he would come to the police station to bail him out. Maezumi drove straight to the station and soon the Bishop appeared before him—in drag.

As Maezumi drove back to Zenshuji, the Bishop clutched his

dress and sobbed loudly and so wetly that his mascara ran down his face blending with his pancake makeup, his lipstick all smeared. He ran into the temple crying and holding his high heels. No one else heard a peep about this and, from then on, things were much more harmonious between them.

Like a Rolling Stone

Tim Burkett stood on the bridge over the small creek watching Suzuki working with Phillip and Bob Halpern. They were shoring up the stone wall embankment close to Suzuki's cabin. In a pause, deciding what to do next, Suzuki noticed a stone up on the steep hillside. He told Phillip and Bob to get another large stone in the creek and bring it over to the wall. It was somewhat buried in the creek. They struggled to move it. They were both strong as heck, but so far hadn't made it budge. Catching their breath, they noticed Suzuki wasn't there. He was up on the hillside with the stone he'd thought might be just right for what was needed next. Tim thought this was strange because the stones on the hill were rough and angular and the wall they were working on was all smooth creek stone. Suzuki had obviously put Phillip and Bob on that impossible task to divert them so he could be alone on the hillside.

"Suddenly," Tim said, "Suzuki Roshi slipped, and started rolling down the hill. I thought oh no, he's old and frail. He'll be hurt! When he got to the bottom, he leapt to his feet, dusted off his robes, smiled, and called out, 'Just like a stone!'"

Second Sesshin Approaching

August 1967 was my first weeklong sesshin. It was the looming culmination of the two-month practice period. I tingled with apprehension at sitting cross-legged from 4 a.m. to 9 p.m. seven days in a row, spending almost all that time in the zendo. The zendo was full, as some students who weren't in the practice period came to the sesshin, including Bill Kwong, Marian Derby, Norman Stiegelmeyer, and Mike Dixon whose wife, Trudy had attended the first sesshin as one of them had to stay behind to take care of the kids.

To us, this room and what we did there were the heart of Tassajara—not the mountains and woods, nor the baths, creek, sky, and stars. The primary function of this room was to have a place to do nothing, to be nobody. There we'd sit, walk, chant, eat, listen to lectures, mainly sit. A place to look at who we were—beyond assumptions and notions. A place to observe body and mind, body-mind, which include each other and the mountains, woods, baths, creek, sky, and stars.

The day before the sesshin, the afternoon was free. Lemonade was served under the grape arbor. "Why are you taking so little," Bob Halpern and I were asked. Each of us took an inch of the lemonade in our glasses. "The more liquids you take in now, the more pain you'll have in your legs during zazen," Bob said. He knew this from past sesshins. I didn't believe it because he said that or because macrobiotic guru George Ohsawa warned against drinking too much water. I'd noticed it in my experience.

"Aren't we supposed to drink eight glasses of water a day?" someone asked.

"Better to drink eight teaspoons of water per day," said Bob.

Dan stepped up to the crock. "Oh boy. I'll have seconds. Good for more pain."

"Pain for a monk is like candy for a baby," said Kobun between sips.

The Big Pain

Just one period of zazen could be painful toward the end. But sitting one after another made the aching come earlier and earlier in the period and more and more each day.

And there wasn't just one type of pain, but sharp, dull, muscle, tendon, back, knees, thighs, neck, small, medium, large, extra-large. The pain was, the pains were, accompanied by sweltering summer heat and sweat running down the entire body, sliding into the eyes, and stinging. Not moving to wipe the brow. Not moving to swat the flies flying around the face, the eyes, landing on the nose. "Don't move" like a mantra that kept being drummed into us.

The lectures and meals were also in the zendo—sitting on a cushion. Meals could last an hour, and Suzuki would not limit his lecture to the forty-minutes allotted in the schedule. He might go on for twice that long which would turn a room full of students eager to hear his every word into one full of students praying he'd bring it to a conclusion.

I think I experienced less physical difficulty in sitting than most. I alternated right and left full lotus, and then half lotus for lectures worked well. But still it took endurance to keep going, and a type of endurance that gave neither gender nor physical strength an advantage. We persevered, encouraged by each other, supporting each other.

This was group practice at its groupiest. We'd sit together like statues breathing together, wipe off our zabutons with our hands and fluff our zafus together, rise together, bow together, chant together. But, as Suzuki said, within this sameness, he could see the distinctness of each.

We'd stand up and do kinhin between zazen periods. I treasured kinhin and every activity that wasn't done at ground level. The brief afternoon and evening services were done standing. Morning service was longer and seated. I'd do it in *seiza*, on my shins, like the Japanese priests did. At least it was a break from crossed legs. The bowing to the floor before and after chanting the Heart Sutra was to me ceremonial calisthenics. Blessed gift was the hour work period outside after lunch. I'd always enjoyed physical labor but had never enjoyed shoveling dirt that much. Walking silently to the baths for a briefer than usual but ecstatic cleansing. The shower beforehand such a relief. Stepping into the hot water of the plunge, feeling it reach higher and higher to the neck and then over the head. The steam room glorious. A dip in the creek a marvel. There was a brief break after the meals. Many would head to bed for a quick relax. I found it worked better not to lie down till bedtime.

The rewards of practicing thus were enough to keep us going.

Our teachers weren't big on the promise of enlightenment to come. The practice itself was enlightenment. Do it and don't think about it. Anxiety and mental pain would drop, and as Richard said, physical pain is limited but mental pain is not. We were there because the big pain in life is mental.

Deflecting Angry Birds

On the second day of sesshin, four young loud guys came walking into Tassajara. Most of us were in the zendo but I was on a meal server's break, hanging up my oryoki cloths to dry on the lines by the shop. I heard them on the road coming in. I went up to them, said hi, and let them know that we were closed for a meditation retreat. That was met with a "So what?" and a defiant stare from one of them. Trying to buddy up to them I learned they were students, inebriated students, from some junior college. I gently reminded them we were having a week of intensive meditation and were closed. They kept walking in.

The one who set the tone and did most of the talking for the group asked, "What's this Zen thing here? Do you have women? Can we fuck them? Do you know karate? Why can't we use the hot baths if you guys are all meditating? Do you think you could stop us?" He kept saying the strange phrase, "You telling us to make our bird!?" Make our bird!?

Silas and Norman Stiegelmeyer came up from the zendo. Silas deflected the hostility by talking to the group of guys in his low key non-confrontational style. The hostile guy was not retreating though. I focused on relating with one who showed signs of embarrassment. Norman started talking to the hostile guy who was still incensed that they were being asked to "make our bird!" Silas shifted his attention to the other two who seemed ready to fight or leave depending on which way the angry leader went.

Norman was an artist and teacher from the San Francisco Art Institute who'd been sitting with Suzuki for years. He was lanky, friendly, and came across so differently, even goofy. His movements were at times jerky. He acted amazed by whatever was happening. And he was fearless. I could see that his presence was throwing mister itchin-for-a-drunken-brawl off balance. At one point he asked Norman, "Do you Zen people believe in god?" Norman scratched his head, turned it from side to side and replied, "Well gee, let me think. No, I don't guess we do."

The ringleader looked startled. He took a step back. "What? Did you hear that guys? They don't believe in god! Let's get out of here! Let's get out of here!" As he ran back up the road he kept yelling, "They don't believe in god!" His relieved friends followed him out. I think he was more afraid of Norman than the no god thing. The sesshin continued unruffled.

I was glad that this altercation was resolved without Phillip getting up from his seat in the zendo. The way I saw it, he could have picked up all four of those guys with one hand and thrown them out the front gate and might have been tempted to break them into little pieces. That would have been an unbecoming thing for him to do with his monk's robes on.

Notable Visitations

On the afternoon of the third day, I compared my present state of body-mind with what I normally would consider the height of pleasure—frolicking in the sun at the Narrows swimming hole with fellow students on a day off. Immediately I was plunged into a replay of the experience and was moved by the depth of suffering I perceived. I could see that I was just telling myself a story that I was having fun. I felt great compassion for myself and for all beings trapped in various degrees of misery. By comparison, I was in a blissful state sitting still and sweaty with pain in my legs. At that moment, I saw the undesirable aspect of pain as entirely mental. When the bell rang, I kept sitting another minute, in no hurry to escape the present situation.

Suzuki gave talks on many of the afternoons and evenings, talks on the Prajna Paramita, the wisdom gone beyond. It's what the Heart Sutra was the heart of. Suzuki's talks included the sounds of the stream flowing, a symphony of crickets, a distant owl.

Suzuki said that nature was the best teacher, that it was actual beauty beyond beauty. Though we cannot escape nature anywhere on earth, at Tassajara she was always there in full force, undisturbed by our presence.

A curious demonstration of the ubiquity of nature occurred during the sesshin. I was sitting near the front by the screen door that was on the path side of the zendo. It wasn't an entrance used formally but was handy during the day for the zendo cleaner. On the evening of the first day of sesshin, as I sat and listened to Suzuki speak, a fat black beetle sauntered in through the generous space under the screen door and up on the tatami. I picked it up with a wiping cloth that was an easily removable part of my oryoki set, opened the screen door as quietly as I could, and let the critter go just outside the door. Suzuki glanced at me and kept on with his talk.

On the next evening as Suzuki lectured, another intruder crawled in at the same place, a fiercer one, a brown and yellow scorpion. Untying the cloth covering to my bowls, I grabbed the middle lacquer bowl, set it over that frightening fellow just as it approached my knee, and slid a sutra card under it. I opened the screen door and went out to let it go on the embankment by the road fifty feet away. Came back in by the same door, sat down. This time Suzuki didn't look my way, but others did.

On the third night, a large hairy tarantula crawled in at the same place. Tarantulas have been used in movies to play frightening, threatening roles, but you can actually pick them up. Even though I knew this, I didn't pick it up, but got the large bowl from my oryoki set, repeated the prior night's procedure, and again went out to take the uninvited guest far off. I tried to be discreet each evening and not distract from the lecture, but I got stern and irritated looks from a few who, unaware of my heroics, were seeing a pattern of restlessness, inappropriate conduct for the zendo, especially during Suzuki's lecture.

I fantasized that each of these visitors came to hear Suzuki preach the dharma like Hyakujo's fox who turned out to be a former abbot of the monastery in the story, something which would be impossible in our case as we had no prior abbots. I also wondered if such visits would continue, but they didn't—until the fox that is.

After dinner on the sixth day, I walked in my thin gray robe down the dirt road past the baths to Grasshopper Flats and stood gazing at the pastel sunset sky where the creek bends. The actual sunset was obscured by the Hogback behind me. The water in Tassajara Creek runs east before joining with other waters that take it in a circuitous route west to the nearby Pacific Ocean. I stood under an oak tree gazing at the sky that glimmered like a piece of ethereal pie wedged into the valley. Beyond the clouds, soft hues were giving way to approaching darkness. Leaves like massive green stars swung from shimmering sycamore branches. Mind not racing, not glommed onto the future. All this sitting, hmm, not bad. How fortunate to be here. I stood there taking it all in. The day cooling, a slight breeze, the complex, agreeable odors of the woods.

Then, from the right periphery of my eyesight, movement. I turned my head and saw a red fox walking down the road. I kept still. It got closer. I kept stiller. The fox sauntered right up in front of me, a few feet in front of me—and stopped. Then it turned around in a circle, lay down, and shut its eyes. It seemed to be sleeping, sleeping at my feet. I continued to stand still. After a few of these unusual minutes, there came the distant sound of wood on wood. The mallet was striking the han, calling us back to the zendo. I was not going to make the first move. The distant han struck again and a moment later again. The fox stirred, slowly stood, and walked back in the direction it came from. I got to my zafu in time.

Sesshin Song

On the last day of sesshin, walking down the same one-lane dirt road, I was alone for the moment but still part of the sangha, the community that makes the effortless effort to wake up to big mind. I hadn't awakened to any big mind, but I felt bigger, and my sense of self was not as concrete. As I passed the spot where the fox had slept, I broke the rule of silence with a little improvised song to express myself and not-self.

> *Walkin down dusty road*
> *Sure am feelin' fine*
> *Finest feelin' ever known*
> *Because it is not mine.*
>
> *Garden grows, river flows*
> *Manzanita, oak, and pine*
> *Finest feelin' ever known*
> *Because it is not mine*
>
> *In the days there are gnats*
> *In the night there are bats*
> *In between suns come and go*
> *The mountains so high*
> *And the clouds they float by*
> *What else is there to know*
>
> *Walkin down dusty road*
> *Sure am feelin' fine*
> *Finest feelin' ever known*
> *Because it is not mine.*

Mantric Awakening

In the zendo, Tim Burkett was sweltering in the summer heat and struggling with pain in his mind and legs. He'd been trying hard to focus, focus, focus.

When it was his turn for dokusan with Suzuki, he was sweating so much that his shirt was soaked with perspiration. Suzuki said, "You've been swimming in the ocean. Go change your shirt."

Tim returned to Suzuki's cabin wearing a clean dry shirt. Suzuki said, "You're having a hard time. Why don't you repeat the mantra '*gya te gya te.*'" This was a surprise to Tim. He'd not heard of anyone using a mantra in Zen Center or in Zen period. Transcendental Meditation did mantras. Tibetans did mantras. But actually, Tim had been reciting this mantra since he came to Zen Center. It's the conclusion of the Heart Sutra.

"Just '*gya te gya te,*' or the whole thing?" he asked.

"The whole mantra," Suzuki answered. "But it's all the same."

The romanization of the mantra on our chant card read *Gyate gyate haragyate harasogyate bodhi sowaka*. The basic meaning, according to the English Suzuki had written above those words on the chant card, was *Gone, gone, to the other shore, gone, reach (go) enlightenment accomplish*. But Suzuki told Tim just to chant *Gyate gyate haragyate harasogyate*—just the *gone to the other shore* part.

Stepping out of Suzuki's cabin, Tim started repeating the mantra to himself. He wasn't thinking about the meaning. He just chanted the mantra. *Gyate gyate haragyate harasogyate, gyate gyate haragyate harasogyate, gyate gyate haragyate harasogyate…*

He repeated it constantly till he fell asleep that night and started again when he woke up. In the afternoon of that day, he was suddenly overcome by a bright openness, an overwhelming sense of relief, a total release from all that he had suffered from. He laughed and cried and left the zendo as quietly and quickly as he could, realizing he was disturbing others. Then he ran into the woods. He was back in the zendo for evening service and dinner. I watched him as he departed the zendo with us. He was, giddy, dancing his way up toward the cabins.

That night he had a dream in which Suzuki said, "You have had a wonderful experience. Not everyone will be able to have that experience, so please do not talk about it with others."

The next day he saw Suzuki in dokusan, and Suzuki said, "You have had a wonderful experience. Not everyone will be able to have that experience, so please do not talk about it with others."

It was hardly a secret though. We all knew something big had happened. Something big as in Suzuki's oft repeated big mind.

Shosan with Suzuki

The penultimate event of the practice period, coming before the closing ceremony, was called shosan. Shosan was a question-and-answer ceremony between students and teacher. Students were lining up to ask a question. Shunryu Suzuki sat on his zafu in the zendo decked in fancy robes, a carved staff in his hand. He spoke.

"According to the teaching of Dogen Zenji, the main point of practice is to listen to your teacher and to practice zazen. You have practiced zazen and studied the Prajna Paramita Sutra. If someone asks me: What is Prajna Paramita? I will answer—practice of zazen. If someone asks: What is the practice of zazen? I will answer: To open Buddha's eating bowl and to take a bath in the evening. If someone understands what I said right now, come and express your way to me in the form of question and answer."

Richard walked forward, hands in gassho, and called out, "Docho Roshi!" (*Docho* meant the abbot.)

Suzuki responded, "Hai!"

Richard dropped to his knees while remaining upright and spoke: "For the big mind, the bridge flows. If everything has such independence, how can we find our own responsibility?"

Suzuki responded: "Your responsibility is under your own feet."

Richard stood, bowed, and said: "Thank you very much."

My gaze was down when the next, "Docho Roshi," came much softer than before and then, after Suzuki's "Hai!" a shriek of "Eeeeeeeeee!" startled me. Oh. It was Bill Kwong who'd come from his Mill Valley zendo to join the sesshin.

Suzuki responded: "What is that?" He paused. "What is that is the question and at the same time the answer. That is what."

Bill Kwong bowed and said: "Thank you very much."

Linda Burkett was next. She asked: "How should we practice negation?"

Suzuki answered: "Negation means liberation. Negation after negation you attain, step by step, liberation."

"I am deeply grateful," she said and returned to her seat.

Tim Burkett said: "Using the mantra you gave me, I broke through one dam of spiritual tension. Should I continue using this mantra to break further dams?"

Suzuki answered: "As long as you are devoted single-heartedly to your attainment, you can use that mantra. You cannot use it for another purpose."

Kathy Cook asked: "Why is it necessary to have some kind of unusual experience in order to practice Buddhism?"

Suzuki answered: "To open up your mind wider and wider."

Mike Dixon asked: "What is the difference between sesshin and everyday life?"

Suzuki answered: "Of course sesshin is everyday life. Everyday life is sesshin. Those are different expressions of our practice. Form is emptiness and emptiness is form."

Peter Schneider said: "Docho Roshi, do you have some question?"

Suzuki answered: "Yes, I have a question. Why are you so serious?"

The room was quiet and then Peter laughed and then everyone laughed.

Suzuki said: "If you start to laugh, that is all right."

Peter said: "I am deeply grateful."

Silas asked: "Docho Roshi, on the mountain-top, what about desire?"

Suzuki answered: "On the mountain-top, where you can see everything, there should be no desire, but there is."

Silas asked: "How coming down?"

Suzuki answered: "Coming down will be your desire. You cannot, you should not, stay on top of mountain. That is not fair. So, to come down is the most important practice, actually. That so-called form is emptiness and emptiness is form. Up and down, back and forth, as you are every week coming to Tassajara and going back to San Francisco. Back and forth, while you are doing your way, your practice will be matured enough."

Marian Derby said: "Great stress seems to have been made on

sitting quietly, and yet Buddha gave up asceticism. I can't reconcile the two, because there is so much pain in sitting quietly."

Suzuki answered: "Just to sit in a squatting position is not zazen. Zazen practice is supposed to be the easiest way to practice and to understand our way. So you should practice it when you really want to, but for a while until your real way-seeking mind arises, zazen practice will be forced on you. The true way at first looks like some morality, or something which was forced on you. This is quite usual, but it will not be so forever."

Ed Brown said: "I don't understand what I have done."

Suzuki answered: "Why is it necessary to understand what you are doing? Buddha knows. At least I know, and people know. When you bow in the zendo, when the food is ready, everyone knows. So find out what you are doing moment after moment. When you bow to me, when you hear the bubbling sound of the rice. There you will find yourself. That is to call your name, to address yourself."

Ruthie Disco said: "What do you ask a sweet potato?"

Suzuki said: "A sweet potato? Many questions. May I eat you? Many many questions."

I asked a question. He answered. I appreciated what he said so much at the time, but afterwards, I couldn't remember what was said between us.

When the last question was asked and Suzuki had given his response, he sat on his zafu looking out at all of us assembled and he spoke: "As I said this afternoon in my lecture, the second master of my temple in Japan was studying Zuigan's addressing his own name for six years. Zuigan. Hai! Zuigan. Hai! But it was not enough. After he found out that the truth of addressing himself is addressing his Buddha nature, the true practice started in my temple. Sometimes there were many students, sometimes few students, but that practice incessantly continues. This practice will continue forever and pervade the whole world, the whole universe, because this is the truth of how everything exists in each world without any contradiction or disturbance existing at the same time in the same way. As I believe in this truth, I am here now in Tassajara practicing our way with you. This is not Japanese way or American way or Japanese way and American way. I don't mind which is which. May we continue this practice without any misunderstanding forever with all sentient beings.

"And on this occasion especially to Maezumi Sensei, Chino Sensei, Phillip Katsuzen, and especially Richard Baker who is in the position of Shuso—with all their effort which has helped our practice—this is my gratitude indeed. I am very much grateful for their effort and the effort of all the students who joined our practice and encouraged our project at Tassajara. This is the most wonderful event which we have had and which you had first in America. I am very grateful for your effort. Thank you very much."

Great Treasure

Maezumi had helped to lead the first month of the practice period and had gone back to L.A. after that. He'd returned to Tassajara for the seven-day sesshin culminating the practice period. He'd made some overtures to students there to come practice with him in L.A. He'd said to me that students progress faster with younger teachers, that the old ones like Suzuki get too soft.

Before he left, he spoke to Bob Halpern and asked him if he'd come to L.A. to help with a sesshin. Bob sought permission from Suzuki to do the sesshin, saying that after two years his practice was not improving. Suzuki told Bob he should stay and not stray, that he'd made significant progress in his time at Tassajara, but it hadn't set yet. Maybe Bob didn't realize, Suzuki said, how pompous he was when he arrived.

To Tim Burkett, Maezumi said, "You had a good experience. I've had many experiences like this. You should come join me and help with my new center. I know how to work with someone like you."

Tim wasn't sure what to say. It was an interesting offer, but should he do it? He felt confused. He didn't mention it to Suzuki, but not long after that Suzuki took him aside and said, "You have a great treasure within you. Someone may try to take it from you. Don't let anybody take it from you."

Neither Bob nor Tim went to L.A.

— CHAPTER FOUR —

RESUMING

Noah the Noble EARLY SEPTEMBER 1967

We had a few days until the second round of the guest season would start. I wanted to get out, but not to the city. So I hiked to Big Sur with our dog, the dirty blonde, medium build, slight frame Noah. Noah came from Big Sur with Nancy Lay back in the spring. When she left, Noah stayed. Noah loved all people and dogs—never barked at a human or canine guest that came in. But he enthusiastically tried to kill anything else small or large. I saw him take on a ten-point buck at Grasshopper Flats. The buck walked away.

I had no map. Putsy, the ranger who'd been tending to the trails for decades, said take the Tony Trail and just keep going west. I figured since Noah was from our destination, he could be the navigator.

We headed up the Tony Trail near the waterfall, scooting along with help from a cable fastened to the steep hillside for a stretch with minimal footing. Then up the trail so steep I worried I'd fall backwards. I got down to Willow Creek. Sank to my knees and drank desperately from that and every creek crossed that day. I hadn't brought water. Noah lapped it up like crazy as well.

I looked up. Struck by the experience of being in a place of such remoteness. I had only talked to a few people who'd gone this way.

This was the spot where Yvonne, lost and exhausted, having wandered up the Willow Creek Trail, met this end of the Tony Trail and, fortunately, took it. I did a double take when I caught sight of a heavy iron contraption. It must have been used for mining. Putsy said they found no gold or silver to speak of. He told me if we ever do find any to bury it— "Unless you want the place overrun and torn up."

Onward toward the Pacific through valleys with giant oaks and meadows. As we walked, Noah sniffed around and occasionally ran barking into a bush or through some trees. We came upon a bobcat. Noah charged it. It ran away, thus saving Noah, in my estimation, from being torn to pieces. Climbing, descending, ascending, descending. Just Noah, me, the birds, and the flies. We got to a ridge overlooking the ocean as the sky was darkening. There was a trail along the top, but I couldn't find a trail going down. It got darker. I picked up a length of rope lying on the ground and tied it to Noah who walked along a while and then led me down blind, through brush, down the steep decline, skirting menacing drop-offs until miraculously we came to a road. We went along the road to the first light. Exhausted, staggering, we climbed the steps to the front door of a home.

A tall, thin old man with a white beard answered my knocks. I knew him. It was Dryden Phelps whom I'd met at Tassajara. He was an Asian arts and religion scholar who'd lived for a long time in China. He went there as a Baptist missionary in the twenties. I stood on his porch parched, just trying not to collapse, as he talked on and on.

His wife appeared. "Who is it?" she asked, and after a look at me,

"Oh, you poor dear. Come in. Have something to drink and eat and rest." She fed Noah and me and gave us a nice place to sleep. The next morning after breakfast and many thanks, Noah and I walked down to Highway 1 and stood on the road with thumb and paw extended.

Dining Room

The boot camp of the first practice period behind us, slightly more sober, we had entered the stage of guest season one, act two. Guests now ate in the brighter new dining room in the old Club House with the deck out to the side and the dorm on top. Paul Discoe had left the cracked but stable dark green paint on the time-worn boards between the ceiling beams. He'd created two openings for windows on the thick back wall. Inside there was now sunlight from three sides and electric lights behind fogged glass in the ceiling for the evening.

"The water's on, the water's on, the water's on, the water's on," I sang as I walked through the courtyard holding high a heavy load of dishes on a large oval aluminum tray. "The water's on, the water's on, the water's on, the water's on," I continued as I opened the door, entered our new, beautiful dining room, and set the tray down on one of the tables Paul and crew had made in the shop using old fence posts for legs.

I continued singing this mantra as I returned to the coffee and tea area, up the steps beside our tiny kitchen and turned off the water before it overflowed the samovar of the coffee machine. Water needed to be added now and then, but there was too much to do to stand and watch the water in the glass tube in the center of the machine rise to the fill line. I'd learned not to trust my memory from a couple of occasions when someone would come up and say that there's something wrong with the coffee machine. I'd run over and see water shooting out of the top and then it would take a long while for the water in it to heat back up.

Caffeine was the drug of choice at Tassajara. There were the tea drinkers, but students and guests drank more coffee, from lots in the morning to a little at night. Guests raved about the food, but there were more serious and mixed comments on the coffee—too weak, too strong, too bitter, too old, not bad, good, excellent. Couldn't get the highest praise from everyone, but we strived for the highest percentage of appreciation. Had to keep it as fresh as we could. We prepared fresh batches for each meal.

We'd open a bag of Farmer Brothers coffee and pour it into a filter nestled into the aluminum container on top, then slowly add a couple gallons of hot water. The coffee would drip into the stainless vat and the coffee pots and cups would be filled via a spigot at the bottom. When the vat on that side was getting low, we'd make coffee on the other side. The hot water in the samovar surrounded it. So there was a spigot on each side for the coffee vats and one in the middle for hot water that was used for drinking, making tea, and coffee.

A major discovery that increased the number of positive comments about the coffee was to start with fresh cold water, not hot water from the samovar, which was best used just to keep the coffee hot. An alert student had noticed the uptick in approval following one of my memory lapses that flooded the samovar with cold water, necessitating quickly heating substitute water from the kitchen.

One of the last things the dining room crew did at night was to turn the heat down low on the coffee machine. The zendo cleaner, who woke an hour before others, would turn it back up. Sometimes there would be a slipup resulting in tepid brew in the morning or awful dregs that had been hot all night. Regardless of quality, before zazen there would be students stopping by the kerosene lamp-lit coffee-tea area draining off the remains of the night before, a few making individual cups, drinking tea, and for a very few influenced possibly by Chinese mentors, plain hot water.

In a lecture, Suzuki advised us not to drink before zazen. I took that to mean not to drink stimulants before zazen and thought that advice was possibly aimed at Phillip Wilson whom I'd see drinking three cups of coffee in a row before morning zazen. I followed Suzuki's advice and ceased imbibing caffeine before sitting.

Fly Herding

Sugar was a drug-like condiment of choice for many, including the abbot, but for flies, it was the main course. We had to be careful not to leave any sugar or honey exposed due to the fly population. At the samovar this meant well-sealed containers never left open and in the dining room sugar in packets put out in little bowls on the tables. Then we learned we had to keep these packets hidden between meals to guard against invading guest youngsters, many of whom were driven to gobble down one packet of sugar after another, some with extra ferocity as a result of being denied any amount of sugar by their protective and well-meaning parents.

We'd leave the windows and doors to the dining room open till mid-morning, then close them to keep in the cool till later in the day. After lunch cleanup, we'd sweep and mop the ever-dusty dining room floor which was then so clean and cool it invited one to lie down for a nap after work was done.

Robert Beck taught us fly herding. It became a standard pre-meal ritual in fly season, which included the guest season. There were screens on the dining room windows and doors, but those pesky little houseflies would regard any seconds of open screen doors as an invitation to enter. After the first ring of the railroad bell announcing fifteen minutes to go, we'd open the screen doors and windows facing the courtyard and issue clean dish towels to a row of students and guests on the opposite side of the room. The towels would be held out gripped by the top corners and on command we would hold them up, then snap them down hard so that they made a sharp popping noise propelling waves of air and sound forward. We'd march ahead, working our way around the tables and chairs and successfully drive most of the varmints out, then close the screens on the windows and screen doors again. Fly herding was soon applied in the zendo as well.

Routines and Surprises

For dinner we put the salad out first, brought over in two huge stainless bowls. We'd add the dressing and toss. Cradling a bowl in one arm, two of us would walk around placing handfuls on each salad plate. I found it uncanny the way the salad almost always distributed evenly with the last handful going onto the last dish. Ed Brown cautioned that if there was a pool of dressing at the bottom of the empty bowl, we'd used too much.

After the second ringing of the railroad bell, we'd open the doors. There were no menus and no reserved seats. Usually around sixty but up to eighty people would come in and sit wherever they wished. The eats would already be set out on platters and baskets on the tables. But first the guests had to find their red cloth napkins which were placed inside napkin rings with guests' names on labels. They were spread out in alphabetical order on a table outside the entrance doors.

The napkin rings were made of bamboo I'd bought at the docks in San Francisco, sliced up in the shop, and soaked for a week in linseed oil. Small Avery Removable Labels had the last name of the party written on them, followed by a number if there were two or more in the party. When they departed for the last time, the labels easily were pulled off and new blank ones attached. That was my sole contribution to the aesthetics of the dining room. Ginny Baker chose everything else: plates, silverware, linen, pictures on the wall, flower vases. Our job was to haul plates, silverware, serving dishes, cups, glasses, water, coffee, tea, bread, salad. We'd serve and pay attention. Then we'd haul back the empty plates and so forth.

Guests raved about the whole grain bread and quickly snatched up what little was being sold in the office. The meals were a hearty version of California cuisine, with continual creative additions by Ed and staff, and a nod to Anna Beck. The casseroles were especially popular. When guests asked what their secret was, I'd say, "Judicious use of leftovers."

We had sixty students taking care of the guests, of Tassajara, of the practice. We had a zendo, ceremonies, construction, garden, but still more than half of us were dealing with some aspect of the guest season. Often I'd make an announcement in the dining room toward the end of breakfast that anyone who wanted to cut vegetables for a while, the kitchen could use some assistance. I'd have guests proudly tell me at dinner they'd helped to make the salad.

There were only three of us on the dining room crew and we'd be eager to tie things up. We had to get all the dishes and food back before going to the zendo for evening zazen or Suzuki's lecture. Frequently a selfless student or two would help out so we could get there on time. But often there would be late and hungry guests—a couple, two couples. And every once in a while, there were more.

One night, Ed was getting ready to leave the kitchen, exhausted after spending all day creating his labor-of-love dishes, when I popped in with, "Everyone's gone but you and me. Party of twelve just arrived in three cars. They haven't eaten. What do you think?"

Ed would have occasional fits over what appeared to be tiny problems or no problem. But if there was a real problem, he'd be like Popeye who'd just eaten spinach. "Let's do it," he said.

I got the table set and ran back to the kitchen. He already had casseroles, bread, and salad ready to go. He helped me bring it over. Afterwards we got the minimum cleanup done, and as the bells to end evening zazen rang, we bowed to each other. On the way out the kitchen door, I turned to Ed. "You were there. How the heck did the Becks do it with so few of you?" He just shook his head.

"The water's on, the water's on, the water's on, the water's on," I sang while walking to the dining room with a bundle of clean red tablecloths just in from the laundry service in Monterey. Cut the string holding it together and walked around the room, dropping the fresh tablecloths to be spread out next while singing "the water's on" over and over. I dallied doing little tasks to get the room ready for the next meal, each task accompanied by "the water's on, the water's on, the water's on, the water's on." I gazed out the window while tapping on a table to the tune.

"David!" someone called out from the courtyard, interrupting my song.

"What?"

"The coffee machine is exploding!"

Dharma Combat

Bill Kwong turned his head toward Richard Baker and stared at him. Suddenly he leaped to his feet, faced Richard, stomped a foot on the floor, and shouted, "Kwatz!" Then Bill turned around and started walking down the zendo aisle. Richard, sitting on the altar platform, called out, "Do you have anything else to say?" Bill stopped. Turned around. Stomped on the floor again. Walked back toward Richard, stopped, gasshoed, and returned to his zafu.

The shuso ceremony had begun. It was supposed to happen before the sesshin at the end of the practice period, but the Bishop couldn't come then so it was scheduled for mid-September.

In his right hand, Richard held a bamboo root staff Kobun had made for the ceremony. Richard pounded it down on a wooden block and the next student spoke. "Shuso! What do you make of my transparency?"

"What transparency?" Richard answered. "I can't see the wall through you."

Another student asked, "Why did Suzuki Roshi come to San Francisco?"

Richard answered, "Buddhism neither comes nor goes. What is this 'you' that you think comes and goes?"

In response to one of Richard's answers, a student said she couldn't accept the "if" in his answer. He said, "You're right. No if."

A student said, "Me asking, you answering—is that a comparison?"

"No me, no you," he said. "Just questioning is all that exists here."

After the last question, Kobun said, "In the vale of these deep mountains, a disciple of Buddha comes to teach. Let us hear congratulations." And congratulations there were from students recent and senior, from the Bishop and Suzuki who said that the ceremony was a beautiful expression of his faith in the shuso and Tassajara.

I wouldn't have remembered any of the details about this ceremony except that Trudy Dixon got it all down for a *Wind Bell*. She was good with details and devoted to Suzuki and, to a certain extent, to Richard. She was such a humble and sincere person—beyond what I felt I would be capable of.

On the other hand, Bill Kwong and Richard had not always had a harmonious relationship. Richard was too alpha for Bill who did not like conflict at all. Since a disagreement they'd had in 1963 about who would lead services while Suzuki was in Japan, Bill had been sitting at home in Mill Valley. Once Suzuki returned, Bill had resumed going to Sokoji, but only on the weekends—to hear lectures, sit, and cook. There were others who lived over the Golden Gate Bridge that started sitting with him weekdays—like the Dixons and Norman Stiegelmeyer. And now there was a Mill Valley zendo with zazen at 5:45 every morning at the Almonte Improvement Club. Suzuki and Katagiri were already giving lectures there as close to once a week as they could. In a month there would be an opening ceremony.

I saw Richard and Bill talking most comfortably with each other in the courtyard after the ceremony. Caught a glance of Marian Derby and bohemian artist and musician Mel Weitsman chatting in the background. Ah, I thought—in one frame there are the four satellite zendo leaders. Richard at Tassajara, Bill of Mill Valley, Marian in Los Altos, and since Jeanne and Howard had moved from Berkeley, the venue for zazen there had moved to Mel's house. Four distinct characters. Probably works best, I thought, each with their own territory.

The Clattering Generator

If a generator wasn't running to power the lights in the dining room, I'd dart to the shop and crank one up. I'd never before dealt with an engine that started with a hand crank. When I was shown how to do it, I was told not to grip the crank all the way around using the thumb, so that if it kicked, it would shoot out my hand and not break my wrist or arm.

During the day we only kept the generators running for shop use or long enough to get the walk-ins cool. It was good to have two of them because those old codgers broke down now and then. They weren't complicated, so Clarke could get one running in a jiff.

Then one evening both generators had parts on the floor, Clarke all greasy working into the evening. So we brought out the kerosene lamps. The guests liked the cozy feeling sitting with the lamps illuminating just enough. Everyone in camp enjoyed the silence. So that was the last of the evening generator. No more electric lights with grumble-grumble clankity-clank penetrating the gentle night.

Charlotte Selver

The guests were an interesting mix of those who came for the hot springs and natural beauty, those who'd come in prior summers, those who were drawn because of its Zen aura, and friends of Zen Center.

Charlotte Selver and her much younger husband and colleague, Charles Brooks, were at Tassajara doing a one-week sensitivity training. A couple of Charlotte's senior students came to assist her. Tassajara students could take part whenever they had the time. The sessions were held in the dining room or on the dining room deck between meals. We'd stack the tables and chairs to make an open space. I joined in some. So did Suzuki whom she respectfully treated the same as others in the class.

The focus of Selver's teaching was on body awareness. I liked the session when we were all lying down feeling our feet while listening to Charlotte and Charles talk about feeling feet, then describing what we felt foot-wise.

They had conducted a few well-attended workshops with Suzuki as fundraisers. Richard was in the city, but he'd surely have joined in on some if he were at Tassajara. Back in 1960, new to the West Coast, before he'd met Suzuki, on a whim, he attended a workshop with Alan Watts and Charlotte Selver. He'd heard of Watts, but not Selver. According to Richard, "Charlotte said, 'Please close your eyes,' and I did. Shortly she said 'blue.' 'Blue' proceeded from her lips across the room as a viscous thickening of the air—hitting me, spreading, penetrating, flowing past. Completely a bodily experience and a spectrum of components beyond the bare information of hearing."

Watts's brilliant insight and Selver's focus on practice were inspiring and planted Richard on the path to awakening. Richard wrote a poem about that experience which Diane di Prima published in an issue of *The Floating Bear*, a newsletter edited by her and her mate LeRoi Jones.

"It was their presence together," Richard said, "which located me in the physicality of 'blue,' which helped me to write a poem, and which helped give me permission to enter a life with Suzuki Roshi."

```
            Struggle

    the clouds were just below
       the residential buildings
     on the other side of the street

    they were streaming out
       the sun just below
       houses shining
    the clouds gaining and losing

    the house
       green leaves
       just moving clouds
                    the blue seeming
        to move with them
```

I visited Charlotte and Charles in Stone Room One. Charlotte was in her mid-sixties, German with a charming accent. She was a fixture at Esalen Institute, and her work influenced the human potential movement. Charles was sweet and devoted to Charlotte. She rather sparkled and got a kick out of how much I enjoyed the wine they'd generously offer me in their room after I'd turned it down in the dining room.

We were standing together in the courtyard talking and I told her I had a weird thing going on in the zendo. When I sat, I'd lean to the right. Suzuki and Kobun straightened me up, but soon I'd be leaning to the right again. She had been watching me work and suggested I try carrying the heavy trays with my left arm as well. I started using only my left arm and she was right. Before long, I straightened up. After that I found using both arms to carry trays kept me straight.

In the office I picked up a brochure about Charlotte and Charles's work and found a quote from Shunryu Suzuki who said the work they do "is the inner experience of entire being, the pure flow of sensory awareness when the mind through calmness ceases to work—deeper than mind-made awareness. What is this entire being? If you want to say something about it, you should know how to be it."

Wow. *Well said, Roshi*, I thought. Too well said. I imagine he said something at least vaguely resembling that, but the wording sure smelled like Richard.

The Levitskys

Melissa and Charles Levitsky came from their well-worn two-story redwood cabin home in Big Sur. I paid them a visit. She had a greenhouse with cactus and succulents. I watched a family of raccoons enter their kitchen in the evening to eat a dinner of cat food and leave. I wondered if we could have a more cordial relationship with the raccoons that haunted our kitchen area at night. I recalled chasing them out and across the stones exposed by the low summer creek, the dominant male pausing and glaring at me as if to say, "Watch it buster—this is our territory."

The Levitskys ran a gift shop at Bill and Lolly Fassett's cliffside Nepenthe restaurant, with a Mediterranean menu. They lived a short walk away. She had been a ballet dancer who'd toured Japan in the thirties and hated what she'd seen of the status of women there. She wasn't interested in going back or in anything Japanese. But she liked us, which was good because they'd been coming to Tassajara for many years, and we didn't want to spoil it for them.

Big Sur, I heard, was nine miles as the crow flies from Tassajara. It took the Levitskys two hours to make the drive. She said Highway One from Big Sur to Carmel used to be even windier and narrower, and the trip to Tassajara take even longer—especially before the oft photographed Bixby Canyon Bridge opened in 1932. Charlie added, "In the winter a car a week would go by."

Melissa and Charlie were at Tassajara when Lou Harrison, composer in residence at San Jose State University, arrived with his partner Bill Colvig and an entourage of fellow musicians who gave us a concert of classical Chinese music. I visited their place in the Santa Cruz mountains with a separate structure just for musical instruments from around the world. They were especially fond of those used for their Indonesian gamelan orchestra. I think Lou could play anything. His taste in music was unrestricted. He appreciated what he called "the music of Tassajara" with its meditative spaces between the sounds of the han and bells, chanting from the zendo. Melissa said she used to hire him to play piano for her when she practiced ballet and that he'd read a book while he played.

She knew avant-garde musician John Cage. I told her he was intrigued with Zen and had been around Sokoji in the past. She said, "The thing to know to understand John is that he doesn't like music."

Other Guests

One late afternoon a group came in on horseback from down creek. I only got a guest count before meals for setting the tables, not a horse count, so it was a pleasant surprise to watch as they slowly rode down Tassajara Lane to Grasshopper Flats.

I followed them—maybe ten, male and female, with cowboy hats and boots. *Oh*, I thought, *They must be the Monterey County Rough Riders that Robert Beck had told me about.* They were a fairly young crowd except for one guy who introduced himself as John Stace. He said he'd been bringing groups in for years. Had even thought about buying Tassajara. "But you Zens beat us to it. So let's see what sort of job you're doing," he said in a friendly tone.

"We just bought it to take care of it for you guys," I said. "You probably want to get to the baths. It's student bath time now. The baths will be open by the time you've checked in and put your stuff in the rooms."

"*And* had a drink!" he said. And that's what they did for three days—soak in the baths, hang out at the pool and narrows, booze it up, and eat. At first, they were pretty boisterous, but they toned it down as they gradually harmonized with the place.

I liked having them there. They reminded me of the crowd at the stables in Fort Worth where I'd go after school sometimes to ride a horse in a wooded park. I loved horses but not the cowboy trip. Not the boots and the hats. I went out to Grasshopper Flats and visited the horses. There was one I vibed particularly well with. I put my nose up to his and we breathed together.

Another afternoon, some older guys arrived who were booked under the name of the Watsonville Domino Club. They settled into the Pine and Stone Rooms. Walking by, I could hear voices on the back porches. I went to say hello. They were drinking whiskey and beer and charcoal broiling steaks. "We'd been warned the food here was vegetarian, so we came prepared," one of them said while offering me a drink.

I accepted a shot of whiskey which put them and me at ease. They couldn't understand why I wasn't interested in their steaks. I met Bud who owned Topless Vegetables. I told him that when the town trip truck arrived, anyone around would help unload it and that I'd sometimes carry crates of his produce from the truck to the walk-ins. Then there was Burt, whose family co-owned globally active Granite Construction. He said they were one of the five largest construction companies in the world and talked to me about the evils of the inheritance tax, which he said would not allow him to pass his business on to his kids.

Mr. Porter was the oldest, had a pot belly, spindly legs, and a reddish face. He grew strawberries. He'd brought a bunch of boxes for us. There was an eightieth birthday dinner party for him the second night they were there. We served a dessert Ed made using his strawberries. There was enough to make that dessert for all sixty guests and sixty students that evening. There were eight Watsonville Domino Clubbers at one long table, all fairly plastered by the time the dessert came out. Mr. Porter blew out the eight candles. There were calls of "Speech! Speech!" He stood up. The whole dining room got quiet. Staff stood by politely.

Mr. Porter picked up a large red strawberry from his dessert plate. "This is one of my strawberries," he said wobbling from left to right. "I'm very grateful to these strawberries. We grow fields of them that are covered in plastic so they don't get dirty and are easy to harvest. Then we burn the plastic and prepare for the next planting. Safeway can't get enough of them. They ship all the way to the East Coast and are still big and red and firm when they hit the stores there. These strawberries have made me a rich man." He paused. "And they taste like soap!"

The whole room exploded with laughter. I wondered why he said "soap." To me, they tasted more like cardboard.

The Outside World

There was an education to be had absorbing the news brought by visitors. That was a time of beginnings and renewals, not just for us, but for the whole of society. Some folks who were thus forging ahead came to sniff us out.

I met a blond fellow who told me about a book he was working on, a catalogue which featured tools for the emerging counterculture and anyone else who might benefit. He had a broad definition of tools—books were included, clothes, whatever would help people to do things themselves, live lightly on the land. He showed me a photo of the earth from space and said that NASA had put it together from many smaller images. His name was Stuart Brand. Turned out he was possibly responsible for NASA doing that as he'd fostered a campaign for just that purpose, had stood in the commons of UC Berkeley with a sign reading, "Show us the whole earth."

There was an engaging man named Dick Raymond who was

excited about all sorts of new developments. He'd started a venture named the Portola Institute. Richard Baker was on their board. Raymond wanted to see schoolkids get into computers and what he called simulated games. I understood neither, but I liked his enthusiasm. A project of the institute was a book of sorts. Soon I realized it was the book that Stuart Brand had talked about. Raymond said it was going to be called the *Whole Earth Catalogue*.

Raymond and Brand had both used the word ecology and were not interested in doing anything that was not harmonious with nature. I'd heard that word earlier in the year from Yvonne's friend Sterling Bunnell who had returned with his wife and kids as a guest. I gathered from him that ecology was a science which saw all life as interconnected and the physical environment as interconnected with all life, and, at least for him, it was all interconnected with the entire universe. To Bunnell, nature was everything and then he'd bring in physics and say it all gets down not to tiny things but to tiny events. There was no subject he couldn't speak on and tie into everything else—science, literature, politics, aliens, psychic phenomena, falcons. He'd written an article for *Scientific American* on the pupfish in Death Valley. I'd seen them swimming in Salt Creek, too, but all I got out of it was *Hey look, there's fish in there*. To Bunnell they had a lot to say.

He'd also written an article on psychedelics for that same esteemed publication in 1964 called *The Hallucinogenic Drugs*. Bunnell had taken many psychedelics I'd never heard of, such as one from a South American plant called yage that was combined with other plant products to make a concoction called Ayahuasca. He was the culprit who guided Alan Watts on his first LSD experience. Watts was so enthusiastic about the benefits of that substance that he wrote about it and shared it with friends and colleagues including Timothy Leary and Richard Alpert, already well aware of it. Watts took LSD to Japan, where he visited with Gary Snyder and other Western Buddhists, Japanese hippies, and open-minded intellectuals. By the time I met Bunnell, psychedelics were in his past. His passions were nature and mind, individual mind, interconnected mind, and big mind that Shunryu Suzuki spoke of. To both, nature and big mind were the same.

The Roscoes

"Room inspection!" I called out, knocking on the door to Stone Room One. A minute later, I was sitting with Anna Beck and her friend Nancy Roscoe before a comfy wood fire crackling in the fireplace. At breakfast, Robert had asked me to drop by after they'd soaked in the baths. He was still there. Anna and Nancy were talking about how wonderful it would have been to run Tassajara "with your army of Zennies" as Nancy called us.

"I'm in awe of you for keeping this place going with...with how many?" I asked.

"Let's see. I was just thinking about that today," said Anna. "We had Nino the gardener. We had Ralph who was the caretaker who stayed sometimes through the winter. And his brother would come. At a full summertime we'd have Ray and Jimmy in the kitchen and Ed last year. And then there would be two waitresses who would double as housekeepers and do the cabins—Kathy and Laurie. And me and Robert. And sometimes we had Jim Cook to bartend. There were Bill and Jim on the pipes and wires, stopping the buildings from falling apart. Alan was here for a while working with them. We'd get a kid to do dishes sometimes. People would come and go. Maybe ten at a time. Often just eight."

"I can't imagine it," I said. "It seems impossible."

"It was," said Anna. "But you all have the meditation and chanting. You're all industrious. How I admire you young people."

"How did you get this place?" I asked.

"Well, Nancy knew it far before I did," Anna said, turning to Nancy.

"The way it happened," Nancy said, "was that Frederick was friends with a woman named Maxine Peterine. Her husband was a captain in the Lafayette Escadrilles in Italy during the Second World War, and they married and came to California. According to

Maxine, her husband brought the first wild boar to the Lamberts. But he died before we met her. She brought Frederick down here and then both of us came."

"We were fresh from France and looking for a little place in the country to go on weekends," said Anna. "So you and Frederick invited us down and we fell in love with it right away. When the four of us were here, Frederick and Robert would wax enthusiastic about the place. I remember those two guys saying boy if we owned this place, we'd do it better."

"Yes they did," nodded Nancy. "It came to be not if we owned this but why not own this? We'll do this, we'll do that. Frederick was a persuasive man, and he said, let's buy this place and we'll run it as a resort in summer and then in the winter we'll travel."

"And the next thing I knew we owned it," said Anna. "It just osmosed into ownership."

"And it was so hard," said Nancy, "and it was so wonderful in the early days. It was winter. It was really cold. We lived in the cabins, and we would go every morning to drink sulfur water which would help with some problems I had. And I remember putting up burlap on the walls of the Pine Rooms."

"And the stone rooms too," Anna added. "And the boys put the second roof over these stone rooms because the rooms got too hot in the summer. The bar was in the end Pine Room. We moved it to the main room in front of the offices. We put that huge table in. We could seat twenty-one people at that table. And we built the fireplace on the other end."

"Since we covered that fireplace with our altar platform, this is the only one," I said.

"We cleaned the pool for our first guests," said Nancy. "But there were problems—like those errant lawyers from a well-known law firm and their girlfriends and I guess they thought it was a hidden place which it was in a sense. And there were problems about the dogs. I think our dog attacked Lumpy. And then of course Lumpy killed Simon."

"Who's Simon?" I asked.

"Our little black poodle," said Anna. "We'd inherited Lumpy from the prior owners who'd inherited him from the ones before them."

There was a moment of quiet. Nancy broke the silence with, "Lumpy was a crazed dog. Anyway, there were disputes about dogs, and about tools. Anna and I got along just fine, but the buddies, the life buddies, they had issues."

"But it was not just all that," Anna said. "It was the fact that you had the coffeehouse, Frederick had the bookstore."

"Frederick and I had very legitimate problems yes, and well, my coffeehouse was going broke," Nancy said. "I didn't really care about it, but I was twenty-one and liked the city lights." She sighed.

"And then," Anna said, "you discovered you were pregnant."

Robert Remembers

"When we first visited here, the place was having a terrible time," said Robert. He closed the door to his storage room in the lower barn. "I remember one morning we were waiting for breakfast, and it didn't come, and it didn't come, and finally the cook came out and his face was covered with soot. He said, 'Sorry folks, the stove blew up again.' There was an old stove that was fired with some kind of oil. And when the wind would stop twirling the fan on top, it kept that oil coming out, it would blow the lids off the stove. So we were sure that with the condition the place was in they would sell it. And Frederick kept saying we should buy this place. The plan was that one couple would be running the place, and the other couple would be traveling in Europe and spending money and gambling. All that sort of thing. So Frederick just kept saying we could do this, we could do this. So we approached the Hudsons and bought it. A little bit down and payments of so much a month. The Admiral just wanted enough down to buy a Rolls Royce."

"How much did you buy it for?" I asked.

"About $150,000. And we started moving in here in the winter of 1960. We'd get stuck in mud and snow bringing stuff in."

"Nancy had the coffee shop at that Columbus tower, kind of angled building just down from Frederick's Discovery bookshop in North Beach. Nancy sold the coffee shop, but Frederick couldn't sell the bookshop. No one wanted to buy all those used books. It was all used books. Have you been there? Ever met him? He's a real character."

"Yeah," I said. "It's right next to City Lights. When I'd go to North Beach, I'd go to both places. And I'd talk to him. I saw him last February right before I came here for the first time. He said he's the one who told Richard that Tassajara would make a perfect retreat for the Zen Center. He said Richard came into his store now and then to buy used books and they'd talk. And he kept telling Richard that and finally Richard came down here."

"Yeah, the first thing that I remember about the Zen Center getting involved was through Frederick." Robert said. "They discovered that Nancy was pregnant, and they backed out. They just said, we can't do it. And we were enemies with them for a long time because we had already sold Anna's antique shop. And I had resigned from teaching math in a school in Chinatown. We were committed. And so here we were, back in these woods, getting ready for the opening of the season. We had no experience with that sort of thing. And they were gone."

"Oh really," I said. "The way Nancy talked about it; I thought they'd been part of it all for longer than that."

"It's what she wishes they'd been able to do. But they weren't and they were gone. And then one day a few years later I was driving my Bentley in North Beach and saw Nancy on the sidewalk with a baby buggy. Before long they were coming back down, and all was forgiven."

Robert and I were welcomed back by Anna and Nancy. We went straight to the sink and drank water from the tap. "Best water in the world," he said.

"Why isn't Frederick here?" I asked.

"You can't get him away from his bookstore," said Nancy.

"I've got to set up for lunch," I said. And then to Nancy, "Glad you kept coming—after a little break I understand."

"Oh yes," she said. "But I was back. Brought my babies, brought my mama, and I loved Tassajara when the Becks had it. I love it with the Zens now but it's a different feel. When the Becks were here and Anna supervised the kitchen, it had a French feel. It was nice."

The Zapper

I was sweeping the floor in the dining room when Tim Buckley came in. He was all shook up. Sat down. He said a crazy guy with psychic power had come into Tassajara and not to let him get hold of my mind or freak out any guests. "The guy was into kundalini," Tim said, "and it made him go psychotic. He's been instantly hypnotizing everyone he walked by. He went through the shop and garden zapping everyone there first."

Someone had run to the office to tell Tim there was a guy on a weird power trip walking around. As head of the office, he was in charge for the day because Suzuki, Richard, Peter, and Silas were in the city for a board meeting. "He came to the office," Tim said, "Right away the guy was literally raping my mind. I started chanting the Padma Sambhava mantra and clung on to it as hard as I could. He got angry and said I was the weirdest person he'd ever met. I told him we don't do that stuff here and that he should leave. The guy said, 'Just try and get rid of me' and walked away."

Kobun came back from a dental appointment. Tim told him about the strange visitor. Kobun spent time with him. The guy was respectful of a Japanese priest and agreed that he'd leave. Bob Watkins and Kobun drove him out, but when they stopped at the first ridge to look at the view as the guy had requested, he jumped out of the car, down into the chaparral, and disappeared. Later in the afternoon he was back at Tassajara. Kobun suggested they give him a room and wait for Suzuki.

The next day, Tim caught me setting up the dining room for

lunch. I knew Suzuki had arrived because I'd heard the han hit one time, which was done when he arrived or departed. Tim was waiting for Suzuki when he walked out of the zendo after offering incense and bowing. They sat outside the office and talked for a while. "I went back inside to answer the phone," said Tim, "and from there I saw that madman run up to Suzuki Roshi. I don't know if Suzuki Roshi even said anything, but their encounter was incredibly brief, like five seconds. And the guy turned around and ran up the road."

Pecking Pigeons

Pigeons were an inescapable part of daily life for me as I spent so much time on the deck outside the kitchen in the coffee-tea area. I'd leave the kitchen with a heavy tray of dishes and before carefully descending the steps to cross the courtyard, I would have to make sure not to trip over a pigeon. There were about twenty of them who hung out around the food area.

Robert Beck said previous owners used pigeons to communicate with the outside world when the road was blocked. I assumed that was a different type of pigeon. Ours didn't offer us any services.

They'd gather around our feet and eat any crumb or edible that fell onto the deck or was left on a counter. Every once in a while, one would peck at my toes. To me they exhibited a sort of creepy greediness. *San Francisco Chronicles* would show up almost daily, brought in by guests or our town tripper and they'd end up on a table in the courtyard. I understood completely when, sitting in a redwood chair there, I read Herb Caen dub pigeons "rats with wings" in his famous daily column.

Suzuki emphasized adjusting oneself to one's environment rather than trying to adjust the environment to oneself. I applied that teaching religiously, but I decided we would appreciate another type of environment to adjust to—one without pigeons. Due to their general unpopularity, I didn't think I had to ask permission and didn't want to anyway, as that can interfere with getting something done. So one morning after guest breakfast was over and the dining room was all clean, I put out a jumbo cardboard box propped up with a stick. I sat still, holding a string tied to it, a plate of their favorite dried cat food inside, and waited. Not long. They were really stupid. One by one caught them all, put them in other large boxes, and before time to set up guest lunch, the task was done. After guest lunch cleanup, I loaded the boxes with all of them in the shopping truck, a box truck with a roll down door in back and drove them out to Carmel Valley. They got back before I did.

Later I selflessly offered to drive on my day off to the Koda Brothers Farm in Dos Palos to get several tons of organic short grain brown rice, a few bags of white rice and one of gluten rice for baking and making mochi at New Year's. I brought some passengers with me, the pigeons re-caught and boxed gingerly for the trip. Dos Palos is between Interstate 5 and State Highway 99 north of Fresno. The road there through Los Banos has a windy stretch that was acting up, making me fear a Volkswagen bus ahead would blow over. Big box trucks do that there. There are billboard-size warning signs.

At the point that I was furthest from Tassajara, I pulled over, slid the back door up, brought the boxes out, and released the pigeons into a new wind-blown realm. I was about a hundred forty road miles from Tassajara—seventy-five as the pigeon flies. They must have decided they liked it there because they didn't come back.

Aphids and Ruthie

Students were concerned. What to do about the aphids that liked to munch on the vegetables growing in the garden? Ruthie worked in the garden. She said you have to kill the aphids. Others didn't want to kill the aphids as Buddhists took vows not to kill. After work meeting one morning, Ruthie invited Kobun to join them in the garden. She showed him the undersides of leaves with aphids. He reached down, took one between his index finger and thumb and squished it while saying, "Become a Buddha."

Ruthie walked up behind me one day and poked me in the ribs.

I hurled around and grabbed her hands and said, "Don't do that to me."

She said, "Ouch! That's too tight!"

"Sorry," I said, "But I can't help reacting like that. I've got some weird condition. It's more than ticklish. Doing that to me sends an electric jolt through me. I've had this all my life."

Ruthie decided we should cure this malady. She got us about five feet apart and told me to stand with my arms up. Then she walked toward me slowly with her hands extended making tickling motions. I could hardly take it without even being touched. Then she touched my ribs just a little and I jerked around.

"That's tickling," I said, "That's hard to take but it's the jabbing that really gets me—especially from behind."

So we tried that. She'd stand behind me and without warning poke me in the sides. I'd shriek and jerk. Rest a minute. She'd do it again. I'd yelp and spasm. After some days of these unusual therapy sessions, I was able to adjust some. I didn't automatically scream or turn around to defend myself. After that, she'd instigate impromptu jabbing attacks now and then to test my progress. Anyone who noticed must have wondered what the heck we were doing.

Ruthie was so uninhibited. She heard students saying something about homosexuals and laughing. She stepped up to them and said in a cheerful tone, "I'm queer! I'm queer!" Bravo.

Robert Beck and I were talking about critters that annoyed us at Tassajara. There were the flies that gathered where there was food and compost. Mosquitoes weren't a big problem, but their relatives, the tiny no-see-ums, might ruin a picnic by the creek. They could bite, but what would drive me crazy was the way a flock of them would gather around my eyes. When that happened, I had to get away. Fortunately, they were only around sometimes and mainly near the creek at dusk. There were few complaints from guests about them. But I heard that construction projects by the Carmel River had shut down when the no-see-ums were bad.

Robert said ladybugs could bite too, but that was rare. They were a blessing for the garden because they loved to eat aphids. I said one day in spring there were zillions of ladybugs in giant clusters all over the valley—on logs and tree stumps and stones—like red blankets. It happened all at once. Robert said that happened every year and that long ago, Andrew Church used to gather them up into jars and sell them to farmers in the surrounding area, even ship jars of them to the East Coast and England. I wondered if there would be a way to farm ladybugs to keep the gardens aphid free.

Esalen Institute

Michael Murphy and Dick Price were Stanford alums and psychology majors who'd had pivotal experiences in meditation and wanted to explore ways to deepen their understanding and share it with others. Murphy had spent a year and a half at the Sri Aurobindo Ashram in Pondicherry, India. Aurobindo's dynamic and positive teaching emphasized our individual and collective spiritual evolution. Price had been influenced by Aldous Huxley's ideas on human potentialities. Murphy and Price were introduced by influential Stanford professor Frederic Spiegelberg under whom they'd both studied Asian religions. They attended Spiegelberg's and Alan Watts's classes at the American Academy of Asian Studies in San Francisco.

Murphy and Price mind-stormed the idea of creating a center for the exploration of ways to awaken our human potential. Murphy's family owned a hot springs resort in Big Sur on the edge of a cliff overlooking the ocean that, like Tassajara, had been used for thousands of years by the Esselen and other Indians. There they founded Esalen Institute in 1962. Alan Watts gave the first lecture. Spiegelberg and a formidable cast of visionaries contributed spiritual nourishment to Murphy and Price's new venture, among them Aldous and Laura Huxley, Gerald Heard, Gregory Bateson, Abraham Maslow, Gai-fu Feng, Charlotte Selver and Charles Brooks, and Fritz Perls who led encounter groups there for five years.

Michael Murphy and Richard Baker had a close relationship,

which is surely one reason Tassajara had a close relationship with Esalen. Mainly we did our thing and they did theirs but there was a fair amount of interaction. Tassajara students went there for brief stays and participated in workshops. Eighteen Esalen staff and residents came to Tassajara to be guest students for a week. Suzuki met with them in the dining room before they left. I was going in and out of the room while they were meeting. I didn't know what they were talking about, but there sure was a lot of laughter.

Suzuki mentioned his discussions with those Esalen staffers at a Zen Center board meeting. In that meeting there had been talk about translating Dogen's masterwork, the voluminous *Shobogenzo*, no simple task. Someone asked Suzuki how he felt about the exchange with Esalen. He said he was amazed at how well they'd done. "Maybe our practice is not so difficult," he said. "It's not a matter of translating the Shobogenzo. It's how to hit the han. How to do zazen."

Joe Kamiya from the Langley-Porter Neuropsychiatric Institute was conducting electroencephalogram (EEG) biofeedback tests on people's brain waves during meditation at Esalen and with Zen students in the city. Kamiya came to Tassajara as a guest. He said that Shunryu Suzuki and Dainin Katagiri both just slept during their tests, but that Michael Murphy and Richard Baker registered theta waves indicative of deep meditation.

Mike Murphy came to Tassajara with his wife Dulcie and George and Lillie Leonard. George Leonard was the West Coast editor of *Look* magazine and an enthusiastic participant and contributor at Esalen with a passion for Aikido. I gave them a pitch for a workshop I could do called *Dig a Ditch, Fill it In, a Week of No Content*. Murphy, congenial and accepting, told me to name a date. I was tempted.

One day I was out at Grasshopper Flats chopping wood when Dick Price sauntered in at about 11 a.m. Price was lean and in good shape. He'd left Esalen at daybreak. That's quick going for that much mountainous trail. I offered him lunch but he said he'd just nosh on some trail mix. I thought of it as a challenging all-day hike to go one way. I told him how walking there from Tassajara I hadn't been able to find the path down from the ridge and had to rely on our dog to find the way.

Bob Halpern and a student named Walter had the same problem and decided to follow a stream down. It led to a series of waterfalls, the last of which offered no option but to leap into the pool way below hoping not to smash into rock just under the water's surface. The deep pool saved them.

Price said he took a different trail to and from the ridge as Esalen was south of the center of Big Sur. He suggested getting to the ridge with plenty of daylight left. He spent a while in the hot spring water and headed back.

I was at Esalen for a few days. It was good to have the opportunity to check it out because it was too pricy otherwise. It was a much looser place than Tassajara. Nothing was required of me. I got up early and sat looking over the ocean as the sky lit up. Dick Price was down in a ravine meditating on a great stone that he sat on every morning. I got a most pleasant massage from a resident and gave her one in return. There were people meditating in the hot spring plunges and a couple being quite amorous. I admired the naked vegetable gardeners against the background of the Pacific Ocean.

Price invited me to join in a dream workshop he was leading. In it, one by one, people talked about some significant dream. He'd encourage them to go deeper, and they'd respond. He'd push them to discover more. Every one of them ended up sobbing. It was my turn. I told about a really yucky and scary claustrophobic dream I'd had where I was trapped in some enclosed space with some creepy, threatening chicken-like beings, a feeling of suffocating in their freaky feathers. Dick asked questions and I answered, and he pushed and pushed and tried to get me to go deeper but to me it was just a dream, and I'd processed it by dreaming it. A heavy dream but I just wasn't into their trip. I think I might have failed in the eyes of my fellow workshoppers when I didn't break down sobbing, but not in Price's. He was an open-minded, non-judgmental person. He gave me a card signed by him that identified me as his guest. He said it would not expire—a lifetime pass to Esalen.

Barry and the Barb

Ernie Barry from the lefty-hippie-counterculture weekly *The Berkeley Barb* hitchhiked in. I always enjoyed glancing through that irreverent rag. It was the first place I saw sexually oriented personals, some of which were audacious eye-openers. One that stuck with me simply read, "You name it, I'll do it."

Barry ate lunch with the students and breakfast and dinner with the guests. He told me he'd gotten permission from Richard to write an article. I told Ernie I was glad Richard did that, that he'd turned some publications away, but said we had to let some media in, especially local media.

Barry met with Suzuki in his cabin and described him in the article as "a short, gentle man with an air of tremendous serenity about him." Barry hated "the so-called Zen macrobiotic diet." He said that apart from being a pile of nonsense, macrobiotics made people gaunt and rigid. He tried to get Suzuki to deny any connection between macrobiotics and Zen, but Suzuki wouldn't bite, said there is some overlap. About LSD, Barry said Suzuki left him completely bewildered. The only thing clear to him was Suzuki regarded LSD as completely irrelevant to anything. But Suzuki did tell him that people who'd taken psychedelics were open to looking for something deeper. Suzuki told him he had nothing against long hair but that he preferred his male students at Tassajara have shaved heads. Suzuki said he was "very sympathetic with young people here in America. They're tired of the civilization we now have."

Barry talked to our innocent priest, Kobun Chino, who didn't know anything about the counterculture. Barry said Kobun spoke some English haltingly and had never heard of LSD. He added that for Kobun everything American seemed irrelevant. He'd come from temples and monasteries in Japan and had almost immediately been driven to Tassajara. Barry asked Kobun what he thought of "America's first actual Zen monastery."

Kobun said, "This place should perhaps be called Zen Village. I sometimes call it Zen Children Village. There are almost no rules. It is a very rare type of monastery. It needs unimpeded growth like most things young."

I made a highly optimistic and questionable contribution to his article by saying, at a time when we were just getting going, that Tassajara was "one of the only successfully functioning utopian type communities in the United States." Then, the not so embarrassing, "Suzuki Roshi's spiritual presence provides the inner harmony to keep the community operating."

I know why I'd said that utopian thing. I'd been talking with Paul Kagen who'd come to study us briefly for a book he was writing about utopian communities. Kagen said that communities often break up due to tensions over food and sex. He told me that secular communities tended to last about five years and spiritually oriented ones about ten times that long. Fifty years seemed like forever to me, so that gave me confidence Tassajara would sail smoothly into the distant future.

Kobun Chino

I showed Kobun a letter I'd written to my sister. He said if he sent something that messy to his brother, it would go unread into the wastebasket. I should have known better. Everything he did had style, and he brought that artistry into our daily life. He fine-tuned the services, was an exemplar of how to chant, hit the bells, and use the oryoki bowls, cloths, and utensils, trained us in form yet was informal. He taught us a great deal about what the words meant—of the chants, objects, monastic positions. There are tons of technique in all that stuff, but he said good technique must have the right spirit. One can never get it all down, but he got us deeper into it.

Kobun brought with him a bit of magic and animism from the old country. He talked of spirits and when we laughed, he asked then why were we afraid to walk in a graveyard? Driving him out of Tassajara he had me stop. He moved a dead rabbit off the road, gently placed it on an embankment, covered it with leaves, and said, "Or else he cannot become Buddha."

As I drove him back in from town, he asked me to stop at a shady spot approaching Chews Ridge so he could pick ferns to cook for a unique day-off dinner side dish. He taught us how to make traditional Japanese daikon pickles and pickled cabbage. I found it curious he thought white noodles were healthy. On another day he gathered mushrooms from the woods and prepared them as his mother had. Some of us were nervous that he might be poisoning us. Envisioning a zendo full of lifeless bodies fallen over their bowls, strewn down the aisles, out the door, on the path, I suggested we need someone to be the official taster and offered to sacrifice myself in that role. Others, I guess, who knew more about fungi identification, were not worried—and they were right. Tassajara was not strewn with corpses after the meal.

Kobun extolled the virtues of an occasional cigarette which gave Bob Halpern and me the opportunity to join him. One day Kobun had to go to San Francisco on visa business. Bob finagled his way into the trip so he could be with Kobun. In Suzuki's office, Bob pulled out a pack of Camel non-filters and offered one to Kobun who accepted until Suzuki said, "No, Chino Sensei doesn't smoke."

On another occasion, I drove Kobun back to Tassajara from San Francisco. I couldn't get him to wear a seat belt till I had to slam on the brakes on the freeway, smashing him into the dashboard. He quickly buckled up after that.

I felt it wasn't right for him to be in America and to experience so little of what was here outside of Zen Center. So we strolled on the boardwalk and ate seafood in Santa Cruz, and in Monterey saw Peter Sellers in *The Party* which brought us to tears laughing. He kept slapping my thigh to share his delight. We got back to Tassajara six hours later than expected and Richard was miffed. He said he felt sometimes he couldn't trust me. I said, "That's okay, Kobun can."

Kobun was patient and understanding. Serving soup in the zendo one lunch, there were so many people that we had to fill the four large steaming tureens to the top. Suzuki and Kobun were served first. Holding the heavy pot high, I walked down the aisle and clumsily placed it before Kobun with a thump. A tidal wave of sizzling soup sloshed into his lap, drenching his sacred kesa and surely burning his body under the cloth. He didn't flinch. After the meal I ran to his room to apologize and offer to clean his robes. He let me follow him to the creek. He took his kimono and koromo apart at the seams and washed them and his tablecloth-shaped kesa in the flowing water. They were dry in a hot summer hour, and he sewed them back together with long running stitches.

Kobun spoke very slowly, especially in lectures. His voice tended to tremble. Like all the Japanese priests I'd been with, Kobun would sometimes sleep in zazen. He loved his private time, and his cabin light would shine so late he'd often be sleepy the next day. Once during the guest season, as he gave a lecture to students and a number of guests sitting in chairs, he spoke slowly, softly, long spaces between words, then a longer space till his head dropped and then drool slid from his open mouth finally waking him up when it landed in his hands. He composed himself and continued the lecture.

Dealing with Demons

I was sweeping the dining room deck one day and heard Ed yelling. He came out of his cabin and threw some objects into the small creek. I looked down. It was his pipe collection. Later he went down, gathered them and put them in the trash. Very good, I thought. He's quit smoking and littering at the same time.

I sat next to Ed in the zendo. He would shake when he sat. His shaking would start as a low vibration and often increase in magnitude as the period progressed. At times he'd thrash about like in a hurricane—side to side and back to front. I worried he'd smash his head on the irregular stone wall before us. It was a bit of a disruption in the zendo but Suzuki and Kobun would sit up there on the altar platform placidly and not interfere.

Suzuki had told Ed that a hindrance was an opportunity to practice so it was an opportunity for us too. Ed said he got some complaints, but I never heard any. One student suggested it was kundalini energy shooting up his spine and hitting blockages and that he would soon be enlightened. I thought there may be someone inside him trying to get out. Anyway, it was clear he was dealing with his demons, whatever they were. Funny thing was that he didn't shake during meals which were also seated.

Ed knew what the source of his shaking and emotional outbursts was. He told me one day how he'd been a preemie in an incubator for three weeks not being touched, being alone in a glass box. At three his mother died. His father couldn't handle him and his brother, so he put them in an orphanage. Then the orphanage separated them. His father would come to visit them and find Ed sitting by himself staring while the other kids were playing.

Most of the time, Ed seemed to have found a way to deal with the pain—service. Ed was always giving. The meals he prepared and supervised for students and guests were an offering from his heart. Dogen said the head cook is serving people his mind. But it didn't make us shake or be anguished. We felt nourished and at peace. That's because Ed kept his turmoil to himself while his better angels prepared the food. He was serving us his heart.

Ed's generosity didn't end with the meals and bread. I'd see him put together a small gift for someone he saw suffering and wrap it artfully. In his core he was sensitive and compassionate with others. I realized he was someone who could feel their pain whereas I would tend not to notice it. He gave loving care to the mini garden outside his room, tending to plants and stone. One day when he was having a particularly hard time, Suzuki came over and set a steppingstone before Ed's door, a stone he knew Ed had admired. Suzuki had requisitioned it from in front of the office door. They could find another one.

During the sesshin, Ed couldn't take it anymore and pulled his knees up. Kobun came to Ed on his zafu and suggested he take a rest. Tears ran down Ed's face so voluminously that he had to hold on to Kobun to find the way. He lay down on his futon and started to sob and shake. His shaking turned into flailing about. Kobun massaged him and softly told him he was alright, and this would pass. And it did.

One day Ed blew up and yelled at a shy young kitchen worker. She started crying. Then he went outside, sat on a bench, put his head in his hands, and sat there looking miserable.

Kobun and I stood on the road above looking down on Ed still with his head in his hands. I asked if we should do something. Kobun said it would probably be best to leave him alone now. Then he sighed and said, "In the eight-hundred-year history of Eiheiji monastery, no monk has suffered more than Ed Brown."

Bookmarked Path

I was tapping my foot on the floor. Bob Halpern asked why I was doing that. I said, "No reason."

Bob said, "Things arise due to the conjunction of causes and conditions. They do not arise without a cause."

I looked at Bob and said, "Them's highfalutin' words there mister."

"They're not mine," he said. "They're Buddha's—from the Lankavatara Sutra, the only sutra Bodhidharma brought with him on the boat from India to China."

Sutras are supposed to be the words of Shakyamuni Buddha, but all these Mahayana sutras that came much later are just pretending that part. Bob had read some of the original sutras as well. Zen had long ago been dubbed the way beyond words and letters, and I defended my ignorance invoking those words. He said, "Yeah—but the lineages that took that illiterate approach literally all died out."

I hadn't read much Buddhist stuff, but I knew I wouldn't be there if not for words and letters. My father's interpretation of the Gospels cued me in with words that said the *Word* was mind-only. I got my first hint at emptiness when he told me that matter doesn't really exist. That led to my sister and me repeating the mantra with our friends at the tennis court, "Does matter really matter? Or does it matter?"

My father said, "Davey my boy, you don't know how lucky you are you weren't taught to believe in god." Now he meant god as an individual being. God in my family was not a super-being to believe in but a word that stood for mind and not mind as in brain but something vast and mysterious. We read the words of Jesus as lessons from an enlightened person on the nature of mind. One time he looked up from a book and said to me "God is thought." Daddy, as my sister and I called him, resigned as a reader in the Christian Science Church because he said they'd elevated Jesus to be more than a human being. I got a better grip on what I'd gathered at home reading Emerson and Thoreau in the eleventh grade, unaware of any influence from Buddhism and Hinduism.

I first heard of Zen when Charles Nunn walked up to me in the hall of Fort Worth's Pascal High School and said, "Look at this." He showed me the cover of Paul Reps's *Zen Flesh, Zen Bones* with an old bald-headed Chinese monk riding an ox on the cover. Intriguing. With a gleam in his eye and a wicked grin as if he were sharing some hidden secret, Charles slowly opened it to:

> *The emperor Goyozei was studying Zen under Gudo. He inquired: In Zen this very mind is Buddha. Is this correct?*
>
> *Gudo answered: If I say yes, you will think that you understand without understanding. If I say no, I would be contradicting a fact which many understand quite well.*

John Blofeld's *The Zen Teaching of Huang Po* had somehow come into my hands before I had any inkling about Zen. I chewed on Huang Po's advice.

> *Mind is the Buddha, while the cessation of conceptual thought is the Way. Once you stop arousing concepts and thinking in terms of existence and non-existence, long and short, other and self, active and passive, and suchlike, you will find that your Mind is intrinsically the Buddha, that the Buddha is intrinsically Mind, and the Mind resembles a void.*

I got the idea from that book that if I just walk when I walk, stand when I stand, sit when I sit, and lie down when I lie down—that in ten years I'd have a good start.

There were Alan Watts's *The Way of Zen*, and D.T. Suzuki's *The Training of a Zen Buddhist Monk*, which I gleaned some teaching from and respected, but they didn't move me to do anything.

A book on the *Tao Te Ching* by Lin Yutang was simple, direct, wonderful.

> *Oftentimes, one strips oneself of passion in order to see the Secret of Life. Oftentimes, one regards life with passion, in order to see its manifest forms. These two are in their nature the same.*

The Psychedelic Experience by Leary, Alpert, and Metzner gave me their take on *The Tibetan Book of the Dead*, the Bardo Thodol, which I gathered was more accurately titled in English, *The Great Liberation through Hearing*. I digested *The Psychedelic Experience* thoroughly and used it with a human guide for the first LSD trips I had. It was most helpful. These books, LSD, mixed with home influences definitely got me motivated to find a teacher and community to meditate with.

Ah yes—in 1965, I greatly enjoyed reading a book in San

Miguel de Allende in Mexico named *Buddha's Law Among the Birds*. In it Avalokiteshvara as a cuckoo preaches a compassionate dharma to a host of birds. The other birds speak up with lines such as "Leave behind that pious talk which leaves your own nature unchecked!" and "Leave behind those religious acts which are mere hypocrisy!" It was written by an anonymous Tibetan lama for peasants.

Two and a half years later at Tassajara I was studying Edward Conze's *Buddhist Wisdom Books* with the Heart and Diamond sutras and saw in the back a list of other books by Conze and there it was: *Buddha's Law Among the Birds*. Then I heard Conze was coming to Tassajara to give a few talks. Oh goody, I thought. I'll ask him about the birds. It was disappointing when I learned he wouldn't be able to come. But then I was most fortunate to hear Conze speak in the city on a brief excursion there. He was expressive in his delivery, peppering what he had to say with anecdotes and strong opinions. He seemed to be British, but he said he had left his native Germany for England in 1933 after publishing a book on Marxism which he said was identical to Buddhism in theory but not in practice.

Conze looked like a stogy old professor, but he brought up his own sex life several times, one I recall being about "having sex with a Jewess in full lotus." That was something I couldn't picture. He said that Buddhism had no racial prejudice, but that he did.

Conze told about climbing a mountain as a young man and accidentally breaking his glasses at the top in a fall. He couldn't see a thing without his glasses. It was getting colder, and he figured he'd freeze to death up there, so he decided to kill himself with his pocketknife. He was just about to do so, he said, when he remembered he was destined to be the greatest Buddhist scholar in the world. He put away his pocketknife and blindly hurled himself down the mountain. "I somehow survived and did go on to become the greatest Buddhist scholar in the world," he said. Maybe it was magic that saved him. He said there's no religion without magic.

Conze said that Mahayana Buddhism and Roman Catholicism were the two great universal religions because they weren't constrained by narrow cultural imperatives—and they had a woman at the top—Mary mother of Jesus and Avalokiteshvara who is the principal character in the Heart Sutra. He scoffed at the vapidity of a wide swath of current popularizers and translators of Eastern wisdom. He also mentioned he'd read a recently published book called *Emptiness*, Conze's prime territory, and suddenly his mood changed to what seemed to be anger. He ranted that "A Methodist minister from Texas, a professor at Southern Methodist University, has written—the best translations and commentary on Nagarjuna that I have yet to see!" Excluding his own, I assumed.

One day a few guests from Dallas arrived at Tassajara. One was named Fredrick Streng. I recognized the name right away as the author of *Emptiness*. Streng was a warm, friendly guy. We talked about Texas and the Dallas Cowboys. I told him what Conze said. High praise indeed.

When I first started sitting at Sokoji, I read two books that clued me in about Soto Zen. One was called *The Way of Zazen* by Rindo Fujimoto. There was a charming photo of Fujimoto on the back cover. It was published by the Cambridge Buddhist Association. I learned that Suzuki thought of Fujimoto as one of few great living Zen masters. The book, or rather the booklet, was about twenty-five pages and was available only in Suzuki's Sokoji office.

Reiho Masunga's *The Soto Approach to Zen* brought home the teaching that practice and enlightenment are one. Indeed, the most repeated theme around there was that it's best to forget about enlightenment and concentrate on practice. So all I needed to do was figure out what practice was.

Richard had talked to Suzuki about ordering books cheaply from an outfit in England, but Suzuki said we should buy locally. I'd never thought about shopping that way and took it to heart. As a result, there was one thing that bothered me about Conze's book on the Heart and Diamond sutras. Rather than buying copies of the book, we each got a cheap photocopied version. That type of technology was not widely available, but UC Berkeley had it and

Richard had worked there until a year before. Maybe better Conze didn't come and learn that we'd ripped him off. Bill Lane said it was okay if we used a Xerox machine to make the copies because Chester Carlson, the inventor of that process and head of Xerox Corporation had been the largest donor toward the purchase of Tassajara.

Three Scholars

Other scholars and writers arrived at Tassajara as guests or as our invited guests. A scholar named Ernst Benz of the University of Marburg in Germany read papers on the early history of Buddhism in Europe and America. Jacob Needleman came to do research on a book to be titled *The New American Religions*.

World religions scholar Huston Smith came with his wife and daughters, one of whom told me she favored Islam. Huston taught at MIT and was an engaging, highly respected figure. His *The World's Religions: Our Great Wisdom Traditions*, published in 1958, had been well-received and widely read. He and D.T. Suzuki became friends when D.T. Suzuki was also in Boston lecturing at Harvard and MIT. They were both on the board of Elsie Mitchell's Cambridge Buddhist Association. Huston spoke of the way the two Suzukis complimented each other—Daisetsu the public, prolific scholar. Shunryu the quiet, low-key master with a "wonderful aura, the peace and presentness of the man."

Huston had returned from a trip to India with a recording of the throat chanting of the Gyuto monks in Dharamsala where the Dalai Lama lived. He played the tape of the Gyuto monks chanting for us. Such an unusual sound, mesmerizing. Huston said to him it was like a somewhat eerie, avant garde piece by a chorus with extremely low bass, middle, and treble voices blending together. Then he said that each monk was somehow chanting the three parts simultaneously. What? Huston said when he took the tape to an audio engineer at MIT, the man replied, "This isn't humanly possible."

Margot Patterson Doss

Margot Doss was an author of books and articles about the myriad places one could go walking in the Bay Area. In the '50s, many of the Beat writers frequented her and her husband John's home in Russian Hill. She wrote regular *Chronicle* columns called "San Francisco at Your Feet" and "Bay Area at your Feet." She didn't write about Tassajara although she was an occasional Tassajara guest who knew the surrounding trails. She was an effective crusader in local environmentalism, using the power of her popular columns to garner support for preserving space for the public good rather than the top bidder. One of her first articles, in 1961, described a walk discovering Japantown.

"Initially, it was Suzuki Roshi who showed me around Japantown. It was wonderful. He couldn't speak very good English at that time. But he could certainly make himself known. It was so interesting. Here was this church which didn't look Japanese at all. I walked up the steps, and the door was open. I went in. I was trying to figure out what denomination it was. I heard someone upstairs. I called 'hello, hello,' and Suzuki Roshi came out of his office. I said that I was exploring around the town. I asked him a few questions about the building. He told me that it was Zen Buddhist. And of course it wasn't Christian. It had been a synagogue. That whole area had been a Jewish community at one time. There had been a Jewish shopping street nearby that had all kinds of second-hand stores. It was a little like going to London and seeing all those shops of all kinds. The Jewish people recycled a lot of things. Also the Ukraine Bakery was in that area.

"I started asking some questions about Japantown. He said, 'Let me take you.' So he walked around with me on that very first walk, pointing out the things that were intrinsically Japanese. It was a wonderful walk. I liked it so much. There was a wonderful shop that had Japanese antiques—Honnami. He took me in and introduced me to the owners. We did Soko Hardware last. I remember the proprietor came out and bowed and said, 'Sayonara,' to us as we left. It was really lovely.

"After doing the walk I was so pleased I sent Suzuki Roshi an orchid to say thank you."

Doss said that Suzuki asked both her and Don Allen where a good place for Richard to scout out for a retreat might be. A close friend of Richard from East Coast days, Allen was an editor for Grove Press who specialized in Beat poetry. And he was the editor of Margot Doss's first book, *San Francisco At Your Feet*. He suggested a good place for a retreat would be the first valley north of San Francisco on Highway One, a valley that ran down to the beach, Green Gulch. Margot suggested Tassajara. She'd first seen it after a trip to Japan as a guest of American President Lines in 1962. She thought Suzuki would like it as it reminded her of Japan.

Doss said that during the initial fundraising drives for the first payments on Tassajara, Richard called her frequently asking her to suggest people who might donate money. She'd give him a list of names, addresses, and phone numbers every time he called. "Journalists, especially columnists, which I am, have access to a lot of people that Richard wouldn't."

Doss and family came back to see how Tassajara was doing after Zen Center had acquired it, staying in the most spacious Stone Room One. She was pleased to see Ed Brown was still there, loved the food which had built on what she remembered from the summers before when the Becks owned it.

After dinner she, her husband John, and their four boys were all submerged in hot springs water when a family with two little girls joined them. She was proud of how well-behaved her boys were in the midst of all that nudity. As a result, the parents of the little girls who wanted to go to Suzuki's lecture asked Margo if her oldest son who was twelve could babysit her children. He said sure.

"After the lecture, I asked my son if there had been any visitors. He said yes, the roshi came in for a few minutes. I asked, what did he say? He said, 'Goodnight.' It was so innocent. That was the feeling about it. There was that innocence in Tassajara too. I remember all the hikers coming in from the trail that went along the creek.

They'd stop and leave their backpacks by the bridge to the baths. I don't recall anything being stolen.

"One of the memorable things about that trip," Doss said, "was the flies. There were lots of them. There were flies around the dining room. We were all chasing flies off ourselves. But not Suzuki. I looked at him and asked, 'Why don't the flies land on you?' And he said, 'I tell them to go away.' Very cute. We loved seeing him there. Suzuki Roshi seemed too down-to-earth to be saintly. But saintly was an impression that I got, along with his down-to-earthness."

Ruth Fuller Sasaki

One morning the chanting of the Heart Sutra was dedicated to Ruth Fuller Sasaki, a Zen scholar, practitioner, and matriarch of twentieth century Zen Buddhism. She never stepped on Tassajara soil but the influence of her life and work had been key in fertilizing Western minds to be open to and supportive of the dharma. Her voluminous *Zen Dust: The History of the Koan and Koan Study in Rinzai (Linji) Zen* had been released in January. It was one of a number of her books in the Zen Center and student libraries. My favorite was *Cat's Yawn*, a collection of journals edited by her, authored by her teacher Sokei-an Sasaki, and published by the First Zen Institute in the early 1940s—with playful sumi ink art—like that of a cat yawning.

I first heard about Ruth Fuller Sasaki from Claude Dalenberg. He said Gary Snyder was among those who worked on her extensive Zen text translation project in Kyoto. She had become a Rinzai Zen priest and had a subtemple at Daitokuji, Ryosen-an.

Her Zen studies began when she met D.T. Suzuki in Japan in 1930. He introduced her to the abbot of Nanzenji in Kyoto where she first practiced zazen and worked on a koan—with D.T. Suzuki as translator.

She was a prominent member of the First Zen Institute in New York City and married the institute's founding teacher, Sokei-an

Sasaki, to get him out of interment in 1944. For a decade she was Alan Watts's mother-in-law. Fuller Sasaki died shortly after returning from a trip to the U.S. Her last stop on that trip was a visit with Shunryu Suzuki. They talked about the fundamental similarities between Soto and Rinzai Zen. Suzuki was surprised to learn she'd met his second teacher, Ian Kishizawa whose temple was close to Suzuki's Rinsoin in Yaizu. Kishizawa was the leading interpreter of Dogen's Shobogenzo. Suzuki mentioned meeting with Fuller Sasaki in a lecture and spoke about how impressed he was with the clarity of her thinking and freedom from unnecessary discrimination.

Dorothy Schalk

Dorothy Schalk had studied with Fuller Sasaki in Kyoto. Schalk spent a few days at Tassajara with us in October. She said she would love to stay longer but she was on her way to Japan and knew it was important she arrive exactly when she said she would. Schalk was the founder of a sitting group in Northampton, Massachusetts where Suzuki had visited several times since 1965, led sesshin, and given talks.

Phillip Wilson had led a one-day sesshin there earlier in the year and given two talks, one on the kyosaku and one on breath. He was from that area and was visiting his wife J.J. who was teaching English at nearby Smith College. She was also treasurer of the Northampton Zen group.

Schalk and her husband owned land in Vermont where they planned to create a *Zen House* for daily practice and sesshin. Of all the East Coast connections that Suzuki had, Dorothy Schalk was the most gung-ho about zazen. Two years earlier she'd come to San Francisco to practice with Suzuki for a month. She sat every period, went to every lecture. After that she'd returned a couple of times for weeklong sesshins. Before Tassajara became an item, it looked like Suzuki would send Phillip to help with her group and Suzuki would be spending more time in New England, the home of transcendentalism. Now Schalk could see that wouldn't happen any time soon. She was on her way to practice at a temple in Japan. Maybe she'd meet a priest there who would be their teacher.

Diamond Sutra

One morning Richard and Suzuki had breakfast with elderly, rather proper-looking couple who had driven a big black Cadillac all the way in. They'd been sent by Elsie Mitchell of the Cambridge Buddhist Association. I sensed in Richard a managed, somewhat nervous vibe that comes with wanting everything to go smoothly.

I brought the food and drinks from the kitchen across the courtyard. At that point I was the entire dining room crew, as all the other guests had left. October was almost over, and this would be the last meal of the 1967 guest season.

The woman told Suzuki she had a question of which she was most eager to know the answer. She had been looking at a copy of the Conze book that she found in the reading area, the one we'd shamelessly photocopied for study periods. She was concerned about something she'd read in the Diamond Sutra translation.

"Now, I've read a great deal about religion," she said, "and I consider that I know quite a bit about the different spiritual paths. But I have never, ever read or heard anything like what I read in that book. It said that there is no self, no being, no person, no soul. What is that all about?"

I stood nearby listening to her heartfelt question about the dharma which was, to my mind, more to the point than most of the questions we students had asked him all summer.

"That is fundamental teaching of Buddhism," Suzuki began, and he was about to continue when Richard interrupted with, "And how are the colors of the leaves in Massachusetts this fall? I do miss that here on the West Coast." And he successfully diverted the conversation to a less challenging topic. Suzuki poured syrup on his pancakes.

Breakfast over, those East Coast folks wanted someone to drive their big black Cadillac out of Tassajara. I told them I was experienced and available to do so. I quickly got the dining room cleanup done, informed someone not too high on the authority tree, and waited for the guests while I sat outside the third stone room reading the Diamond Sutra.

Rather than get out at Jamesburg where the pavement begins and take the next ride back in as would be expected, I continued with them to Big Sur's Nepenthe Restaurant where they treated me to a delicious hamburger. On the way I brought up the woman's question to Suzuki and went on about no self, no being, no person, no soul for a great deal longer than the minute or so Suzuki would have. "It is written," I said when we parted, "that the sixth patriarch got enlightened by hearing a monk recite the Diamond Sutra at the point that it said there is no abode. That's something to chew on, huh?"

She smiled. Her husband smiled. I thanked them for the ride. They thanked me for driving them there.

In the Diamond Sutra, written over a thousand years after Buddha's time, Buddha is talking to Subhuti. But Suzuki ignored that and said this is Buddha giving this teaching to Buddha. Not like a person Buddha but a cosmic one—Vairocana Buddha. I loved reading the Diamond Sutra during the practice period, was attracted to the nobody thereness nor anything hereness. In it Buddha would say things like all beings are beingless and therefore they are called beings. It seemed to me that Buddha would then deny he'd even said that.

In a talk he gave at Esalen, Suzuki said:

> In the Zen school, in short, we wipe up everything, all the dust on the mirror. And to see everything in the reflection of the mirror is our way. Or to write and erase everything from the blackboard is Zen. And we continue this kind of activity—write it, wipe it up and write something else on it and wipe it up. This is, in other words, detachment.

I could easily see how this kind of teaching might disturb someone with a more sensible way of looking at it all.

After the Cadillac

I got a ride with some hippies in a VW bus and ended up in Palo Colorado Canyon getting stoned in the redwoods with folks I'd met at Tassajara in the summer. Into the night with welcoming revelers, ecstatic music, dancing around, warm libertine openness. Dozed off in a tree house.

Hitchhiking back to Tassajara the next morning, I immediately recognized the driver of the car that pulled over as Lou Gottlieb, the eloquent bassist for the folk group, The Limeliters. I loved The Limeliters when I was in high school and played a number of their songs. I heard them perform in 1963 at a well-attended concert in a basketball stadium at Texas Christian University in Fort Worth. This was the third time I'd actually met Gottlieb. The first was in 1964, backstage at a New York City night club where my mother, sister, and I had gone to hear them at my urging. The second was at Tassajara soon after we'd opened for guests. I was delighted to find him at the coffee machine and introduced myself. He was most friendly and talkative.

Gottlieb was famed for his commune, Morning Star, in Sonoma County. He'd deeded it to god and let anyone come live there who wanted. I asked him about a fellow who'd been with us for a few weeks and told me he was headed to Morning Star next. Gottlieb said, "Ah yes, Larry is there. He built a little mini-zendo on the land where anyone can do zazen whenever they want."

Amelia Newell, with flowing white hair, was in the car with Gottlieb. She lived above Deetjen's Big Sur Inn and had a nursery there full of succulents. She had turned several hundred acres south of Big Sur in Gorda into another hippie haven. A few years prior, she'd offered that land to the Zen Center. Suzuki, Richard, Ginny, and Henry Shaeffer visited. She showed them around. Suzuki said the pines on the slopes reminded him of Eiheiji. They were offered homemade bread and marijuana. They accepted the bread.

Gottlieb and Newell were sweet, cultured, adventurous Bohemians with the best of intentions, but their rule-free communes, each with over 200 hippie homesteaders, were not appreciated by their neighbors and local health departments for the anarchy, shocking squalid unsanitary conditions, rampant drug use including injected meth and epidemic hepatitis. But of all the rides I had ever gotten hitchhiking, that was the one I remembered most fondly.

Back at Tassajara, I went to Suzuki's cabin to pay respects. He was in his garden working. He said hi and kept working. Then he remembered something and changed tone, scolding me for leaving and staying away without getting permission, saying that monks don't leave monasteries on their own. I snapped at him that I had told someone.

He said, "Oh okay. I see." There was something about the way he just politely dropped out of it when I resisted. For a second, I didn't know where I was. I'd expected a counterattack. He'd made his point and didn't pursue it further, instead tripping me with kindness. But what he'd said sank in and I was less sneaky after that—a little less. Suzuki would say he'd only be strict with or hard on someone if they were a good student. He was not strict with or hard on me. But still he left me with a feeling of not being so sure about where I stood. No abode.

Elsie Mitchell

It wasn't just those guests that Elsie Mitchell had connected us with. When Suzuki and Richard went to the East Coast to raise money toward the purchase of Tassajara she arranged for them to meet her father, Edward C. Johnson II, the founder of Fidelity Investments. That meeting went very well. Johnson was taken with both Shunryu Suzuki and Richard Baker and became a major contributor.

Elsie first met Suzuki at Sokoji in 1959 and again in 1963, both times when she was on her way home after visiting Eiheiji and her teacher Rindo Fujimoto at his temple. She and her husband John had recorded the ceremonies and sounds of Eiheiji, which Folkways Records had published as *The Way of Eiheiji: Zen Buddhist Ceremony* in a two-record set with a twenty-five-page booklet. There were not many Buddhist groups in the United States at that time that catered to Caucasians, and just a few small Zen groups—the oldest being the First Zen Institute of America in New York City. The Cambridge Buddhist Association had no priest. Buddhist scholars D.T. Suzuki and Shin'ichi Hisamatsu were both on the board and Hisamatsu lead the zazen.

Elsie had the Soto Zen ties in Japan, but the Cambridge Buddhist Association was not associated with any sect. It was surely the only group outside of Suzuki's own Japantown territory that he had joined in America. The main glue was that he and Elsie had made a personal connection. He appreciated how she committed herself to Buddhism and to helping to establish it in America step by step and without making a big deal of herself. She admired his low-key, open-minded style, that he had worked so hard on his English, and how well he had adapted to American life. She found him less culture-bound than other Japanese priests she had known. She had been "greatly impressed with his integrity, his goodness and particularly his willingness to work out ways of traditional Buddhist practice really suitable for contemporary Westerners."

Suzuki had led zazen and given a talk at Elsie and John Mitchell's home during both his spring '66 and '67 trips East. They always enjoyed meeting each other, but the time they each held most dear was Suzuki's extended 1964 visit to Cambridge when he had no other commitments.

Grand Occasion

On September 9, 1964, Suzuki sent Elsie Mitchell a letter.

> Whenever I receive your letters, I find great encouragement in them. Now I have decided to visit your home after the 20th of this month. Please let me know what day is convenient for you and where and how I can meet you. I think I can stay there more than one week. I have no idea of forcing our way on anyone, but I want to be sincere enough to accept people and help people improve for the better. I am sure we will have interesting talks about the matters that concern us most.
>   With gassho, Rev. Shunryu Suzuki
>   I am always in black robe with Japanese kimono.

Elsie Mitchell enlisted the help of members of the Cambridge Buddhist Association to prepare for Reverend Suzuki who was scheduled to fly in the following evening. They were cleaning up the library-cum-meditation hall, his bedroom, the kitchen, the living room.

On a table in the entryway, there was a recently received card from the soon-to-be honored guest giving his time of arrival and flight number. "Since I bought the ticket," he wrote, "I have started to feel excited. I can hardly imagine how I'll feel when I meet you at the Boston Airport, at the other end of this continent."

Everyone was wet with sweat or mop water in old work clothes, feeling rather dirty and unpresentable, when the doorbell rang. John stopped his dusting, stepped down from his ladder, opened the door, and Shunryu Suzuki was standing there with traveling bag and grin as a taxi behind him drove off. They had been so sure he was coming the next evening, and they were absolutely nonplussed by his arrival.

"Oh, we didn't think you were coming until tomorrow!" said Elsie.

Oops. He'd obviously written the wrong date on the card, he admitted and laughed unashamedly and most amused at the situation. "Well, let me help you prepare for the grand occasion of my arrival," he said, tying his traveling robe sleeves behind his neck.

Everyone protested *no no no no no you can't work!* and bid him to rest after his trip, but there was nothing he would rather have done than to join in with them in cleaning. They cleaned and cleaned until it was past bedtime. Suzuki was completely at home in his new surroundings, and everyone was charmed as could be.

The next morning after breakfast, Elsie told Suzuki to take it easy for a while, that she had to go out and do some shopping. When she got back with her groceries, she found him outside on a tall ladder cleaning windows in his white long underwear and in plain view of her most proper neighbors.

The Mitchells took him to their country place at Cape Cod and let him be alone whenever he wanted. He sat sunrise zazen on a large rock on the beach, chanted with the waves, and walked back to the house as the sun came up. He called that his secret hobby and said his wife wouldn't have let him do it because it was too cold and wet.

He weeded around the house, adjusted a few stones in the rock garden, raked leaves, and trimmed their bushes. There were boulder-size stones in the garden. He climbed on them and jumped from one to another which made Elsie gasp and worry. Suzuki made a miniature garden of moss, berries, and sand in a large shell so he could "take a bit of New England back to California with me." John put his mini-garden sideways into a wide-mouth jar to protect it.

They talked about Buddhism and Christianity, Japan and America, about Fujimoto and Fujimoto's dharma brother and polar opposite, the spirited Hakuun Yasutani who used koans and was conducting sesshins for lay people, including Westerners, in Japan.

Walking around outdoors Suzuki got down on the ground for a close look at what bugs and rocks and plants were there and then he rolled over and peered up at the trees. Elsie said he was almost giddy, that she had to keep pulling him back from wandering into poison ivy. He took some of it and planted it in his garden-in-a-jar.

He kept remarking at the beautiful colors of the fall leaves on the deciduous trees. Not much of that near San Francisco—there were seasons here. So much reminded him of Japan—especially the pines. And parts of old Boston were like areas of Tokyo. He felt quite at home and said he looked forward to returning.

That same month, Elsie received another card from Suzuki.

> *Tues. Sep. 29, 1964*
> *Dear Mr. Mrs. Mitchell, I have just come back without the beautiful but poison oak-like-plant and my Japanese coat. I told my wife all the rest of the things which I did at your home, except my secret hobby. Will you please keep my coat till I visit you next time?*
> *With Gasho, Rev. S. Suzuki*

Elsie sent his coat back in a wooden box with a donation for the Zen Center which Suzuki set aside for his next trip to Boston.

Landmarks on the Road

One day Fred Tuttle drove unannounced into Tassajara. He just came in for a visit, but a visit from Fred would always include some helpful education. It was my day off, so Tim in the office asked if I'd take care of him.

Fred said he wanted to show me something. I followed him up the road to the cold-water spring. Where the road was wet, we climbed through bulging greenery toward the source. He said the dominant plants around the spring were giant chain ferns. They led to the catchments.

Fred told me we should check the catchments frequently to make sure they were clean and uncluttered with debris that might stop the flow and to make sure they were properly screened so that there would be no dead rodents that got trapped. According to Fred, the spring water originated in the Sierras, and he could tell because it was so cold. Pipes from the catchments ran under the road to two cement reservoirs, the second one larger and built by Paul Discoe and team to allow more water to be stored. From there a series of connected pipes ran to Tassajara in the small creek by the road. That made sense in the months it was dry, but it was a choice I would question when working on it wet and shivering in winter's icy cold.

Fred had to get back to the lookout tower. We walked down to his truck. I asked if he'd give me a ride to the first ridge. I wanted to hang out there a while, look at the view, eat my bag lunch, and walk back down.

We'd only driven up the road for a minute when he stopped just a little beyond the cold spring and asked if I'd noticed the Indian maiden painted on the boulder to the right. The painting had faded, but I could see her. Fred said that Harrison Fisher, a famous artist, had painted it half a century earlier. At the second switchback, he pulled the truck over and we got out. He said that was Echo Point and told me to yell something. I uncreatively yelled "Echo" and indeed it did come back at me—multiple times reverberating from that narrow canyon. The creek went under the road again just before the Church Creek Trailhead on the left which was just before the Horse Pasture Trailhead on the right.

At the third switchback, Fred said that's where the small creek crossed the road the first time. We'd already passed five crossings. I thought it would be neat to walk up creek from there to see if I could get to a place where the creek disappeared. As he drove up, I kept learning about the landmarks of the road. On the fourth switchback we had a view of the formations at Lime Point and below that, The Pines, which was in a 160-acre inholding the Becks owned. He said you go through it on the Church Creek Trail.

At the next switchback, there was a deep cast-iron bathtub at Wildcat Creek crossing below Bathtub Spring. The bathtub would fill with water coming down the ravine. It had been used in earlier times to fill overheating radiators. Fred told me to keep a branch or piece of rope running out of it so rodents wouldn't get trapped. He said he'd found as many as twenty dead mice in it when there was no exit.

Fred said parts of the road used to be paved with asphalt before the war, which meant World War II for anyone his age. He said it wasn't maintained for a few years during the war. It washed out and Tassajara was closed. I could see broken-up asphalt in places on the side mixed with rock and dirt.

He continued to a place after the last switchback where the road leveled off. Fred called it Black Butte Summit. He said the spot just before the road descended was called Hotel Point because until the late forties the road was one way and there had been a crank phone there to call Tassajara to see if a car was on its way up and to let the folks there know a vehicle was on its way down. He said that phone was first used back when there was still a horse-drawn stagecoach. I got out and thanked him for the tour. He nodded and drove on.

I wanted to say something about the letter we'd recently received from him and his wife Linda, also a fire lookout. It was so heartfelt and he's such a man of few words I thought it best to leave our parting with a thanks and a nod. Also, I thought I might choke up. In it they wrote, "Fire season terminates tonight, for us at full dark. It would be impossible to put into words all the good things you people have done for and meant to us. Somehow you folks have managed to bring here quiet, laughter, a subtle and impressive gravity, and that just plain simple humanness of which so few of us are capable. Thank you."

I walked to a spot a little above the road. After being in the narrow Tassajara Canyon so much, the panoramic views were breathtaking, expanded my sense of being. I ate my bag lunch, sat there an hour, took it all in, and lay down for a nap.

On the way back down to Tassajara Canyon, I spied some remnants of the old bare metal phone line from Hotel Point still running through some trees. Just before I re-entered Tassajara, I paused at the gate to look at the three peaks rising in the distance. Suzuki said those mountains were watching over us and were an important part of the spirit of Tassajara. I bowed to them—and then turning around, bowed to Fred in his tower, also watching over us.

Approaching Tassajara—view from below Lime Point above The Pines. Photo by Shundo David Haye.

― CHAPTER FIVE ―

CONTINUING

Working with Stones   NOVEMBER 1967

Watching Suzuki and Phillip working with stones, it seemed Phillip knew exactly what to do without Suzuki saying a word. Phillip was like a different person when they were together—or maybe no person. Richard said no one bonds with Suzuki the way Phillip does.

Paul said that he'd returned from the city in the Land Cruiser with Phillip driving and Suzuki sitting cross-legged in the front passenger seat. "Phillip was nodding out and I tried to wake him up and he said, 'It's okay—he's driving,' and he nodded toward Suzuki, and he never swerved or wiggled or anything. They had a very special relationship."

Since the guest season was over, my dining room days were too. I was now the dishwasher. I started working right after the meals and had plenty of time off. Suzuki asked me to help him in his garden one day when he saw I was unemployed. Phillip and Bob Halpern were already with him. I wondered what he needed me for. I didn't feel qualified, and I wasn't eager to work on stones with him. But when I got there, he asked me to bring them a wheelbarrow of dirt. Good. I went up to the garden by the shop, got a wheelbarrow, and asked Ruthie where to get dirt. Out past the baths by the compost bins.

I brought them three wheelbarrows of pristine Tassajara dirt.

Suzuki knew what I was good for. And I got to drink tea with them afterwards.

When Suzuki went off for his bath time, I asked Phillip if he'd done stonework before, and he told us about working with a Japanese stone and bonsai gardener in Hayward for half a year. He said, "Rev. Suzuki sent me to him when I said I wanted to learn stonework. That's where I got sensitive about stones. His name was Hamada. He was from a samurai family. He'd hire Japanese guys to work for him and he was rough with them, a brutal guy. I saw him make a guy get down on all fours so Hamada could stand on his back to change a light bulb. He and I were carrying a twenty-foot board. I turned and twisted it to hit him in the face. He asked if I did it on purpose. I did it because of how he treated those other guys.

"I liked him, though. He said he used to be more of a Buddhist, and he appreciated knowing Rev. Suzuki. He visited Sokoji for service one Sunday. Rev. Suzuki would give little square cards with his calligraphy to Japanese visitors. He gave one to me to give to Hamada and Hamada put it on his altar."

Phillip said he'd helped Hamada build Japanese gardens with large bonsai. "He would do a little landscape, whatever the yard needed, pop in some rocks, make a small pond, and stick a pine tree in there. Voila. He would put different kinds of dwarf plants around it for alpine foliage. A little Japanese garden. They were nice. Very fast. This guy loved rocks. That may be where I began to get a rock fetish where the rocks do things."

Phillip made a miniature rock garden in a box and showed it to Suzuki. Suzuki started moving the small stones around and Phillip saw them come alive. "When I saw Suzuki moving those rocks around with his hands, those stones in the box, I realized Hamada was like a child when it came to what Suzuki was doing."

Two years earlier in Japan, after nine months at Eiheiji, Phillip began living near and practicing zazen and tea ceremony at a famous Rinzai temple, Engakuji, in Kamakura, the temple associated with D.T. Suzuki who was a layman. The practice there suited Phillip better. It was simpler and rougher. They didn't sit on tatamis with zafus and zabutons but on hard wooden floors.

When Suzuki went to Japan in 1966, Phillip joined him at Suzuki's Rinsoin temple in Yaizu, a couple of hours by train from Kamakura. "That was the first time we did stonework together. Stones had slipped in their positions above the pond. We worked all around the yard."

There were two enormous stones by the pond behind the temple that Suzuki had placed there in the '50s. Phillip wondered how they got there, especially when Suzuki told him that a good amount of each stone was buried. That reminded Phillip of how Suzuki had shown him to drive incense deep into the center of the bowl of ashes on the altar.

At first at Tassajara, they worked on walls. "He said that one of the most difficult things to do is to repair a wall that's already built. When a wall is finished and something goes wrong in the base, it's hard to replace the stones at the foundation. I reflected on my own foundation or lack of it. I kind of peeked in there but it was too dark. I didn't see too much. So I would work with him on repairing the foundation walls.

"We worked without mortar. He showed me how to put the rocks in at an angle. He would dig holes, and we'd put up some structure to hold the other rocks back. Then he would use a big stick or limb to lift a rock or move it into place. He'd jiggle it around there. He showed me that the rocks have different positions. You can make a rock very stable by setting it. You have a flat surface, then a front, different sides and back. He showed me there were different faces to a rock. He'd put water all around them. Rev. Suzuki said there were rocks that were alive and those that weren't. I came to understand that."

Building Walls

Steel rebar footings for the foundation of the new kitchen were already being made when Harold Dodson, the Monterey County head building inspector, arrived. Paul Discoe, in charge of the project, dealt with him. Dodson looked at the plans that called for steel reinforced stone walls and, even though he was impressed with the project, said you need an engineer to do calculations to ensure that these walls will be strong enough to hold up in an earthquake. Geoffrey Barrett, whose offices were in Mill Valley, was hired. He and Paul went back to the building codebook and came upon a surprising find. If the walls were eighteen inches thick, they wouldn't need any additional reinforcement. That was the traditional method, and it was still to code. Dodson agreed and gave Tassajara three years to complete construction of the new kitchen during which the county would ignore the lack of compliance of the functioning shack kitchen. The rebar footings were used for the walls of a new septic tank.

The old stone buildings had walls of jagged mountain rock. After surveying the mountain and hillsides around, that didn't seem practical. The streambeds, however, were right there and had what seemed like an endless supply of beautiful, smooth basalt and granite stones of various sizes and shapes. Another plus in their column was that Suzuki favored creek stones.

Paul was an admirer of Helen and Scott Nearing's *Living the Good Life*, a classic book on self-sufficient living. The Nearings followed a modified version of the Flagg method of stone wall building. Ernest Flagg was a New York architect who developed a method that could be done by those with limited skills and experience. The Nearings used 18" tall wood forms. The stones were placed in the form against the exterior side and concrete poured behind them. It would form a smooth interior wall and ooze in between the stones to keep them held tightly in place. When a level was dry, the form would be reused for the next level up. Paul followed a modified version of the Nearings' method.

Selecting the stones, getting them to the site, and building the wall was a tedious process. Some were as small as a softball, others too large for one person to carry. Sand and gravel were gathered in the creek and brought up in bucket brigades. The area was in time covered with stones—except for enough of the path left free for passage. That construction site was smack dab in the center of life at Tassajara and was a delightful contrast with the relatively orderly developments elsewhere.

Shunryu Suzuki squatting. Paul Discoe setting a corner stone. Phillip Wilson upper right at the cement machine by the arbor with hanging han and bell. Building upper left is the zendo.

Making Robes

Before the first practice period, Kathy Cook had gone to Suzuki and suggested that we get started making robes for Tassajara students to wear in the zendo. He gave her one of his work robes as an example of what might be appropriate for lay students. She had plenty of experience sewing, but what he gave her was put together in ways she'd not seen. She laid it out to understand how it was made. It had elastic at the wrist of the sleeves, a pleated skirt, and hung straight with a dropped shoulder. She worked hard to come up with some facsimile suitable for us with a slightly different design, used a gray cotton poly mixture, made a pattern, and started sewing. She showed the first prototype to Suzuki. He liked it.

The seamstresses had what to Kathy was a wonderful sewing room in the lower barn by the stream. She felt empowered by Suzuki. She loved her job and was working with good friends. Robes weren't the only sewing that needed to be done so they'd been coming out slowly. Then, while Paul Discoe was in San Francisco with a truck doing some shopping, he got six treadle sewing machines at a secondhand shop on McAlister Street behind City Hall. That sped things up.

Suzuki came up to Kathy one day and said, "You're doing very well, and I don't mean in terms of success and failure."

Kathy was attractive. One day when she brought a sample of her work to Suzuki he told her, "You are too charming." She wondered if she should make robes out of sackcloth and ashes. The one she brought him was a candidate for winter robes, made with a heavy woolen weave.

She tried to figure out designs for zendo wear that made sense for Western bodies. She also worked at making designs for women's bodies that differed from those for men. She tried long skirts and blouses instead of robes for women. I got a thin gray robe in the summer and found it made sitting more comfortable. Kathy thought that by the spring of the following year, there would be enough for everyone. Some students complained about having to wear robes, saying it would be too regimented. Kathy went to Suzuki upset. He told her, "I get angry with the students because you work so hard, and they don't appreciate your effort."

Kathy's mother came to Tassajara. They had tea with Suzuki. Afterwards he told Kathy, "In Japan we say, 'fighting the curtain.' You're still fighting the curtain." And then, "When your mother dies, you'll know how lonely you are."

Kathy told Suzuki that when she first came to the Bay Area, she had a boyfriend who asked her to describe herself using three words. She told him, "Kathy, girl, thinker." After a lecture when students could ask questions, she expressed her understanding of how practice was not confined to any particular activity, that it covered everything "from the heights to the depths." Suzuki said,

"Your understanding is correct, but it's not real—try not to think so much."

Kathy had a chronic problem with pain in one knee when she sat. She'd had an operation years earlier. The pain was greater than the everyday pain that most of us experienced in zazen. Suzuki encouraged her to sit with the pain. She didn't feel it benefitted her, but she did her best "out of faith in Suzuki Roshi's way." Finally, she listened to her body instead of Suzuki and started sitting in a chair. Suzuki encouraged her to go back to cross-legged sitting as a way of strengthening her knee, but she felt he was completely wrong.

Suzuki talked to Kathy about having a farm and said we should go out to the Salinas Valley and do it just the way other farmers do it. We don't need to have some special way. She let him know he had no idea what agribusiness farming in Salinas was like and that we would not be on that scale or doing it that way with all the poisons and monoculture. He said to her, "I can't always be a wise man."

The Banker

Jack Tjeerdsma was a senior at UC Berkeley when he met Richard Baker in 1962. Richard took him to Sokoji. He sat in the zendo, which he found to be an unusual experience. Richard introduced him to Suzuki. The first impression Jack had of Suzuki was that this was a very detached, calm, older Japanese man. After that, he'd go to Sokoji to sit occasionally and would meet with Suzuki when he did. And Jack continued his relationship with Richard.

They worked together to create a magazine focusing on the latest developments in the world of science. Nothing came of it, but they got to know each other better. After graduating Phi Beta Kappa, Jack specialized in the Japanese financial community in America and became a consultant to Japanese banks, especially advising them on their investments. Richard told Jack Zen Center would like to get a loan to cover the mountainous costs of getting Tassajara going. Jack set up a meeting at the Bank of Tokyo. Suzuki and Richard arrived in robes which Jack said, "rattled the natives."

They were successful in obtaining a loan with their presence as collateral. Silas followed up and arranged the details.

Jack had already been following Zen Center's progress. He'd been to Tassajara to check it out back in the fall of '66. Less than a year later, Richard suggested he go to Tassajara for a week. Jack agreed. He met Phillip Wilson early in the morning at Sokoji for a ride down in a pear-shaped Volvo. Jack asked if anyone else was coming. Phillip said yes, one person. Then Suzuki appeared. Suzuki took the back seat next to Jack and bowed to him. Jack bowed back.

When they arrived at Tassajara, Suzuki bowed to Jack. Jack bowed back. Suzuki walked to the zendo to offer incense. Nary a word was spoken the whole way. Jack couldn't figure out how traveling silently with Suzuki for four hours could leave him with such a feeling of amazement. "He was just there in the Suzuki Roshi way," he said. "It was very connected, personal, compassionate."

Phillip took Jack to one of the Pine Rooms.

"What are we doing here?"

"You're going to sit tangaryo."

"What the hell is that?"

"You're going to sit here all day tomorrow."

"You've got to be out of your mind. I didn't come down here to sit all day."

"Well, that's what you've got to do."

"When is there a bus back or when is someone going back out? Cause I can't see sitting here for a day."

"No one's going out, so this is what you have to do. It's what Suzuki Roshi wants you to do."

"Oh my god."

Jack went along with it. He spent the first half of his tangaryo day reviewing his life and finally stopped because he got bored. "I sat there thinking, but my thinking was no longer following a discursive path," he said. He was uncomfortable, but he soldiered through.

Jack was given a robe, an oryoki set, and a seat in the zendo. He received a brief instruction on how to use the oryoki. The next morning, he entered the zendo with the others feeling like an out-of-place commercial banker who'd wandered onto a stage in the middle of some medieval performance.

Jack was overweight and couldn't put his legs in lotus position. He seemed so awkward and clueless to John Steiner sitting next to him that John assumed Jack was a new student who had received no zazen instruction. John leaned over and showed Jack how to put his hands on his knees and rock back and forth in diminishing arcs. He showed him the oval mudra, left palm on right and thumbs almost touching, held at the lower abdomen.

Suzuki entered the zendo, offered incense at the altar, sat on his zafu, and the bell to begin the period rang. John continued whispering his zazen instruction. I was sitting a few seats away and thought that was unusual, a zazen instruction during zazen. Tim Buckley was sitting next to me. Jack was sitting next to Tim and John on the other side of Jack. Tim turned his head to peer at what was happening as John's thorough instruction continued in a low but audible whisper. Tim turned his head again. Finally, Tim leaned back, reached over, and signaled to John his displeasure. Bang! Suzuki leaped off the altar platform and in a flash was striking Tim on the shoulders repeatedly with his nyoi. Tim gasshoed. Suzuki returned to his seat. Jack was shocked and wondered if he would be next for a flogging.

John brought his instruction to a close. I wanted to applaud, but continued sitting silently with my fellow students, all certainly more alert than a moment earlier.

After zazen, Jack started to walk out. Then he realized students were not leaving. They were walking slowly in the aisle. He joined in, copying the others as well as he could. A bell rang. They walked around and returned to their seats. He sat down for another zazen. Then there was service. Jack followed along, bowing down to the floor and chanting the Heart Sutra, reading it off the chant card John handed him. Soon he was raking leaves off the path during morning samu. Back to the zendo. Again? People put their oryoki bowls on the meal board that ran along the tatami. He felt self-conscious being a step behind on everything. In the oryoki meal he couldn't remember what he'd been told. John silently guided him along.

After breakfast, Suzuki didn't leave, and everyone stood in the aisles in front of their zafus. Phillip came over and whispered to Jack that now there would be an entering ceremony for him. Following Phillip's instruction, Jack walked slowly around the zendo, slightly bent over, hands in gassho. As he passed the other students, their hands were also in gassho. Jack bowed with Suzuki, then returned to his seat. A bell rang. All did a standing bow together. The ceremony was over. Jack walked out somewhat dazed, feeling that he'd just gone through an initiation that gave him kinship with millions of monks, nuns, and contemplatives throughout the centuries.

What a great week followed. It was difficult, but every day he got more into it. He made friends with John Steiner who'd been so helpful. They joined Suzuki during work periods, gathering stones from the creek. Then one day after dinner, Phillip told Jack they'd be leaving the next morning at 4 a.m. Jack asked, "Who?" "You, me, and Reverend Suzuki." The next morning, before others had arrived for morning zazen, Phillip and Jack joined Suzuki and Suzuki's attendant Louise while Suzuki offered incense in the zendo.

As Phillip, Suzuki, and Jack drove off in the pear-shaped Volvo, Suzuki asked Jack how his week at Tassajara had been. And they talked and talked most comfortably the whole four-hour ride back to the city.

Jane Runk

Jane Runk grew up on the coast in Virginia and North Carolina where she loved swimming in the ocean. She graduated from the University of Maryland majoring in art and education and got a master's in education at Temple University in Philadelphia. In New York she studied with a master printer, taught poor kids in Brooklyn, and made prints at night. She was a devoted Catholic when she was young, but that had fallen away by the time she was twenty. "And for about ten years," she said, "I felt like I was drifting with nowhere to alight, no sense of security or sense at all of the world." She started finding relief in reading, beginning with Albert Camus. She especially liked *The Plague*.

Jane frequented a coffee shop in the mornings and "rather abruptly" married a guy she met there. She became Jane Westberg and they drove to Seattle where he had family. They planned to go to China, so they took an extremely intensive three-month course in Chinese. They had to learn sixty-five Chinese characters a night and be able to read material with them and use them in conversation the next day. She loved it. Her husband did not. They broke up.

Then a friend gave her *The Supreme Doctrine* by Hubert Benoit. "I started reading it and I couldn't put it down because it was like talking to someone who knew exactly what I was going through. Benoit quoted D.T. Suzuki so much that then I started reading his books. And when I was reading them, I really, really wanted to find a teacher and find out what he was talking about.

"I used to go to the free school and sit and talk to people in the evenings. Someone there said there's a Zen master down in San Francisco. Then I heard about a bus going there to join in an antiwar march. I signed up for it. I met a guy named Bill Lane sitting in the office and he said he was on his way to Japan because he wanted to study at a temple. I told him, 'Well, there's a master in San Francisco. If we go down there, you might get the same thing without having to go to Japan.' So he changed his mind, and we got to San Francisco and joined the march.

"When it was finished, I went over to Sokoji. The door was open and I walked up to the second floor because I didn't see anything. The office door was open and Suzuki Roshi was sitting at his desk. I asked him, 'Could I come in?' He said, 'Sure, come in.'

And I sat and talked to him about why I wanted to study Buddhism. I told him that I was very much afraid of death. I couldn't stop thinking about it and about how we all live a life and do things and struggle and then the only thing at the end is to just die. He was really sympathetic, and he said, 'Let's go sit right now.' I had no idea what he was talking about. I went into the zendo and sat with him. He arranged my posture and all, and then he sat next to me. I was so self-conscious. I thought we sat a really long time, but I'm sure it was no more than five minutes.

Afterwards, we got up and went back to his office and I thanked him and started to leave. When I got to the door, he said, 'I hope I'll see you again.' And I thought, yeah, I do too."

Jane went back to Seattle and gave notice at the preschool where she was teaching. When the semester was over, she took a bus to San Francisco and went straight to Sokoji. Only Richard was there. He said he was just leaving to go to a benefit event. He showed her a poster. *Meditation in Everyday Life. Benefit weekend. Charlotte Selver, Charles Brooks, Shunryu Suzuki Roshi (Zen Master), Katagiri Sensei conduct a seminar of practice with explanation, intellectual silence, and awareness.* Off she went.

When Jane arrived, there was a crowd sitting and listening to Charlotte Selver. She heard Charlotte say, "Just look at the things that are in front of you. I want you to see the power in each one." Jane focused on a red plastic ball. "But no matter how much I tried," she said, "I couldn't see it as something powerful." After the workshop Jane kept thinking about the red ball and thought, "I'm going to see this red plastic ball as something wonderful."

Jane attended both days of the benefit weekend. Bill Lane was there too. He'd been sitting at Sokoji since they first came for the peace march.

Richard invited Jane to come to Tassajara to help get it ready for the opening. She rode there with Nancy Lay and her dog Noah. The first person Jane met at Tassajara was Peter Schneider. "He had a flash in his face like he was really happy to see me," she said. "I thought, 'Oh, I like him too.'"

It was hot during the day. Richard told Jane she'd just need one blanket but the first night she woke up freezing and was too tired to get another blanket. She roomed with Nancy Lay and wanted a sleeping bag like Nancy. She thought it was adorable the way Noah would get into Nancy's sleeping bag and stick his nose out. The lack of electricity was no problem for her. For a time, her father had been a principal at a two-room schoolhouse. They lived in a nearby house without electricity. But they were by the beach.

Jane loved Tassajara, Suzuki, her fellow students, and the practice. She stayed for the practice period and through the fall. She'd found what she was looking for, what had been missing. She didn't want to be anywhere else doing anything else.

A Danish Carpenter

The first time I saw Niels Holm, he was staggering lanky and loud down the road from the parking lot, having hitched a ride in with some hippies headed into the woods to go camping. He'd gone to Esalen but couldn't stay because he couldn't pay. But he could play and by late morning left an all-night party in Big Sur drunk. He got stoned with the hippies who were going to a Zen monastery. He tagged along to check it out.

Niels said he'd been drunk but never stoned before. I took him to the baths for a sobering soak. Richard was there, showing some guests around. He came back in a while and joined us. Saw right through Niels's whacked-out condition to the solid core, found out he had skills we needed, asked him to stay, and even suggested he might want to become a priest. That was not a normal thing for Richard to say to people who'd just arrived or actually to say at all. Paul said that Richard had an uncanny ability to size people up quickly. Perfect time for a Danish carpenter to walk in. There were ambitious plans and much work to do. Right off Niels was working with Paul. And right off they were arguing. Niels slid with ease into the zazen schedule. He sat legs in lotus from the first. He said he'd done a lot of that in India.

Niels had been a sailor and merchant marine. His choice of words bore that out—much profanity. He'd walked across Europe through Iran and Pakistan into India where he gave away his clothes and money. He spent nine months walking from place to place in a loincloth, sitting under trees meditating. There was a shortage of food in India, but Niels said his main problem was people giving him too much. Sometimes the food was too spicy. He arrived at a village one day starving and thirsty and was enthusiastically invited to join in on the festivities of a local wedding. Many little dishes were spread out on tables. He tried one, but it was too spicy hot to eat. Every subsequent attempt was the same. His mouth was on fire, so he started to drink a cup of water, but it was too spicy hot to drink. Somehow, he survived.

From Niels I learned new and impressive facts about Denmark, for instance, "Denmark is one of the biggest countries in the world!"

"Really?" I said.

"You don't know anything!" he chastised then reminded me that Greenland is owned by Denmark. He went on about Vikings too. He'd pronounce it like it was spelled Wikings. "Vikings were the first Europeans in America! They ruled England, France, Northern Europe, and Russia! The Vikings were the Rus! They became the Russian royalty!"

"Niels, you're speaking with exclamation points."

"It's because you are ignorant about the great history of Denmark!"

Niels's father was a beer distributor. Niels was born in 1941 and remembered occupying German soldiers coming into the house to get beer. He said it felt to him like a dark cloud had entered their home.

On a four-and-nine-day, Niels invited me to join him after breakfast to drink some real coffee. He derided the coffee from the machine, calling it no better than colored water. But then he puzzled me when he filled up a thermos with that same weak brew. When I questioned why he did that he told me not to be rude and insult my host and get two cups. He refused to let me bring any powdered milk. Once in his room, he poured two cups of coffee and then brought out a jar of Nescafe from which he added a heaping teaspoon to each of our cups. I declined the sugar. We drank two such cups each.

We started off in a rather philosophical vein, but as the caffeine kicked in we were jabbering away energetically, telling each other whatever stories came to mind. He said that Danes are boring in general but there are some exceptions such as a group that did outlandish political street theater. One of their performances was at a Fourth of July event.

"Fourth of July? In Denmark?"

Yep. He said that Danish Americans had made the Fourth of July a popular event in Denmark known as the Rebild Festival. He said it's celebrated in a hilly nature preserve in northern Jutland. They have a flag ceremony, speeches by dignitaries, music, and a feast. Thousands of people attend including the Danish royal family. One year there was a distraction from the festivities when, at the top of a hill, a long line of horses appeared mounted by what seemed to be American Indians in war paint. After remaining on the hilltop for a half hour, making many people below rather nervous, the Indians swooped down on the gathering whooping like Indians in movies and rode around the attendees with menacing faces, threatening spears and bows with arrows set to fly. Then, from another hill came the U.S. Cavalry which stormed down and slaughtered the Indians in a gory spectacle. Niels said they did it so well that many festival goers were horrified thinking the Indians were really being killed.

He said one year right before Christmas, in a bold statement against capitalist commercialism, a bunch of these pranksters dressed up as Santa Claus, went into department store toy sections and started handing out toys to young children who then had to experience the gifts Santa gave them taken away by confused parents and store employees, the children crying, "But Santa gave me this toy!"

After recovering from those accounts, I asked, "So, Denmark still has royalty?"

"For over a thousand years! They are Vikings!" And then he added the unexpected, "I have often seen the king naked." I asked him to please explain that. Niels said the king of Denmark was completely covered with tattoos. They were not visible when he was dressed because he didn't go around in shorts and a t-shirt. Niels, who had no tattoos I knew of, would walk into a tattoo parlor with a fellow mariner and often see photos of the Danish king naked front and back proudly displaying his tattoos.

He not only sailed and walked around the world, Niels astral traveled. He said mainly he did it when he was younger, but he could still do it. He said he couldn't do it if he wanted to though. It would happen when he was starting to fall asleep. He said he would roll over on his side, get into a calm state of mind, and just before sleep fly off into the room then out of the house and down the street over the cars then above the cars, over the city and into the clouds. He said he didn't really care to do it anymore.

The coffee high was wearing off. We started to crash. While I was telling what I thought was a most compelling story, Niels cut me off with, "Now you're boring me, David Chadowick." That's how he pronounced my last name, with an O in the middle. "Now I'll take a nap," he said. "You go away."

I headed for the baths to cleanse my body and mind—had a bit of a jagged feeling from all that caffeine—but was happy to have a new and unusual friend.

Noh Answers

Bob Halpern was getting bored and decided a visit with Suzuki would kindle his enthusiasm. He asked Kobun what the best way was to announce his presence to Suzuki. Kobun told him, "Maybe better to leave Roshi alone." Bob persisted.

Bob called, "*Ojama shimasu*" outside of Suzuki's cabin, using a Japanese phrase that literally meant I'm disturbing you.

"*Hai!*" came the response.

Bob went in and apologized to Suzuki for bothering him. Suzuki gestured for Bob to sit down. Bob told Suzuki that he was having a problem controlling his greed and pointed out that greed was one of the three poisons, along with hate and delusion. Suzuki remained silent. Bob said that he'd been stealing food from the kitchen and the kitchen storeroom and asked Suzuki if there was some special practice or mantra that he could utilize to deal with this problem.

Suzuki reached behind the low table he worked at and pulled out a little bag. "Here, have some jellybeans," he said.

Bob told me about that encounter which he called "Suzuki Roshi's homeopathic teaching."

It reminded me of an exchange that Fred Stoeber had with Suzuki the year before at Sokoji. Fred wanted to see Suzuki. He said he didn't have a pressing question, but thought he should, so he made one up. As he sat before Suzuki, he asked his question sounding as sincere as he could. Suzuki sat quietly for a moment, then turned and took a stack of envelopes from his table, handed them to Fred, and said, "Would you mail these for me?"

All Shining

After they'd been at Tassajara for nine months, Bob Watkins said that it was time for him and Sandy to move on. We appreciated them with their savvy and good vibes, and we didn't want to lose them, but they couldn't be dissuaded. Richard was angry at Bob for leaving. We weren't just losing friends. We were losing two people who contributed a lot to the day-to-day functioning and flowering of Tassajara.

When I first came, I envisioned each person as a permanent part of the community. But by October I could see that we'd all be coming and going, and we couldn't, we shouldn't, impede this flow.

The night before they left, I paid Bob and Sandy a visit. I told Sandy that not only the people, but the plants would miss her dearly. But I said I bet she'd be relieved to be away from the poison oak. Her arms still showed a few of the red bumpy signs of it. There wasn't any in Tassajara proper, but it was out there whichever direction you went. She'd get it from Noah. She said she thought she got it from the air. "It seems you'd have developed some immunity by now," I said.

"It isn't as bad as it used to be," she said, handing me a cup of chamomile tea. "There's also chamomile everywhere," she added. "Helps you sleep."

Bob Watkins would ask questions in lectures that showed he knew something about Buddhism before he came—but he'd pronounce the Sanskrit words wrong because he'd never heard them. He said it was because he'd just read by himself and never studied with anyone. "Suzuki Roshi," he said, "is the only spiritual teacher I've ever had."

After a while, Bob said, "I'm gonna miss that little guy. I remember the first time I met him. We were digging and I was down in this ditch with a pick and here comes Suzuki Roshi. I said, 'Gee I waited all this time to meet a real Zen master, and I can't think of a thing to ask.' I totally blanked out. I wasn't embarrassed or confused. In fact, I was surprised. It was like somebody reached up and turned off the lights. There just wasn't anything to say. Suzuki Roshi laughed and went on.

"You know how Suzuki and Katagiri sometimes wear white gloves when they work?"

"Sure. Dan says that's common in Japan," I said.

"Reminds me of Mickey Mouse," Bob said. "Suzuki has these little one-liners—like 'Just do it.' Another one is 'little by little.' He uses it like it's how things happen, how you can accomplish something. Little by little you can do it.

"Roshi and I both have a sweet tooth and, early on, after the last sitting period, he'd come to our cabin and sit on this stump and pull some candy from his sleeve. We would eat candy and talk for about ten or twenty minutes. Those times were wonderful.

"We were working on that wall down underneath the bridge and a couple of guys were talking about something and just as they crossed the bridge one of them said, 'Don't make any waves, don't make any waves.' And Suzuki Roshi said, 'What does that mean?' and I said, 'Don't make more of it than it is. Don't excite the situation. Let it be.' And he went, 'Oh,' and continued working. And that evening he used it in lecture."

Bob had shaved his head like most of the men at Tassajara. But not his long red beard. "One night after sitting we were watching the full moon which was very bright and Suzuki said, 'Heads, minds, moons, all shining.'"

Bob and Sandy went to Suzuki's cabin to say goodbye. He invited them in for tea. He thanked them for how much help they'd been. In parting, Suzuki told them, "You may leave the monastery, but the monastery won't leave you."

Bob Watkins with Shunryu Suzuki. Photo by James Hatch.

Evil Desire

Kobun had no defenses against exotic temptations he'd surely never experienced without the pressures and limitations of his home culture. A student who had been away for a week went to pay his respects to Kobun first thing upon returning. He was shocked to see his own wife answer the door. He quickly sized up the situation, scooped her up, drove to the city, and went straight to Suzuki.

The husband cooled off and didn't hold it against Kobun or his wife. I could see how bad Kobun felt about it.

And then there was the sultry woman who'd sold me pot the first time I was in the Sokoji neighborhood. She had come to live at Tassajara. Quite a past. She'd been a Seventh-day Adventist housewife, married to a dentist, living in Loma Linda, and making strictly vegetarian meals. She said she got so bored that one day she just walked out of that life. Before long she was with a new guy and had become a biker chick eating meat, drinking booze, taking speed, and having sex with all the guys in the gang at least once. Her path led from there to another vegetarian community—Zen Center.

She got a job, went to zazen and lectures, but occasionally she'd do something unusual. Like the time she walked into the Sokoji zendo ringing a bell while Suzuki was giving a lecture. He paused and she said, "No longer is it necessary for you to sit zazen—Jesus Christ is now Lord and you'll all be saved."

Suzuki said, "Very interesting, but can you survive?"

She got quiet and sat down. That was just a phase that she passed through. But there were other phases. She'd been fixated on Suzuki, then Katagiri, neither of whom she could get anywhere with, and more recently, while she was a student at Tassajara, Kobun.

One day she entered the zendo completely nude during noon service, walked right past us students who were standing chanting. She stepped up to the altar, sat in the center, and when the chanting stopped, started giving a lecture until she was politely asked by Peter Schneider to stop and was escorted out. She was driven out but not banned. She went back to her apartment and kept sitting at Sokoji and soon all was forgotten. But maybe not forgotten by one person.

After that episode, Kobun refused to leave his cabin. It went on for weeks. I'd go talk to him. He'd stay in his sleeping bag and barely respond at all. I suggested we take him to a doctor. He replied, "No doctor can treat this illness. I am the victim of evil desire."

One morning while carrying the kyosaku, I walked to his cabin and knocked. Kobun opened the door. I gently tapped him on each shoulder. He gasshoed with me and I returned to the zendo.

Bob Halpern helped Suzuki send a subtle message to Kobun by working on a rock garden outside his door. Finally, Kobun agreed to go to the baths with Suzuki. A Volkswagen was driven up the path to their cabins. They both got in and were chauffeured to the bridge by the baths. Forty minutes later, they were driven back.

It wasn't just the two brief affairs and karmic results that toppled Kobun. The first woman, I learned, had introduced him to LSD. The way I saw it, all his assumptions had been smashed. He needed time to grieve the loss of his old identity and sense of purpose alone, time to reflect and rebuild. Finally, one day, Kobun got up, went to the zendo and the era of the cabin hermit was over.

Waterfall Descent

Hiking down from the Horse Pasture to Tassajara Creek, the trail follows a smaller creek that includes a waterfall that dries up in the summer. It's a narrow trail carved into the side of a steep dry, rocky incline with sharp swords of yucca to slip around, like entering a bit of desert. When I take that trail, I'm careful not to miss a step. Then I did that walk with Niels and Dan who scampered down its loose sandy steepness whooping with delight.

On another hike, Niels and I approached the same descent, and I mentioned how he and Dan had been like mountain goats while I hugged the wall. Niels said, "You are right. It's too dangerous to go that way. I will take the waterfall." I looked over. There was a trickle of water still falling about fifty feet onto the stony creek below. I suggested it would be more prudent for Niels to come with me on the trail, which really wasn't dangerous at all. But he feigned terror at the trail as he stepped into the creek bed above the falls.

"Oh come on Niels—please don't," I begged much as Kobun had begged Bob Halpern and me not to jump off the ledge in the cliff wall at the Narrows. It only encouraged Niels to mock me more.

As I walked sheepishly around, he started climbing down the face of the drop-off next to the falls. He called out how safe he felt now that he wasn't on the trail. It seemed only I who stood on solid ground was squeamish. He got to a spot where he couldn't go any further—still twenty-five feet up there. I assumed he was going to give up and climb back the way he came, but suddenly he leaped out at a tree branch, caught it, swung down and dropped from it to terra firma. I about fainted. We met below where he congratulated me on conquering the harrowing trail.

Rohatsu Sesshin

There was a seven-day sesshin Kobun called *Rohatsu*. He said Rohatsu meant December 8th. The sesshin started on December 1st and ended on the morning of the eighth with a ceremony commemorating Buddha's enlightenment. In August, we'd sat for seven days with sweat running down our faces. This time we were sitting hour after hour in the cold cold cold of our unheated zendo. Some people cheated and wore socks. Durand the ship captain wore socks that had battery operated heat. He also kept condiments in his robe sleeve for the meals.

On the seventh day of the sesshin, there was a shosan Q&A ceremony with Suzuki. He opened it up by saying that although it's said Buddha started teaching at Varanasi, he actually started teaching as soon as he attained enlightenment under the Bodhi tree after sitting there for seven days. Buddha was teaching then, he said, without words. He concluded with, "I want to see and I want to hear your true teaching. Now come and show me your teaching."

Oh gosh, I thought, *how do I show him what I don't have?*

In one exchange that impressed me, maybe as much because of the authenticity of the delivery as the words, a student said: "My heart is full of joy. This zendo at Tassajara is like my own home. Sitting in zazen, eating with my fellow monks, trying to follow the way of my Roshi. Word by word, moment by moment, feeling by feeling, my delusion and my feeling are expressed in this moment."

Suzuki answered: "Yes. In this moment is right. Don't live in future or past."

The student said: "Thank you very much," and the next student stepped forward.

Dan Welch said: "Docho Roshi, as the sun enlightens our daily life, as the stars never cease to shine, how is it possible to forget?"

Suzuki answered: "Originally you do not forget."

Another student said: "Docho Roshi, outside I see the trees, and the things that grow, and the rocks seem to do perfect zazen. And I see my own potential for this, yet still I feel great fear. Please tell me what is the true nature of fear?"

Suzuki answered: "Fear has no reason why it arises. So, when the rocks and running water become a part of you, when you become truly their friend, there will be no fear."

A student asked him: "What place is this?"

I expected Suzuki to say "no place" as in the "no abode" from the Diamond Sutra. But Suzuki answered, "This is Tassajara zendo." The student thanked him. *Aha*, I thought, *this is what he meant by going back and forth from emptiness to form.*

Another student asked: "After months of practice and a seven-day sesshin, what am I doing here?"

Suzuki said: "You are doing nothing." *There*, I thought, *now Suzuki goes to the emptiness side.*

Bob Halpern asked: "Are impulses okay?"

Suzuki answered: "Yes, sometimes they are." Bob then turned around without closing the exchange with the customary gassho and thank you, left the zendo, quickly returned to his spot while taking the last bite of a cookie, bowed deeply, and said a garbled, "Thank you very much."

Suzuki bowed in return and the ceremony continued without a flinch.

Liz Wolf asked: "What happens if something happens to you, and you can't be our teacher anymore?"

Suzuki answered: "That cannot happen. I am always with you forever."

A student asked: "Docho Roshi, what is the fundamental cause of the universe?"

Suzuki answered: "Universe. Ah, we do not discuss it because there is no beginning or no end for the universe."

Hmm, I thought, *Buddha would answer metaphysical questions like that with what was called* noble silence.

A student asked: "Roshi, when a person has saved himself or herself, has that person also saved the world?"

Suzuki answered: "Yes. Whole universe will be saved. If it is not so, he did not save himself or save others."

Ed Brown said: "Docho Roshi, I have many questions, but they seem to come and go, and they don't seem very important. And everyone seems to have worked very hard during sesshin."

Suzuki said: "The question should not be about whether it is right or wrong. Right now, the most important thing is to find what is the most important thing. Your question is directed in the wrong direction. You are asking for others, which is not important. The most important thing is to be involved in what you do—what you are doing now, without thinking good or bad. Stop thinking and devote yourself to your kitchen work. Whatever people say, or whatever you yourself say, you should not be concerned about it."

I asked: "Docho Roshi, what now?"

Suzuki answered: "Now. Don't ask me. Now is now. You have now. I have my own now. That is why now is so important. It is beyond question and answer."

Someone asked: "Who are the sangha?"

Suzuki answered: "We are. Those who are in Tassajara are sangha—in limited sense. But all of us, all sentient beings are sangha."

A student asked: "Docho Roshi, if everything changes, why is there always suffering?"

Suzuki answered: "Because of change. Change itself is suffering. Change is the essential nature for everything. Suffering cannot be avoided. Because there is no way to avoid it, there is our relief."

A student asked: "Docho Roshi, neither mind nor Buddha, what is this?"

Suzuki answered: "Neither mind nor Buddha points out the real Buddha because we are caught by the word of Buddha. If we say 'Buddha,' we want to find out where is Buddha, when Buddha is right here. So 'neither mind nor Buddha,' we say."

Suzuki concluded by saying:

> *Yakusan Zenji did not give lectures for a long time. The monks asked him to give them a lecture. Yakusan Zenji mounted on the altar, looked at every monk one by one, came down from the altar, and went back to his room.*
>
> *A monk who was responsible for the zendo asked him why didn't he give a lecture? Yakusan said, 'There is a scripture master or Buddhist philosophy master, but I am a master of Zen. Don't wonder who I am.'*
>
> *Zen monks are Zen monks because they are speaking fluently without saying anything—just by everyday activity. That is how Zen students should be. That is why I said Buddha started teaching when he attained enlightenment under the Bodhi tree in the country of Magadha. We should not forget this point.*
>
> *And we should take care of our practice, not only zazen practice but whatever we do in Tassajara. I am very grateful to you for observing our way in various ways without asking why we do that or why we should do this. Whatever you do, that is our practice. There you will find yourself. Our practice is valuable because we can find ourselves on what we do in this moment.*
>
> *Thank you very much.*

Saying Goodbye

On an afternoon in late December, I was getting ready to go to the airport. I'd come to San Francisco the day before and had slept on a futon in an apartment occupied by the ever-expanding Zennie population. There was always room for one of us passing through. And there was always someone free to give a lift to the airport.

I hadn't gone back home for the holidays the year before because I wanted to get the grooves of the new Zen habits dug deeper. Suzuki had the flu and was in bed in Sokoji. People said he wasn't seeing anyone, but I thought I'd give it a try.

Sokoji had a hollow old funky atmosphere without the usual swarm of warm bodies. Upstairs I put my zoris in the shoe rack and glanced into Suzuki's office. No one there. So I went into the zendo onto the polished wood floor. Even with the large altar and all its bells, statues, candles, flowers, offerings, and alcoves, the room still felt barren. Tatami still lined the sides, but the goza mats with the black cloth ribbon edges were not spread out as they would be for zazen. They were folded and stacked in a corner.

I went into the kitchen and looked at the worn wooden table with the Japanese condiments on it, a pot on the stove, and the stacks of bamboo Chinese steamers on the high shelf. There was an earthen teapot on the counter with little teacups around it like baby ducks. I went back into the zendo feeling uncharacteristically melancholy.

"Excuse me?" I said in a hesitant voice. Nothing. I tried again a little louder, forcing a cough. "Excuse me."

"Hi," I barely heard a voice coming from above. Suzuki was looking down from a window in his room that opened to the zendo. He was in his underwear.

"Hi," I said. "Excuse me Roshi, I'm sorry to bother you. Um, how are you feeling?"

"I'm getting better. I think I'll be good pretty soon."

"I know I shouldn't be bothering you ... but ... I'm going to Texas for Christmas to see my mother and grandmothers, sister, and friends ... and I wanted to come over to say goodbye."

"Oh, thank you. Are you going today?"

"Yes. In about an hour. I wanted to tell you how much I appreciate practicing with you here at Zen Center. It's been a wonderful year—more than a year. I'm only going away for ten days but I thought I should say goodbye to you. I haven't been this close to anyone like this, a spiritual teacher, since my father died."

I could see him melt with sympathy. "I'm coming down. Let's have some tea."

"No no no, you don't have to do that. I just wanted to say goodbye and thank you."

"No, it's okay. I want to. Please wait a minute," and he disappeared from the window.

After a moment he came down the narrow steep stairs from his tiny room in the west tower and entered the zendo wearing brown slippers and a gray kimono. He was still wrapping an obi around his waist. Obviously Mitsu was out, or she'd have shooed me off.

He sat looking at me, smiled, sipped his tea, then slapped the palms of his hands on his knees and made a satisfied sigh. He asked me how Tassajara was, and I said it was wonderful and peaceful. He apologized for his absence from the zendo. I apologized for bothering him again and he repeated that he was getting better.

"Your practice is pretty good," he said. "You've improved a lot." That's the sort of thing I gathered he'd say if someone needed encouragement. But it was nice to hear. I asked him what I could do to help my mother and grandmothers. "Just be kind to them. Don't tell them too much about Buddhism. Just be kind to them."

On the way to the airport, I thought about Suzuki's advice. It reminded me of what Peter Schneider had said back at Tassajara. I'd told him I wanted to give my family members books for Christmas so they'd understand what I was up to and asked what he suggested. He said he used to feel that way too, but he's learned it's better to give them what they're interested in, not what you're interested in.

On that day I'd seen my teacher before I went off on a trip. It was just a brief meeting, but it sealed a trust that had been building for some time. By just saying hello and goodbye and drinking tea together, we deepened our tie, and he encouraged me to continue this way of "seeing things as it is" and being kind to others.

Cowtown Holidays

It was good to be home, spend time with family—and friends who were always welcome. No need to call—just like before. And just like before, we'd play music and talk endlessly about our passions. We could drink as much booze as we wanted, discretely smoke pot, and get loud and crazy. We could cuss but not a shred of racist or homophobic talk or Mother would be in the room reprimanding whatever uninitiated newcomer had uttered the foul words.

I spent time with both grandmothers, each still in their own large homes. My father's mother was sweet and a bit batty. She was still running her real estate business though she couldn't get far from her cluttered desk stacked with back mail and faded manila envelopes. A down-and-out old guy was doing legwork for her. Her business was functioning mostly in her imagination and at a deficit those days. Mother thought it well worth the loss to keep Granmamma, as we called her, occupied and content.

Mother's mother, Granny, was amiable and effusive, a pleasure to visit. She was pleased to see I wasn't shaggy. She asked where my hair went. I said she had a hairdo, and I had a hair-don't. That made her laugh. When I was a kid, she would tell me to save every penny, study hard, work hard, and make the family proud. I'd respond, "Granny, when I grow up, I'm going to be a cabbage." That would make her laugh too.

Fay and Odell were still working for her, as they had for as far back as I could remember. They added considerably to the warmth and good vibes of the home. In the basement, I racked the balls and shot 'em in the pockets one by one. Growing up I could stop by with friends anytime to do that. Had a key to the house in case Fay was off and Odell was driving Granny somewhere.

I stood on the patio out back looking at the rolling terraces I'd summersault down as a kid. An untended wooded area lay beyond the hedges bordering the grass yard. It ended at a tributary of the Trinity River way down below. The goats next door would chase me till I took refuge in a tree. I'd descend and they'd chase me to jump up in another one. Every once in a while I'd meet a hobo in that hidden realm not far from the switching yards, a wanderer of the voluntary homeless, interesting guys.

I took a pee in a bathroom upstairs, put the seat down and sat on it recalling sitting there in the fall of '64 gazing at the fallen body of Papa, my grandfather. Heart attack. I sat with him till medics arrived, confirmed he was dead, and carried him away. I thought at the time that he died after peeing because his zipper was closed and there was just a spot of wetness on his pants about the size of a quarter. I wondered what he was experiencing, surely a surprising transition. He and Granny were atheists.

Mother said she grew up terrified of the thought of death because she was told that all that happened when you die was that's the end, everything goes black and then your body goes into the ground. Meeting Kelly, my father, turned the lights on for her.

Our home was a few blocks from Granny and Papa's. That neighborhood was my playground. We kids were free to roam, go down to the river. We organized our own games, played in the streets and yards. There were few walls or fences. So many butterflies.

My sister Susan flew in. She was living in Washington, DC, and working for the *Mid-East Journal*. She and I had always gotten along well and supported each other.

I noted some of the oriental touches in our home I'd always taken for granted. Paintings of horses with Chinese characters on a mantel in the den, rattan easy chairs, a coffee table book about Japan named something like *They Leave their Shoes Outside*. By my teens, I always took my shoes off as soon as I entered the house. Mainly I went barefoot outdoors and indoors. Now I wore zoris and left them neatly placed by the door. Growing up, most of what had to do with Japan was footwear and art related—or war related.

In the tenth grade, World War II only fifteen years behind us, I had a geometry teacher, Mr. Smith, who was a POW during the war, captured in the Philippines soon after it started. He said a Japanese soldier on a bridge lobbed a hand grenade at him and his buddy walking down below. He immediately threw himself on the ground, but his comrade ran, ran a good distance, he said. He watched him fall. Smith was captured. He said groups of ten prisoners would walk unescorted from the camp to town to work. If only nine returned they'd execute them. He said that if someone got too near the fence, they might get their head cut off and hung on the fence. They'd carry heavy bags of rice dropped onto their backs, and if someone fell, they'd get bayonetted.

One day in the spring of 1945 working at the docks, he heard that Germany had surrendered. Back at camp he told the guards that, laughing and saying Japan would be next. They got him up in the middle of the night and asked who'd told him that—knocking out all his teeth in the interrogation. He pulled his false teeth out and showed them to us while making a big toothless grin. He said he didn't expect to live to come back home, that eighty-five percent of the prisoners in his camp died in captivity. He told us all this in a good-natured way without a shred of anger or resentment in his voice. "Actually, I liked those little guys," he said. "Most of them were good people. We're at peace now." I was amazed at how that horrendous experience that went on for over three years had not embittered him. I learned my first Japanese from Mr. Smith, something he said they'd often say to him—*takusan shigoto*, a lot of work.

The well-lit Christmas tree in our living room was another of Mother's masterpieces, full of antique hanging ornaments, covered in delicate angel hair, gossamer glass, that she had for decades saved from each year's tree for the next season. The front porch was lit with colored lights.

Mother had a boyfriend now, John, a pianist much younger, who specialized in playing the standards. He'd played for many famous singers—Judy Garland for one. Mother met him the year before on New Year's Eve when he was playing at the Fort Worth Club, a downtown businessmen's club where she had a low-cost widow's membership. She'd met my father at the same place on New Year's Eve thirty years prior. In the evenings John would come over after work, we'd get him to play for us, and we'd all sing along on too many Christmas carols.

Jerry Ray and Warren Lynn took me to meet their teacher, Alden Truesdell, founder of the Christ Truth League. His approach was like what my father had been into—New Thought Christianity, or what I called mind-only Christianity—Jesus as an enlightened teacher who showed us how to awaken to our divinity. Jerry told me, "Truesdell's favorite guy is Meister Eckhart."

Jerry said, "Suzuki was the first spiritual person I met. Walked into his office with you and Suzuki Roshi was standing there in robes talking to people—presence that filled the room. Was a short little man. Nothing needed to be said. Before it had all been in books. It was real. I didn't know it existed. I considered going back to Suzuki Roshi to study Zen but then, here in Fort Worth, Alden Truesdell and his wife Nell were the second and third spiritual people I met. So I didn't do the culture switch and stayed here."

Truesdell had an office in downtown Fort Worth where his door was open to anyone who wanted guidance or who just needed to have someone to talk to. I wanted to visit him there, but my trip was so short and filled with being at home and a checklist of visits with friends including Ward, Raymond, Jim and Anne, Frank and Dogie, Barry and Dotty. Mother treated us all to the elaborate Sunday brunch at Colonial Country Club.

I went to Southern Methodist University in Dallas and met with Fred Streng, the author of *Emptiness* who'd been a guest at Tassajara. He asked me to join him for a class on the last day before the holiday break. Afterwards I asked how he survived teaching so many lovely young women. He said, "You get used to it." He'd played college football. I visited him another time and we watched a Cowboys game together, drank beer, and ate chips.

I didn't spend my time trying to convert anyone, but I did hand out *Wind Bells* so people would get a hint of what we were doing at Zen Center. Some, like Mrs. Whetmore, had already received one in the mail from me. Mrs. Whetmore was my sister and my *practitioner*, our spiritual guide when we were kids. When I dropped by to see her, she held up the *Wind Bell* she'd received and said with exasperation, "David! What's this? Body *and* mind? Body *and*

Mind?! What are those people teaching you?" I tried to explain to her that of course they, we, knew body and mind are one, we just didn't use the same language she did. "Nonsense," she said. "If they knew body-mind were one, they would not say 'body *and* mind.'" My attempts to explain to her how much common ground we had fell flat.

The big event, as usual that time of year, was Mother's New Year's Eve party. Sixty or so people showed up plus a number of my sister's and my closest friends. I knew lots of Mother's guests from growing up there. Old friends of hers and my father's, of her mother's, from the opera board which she'd been on since the mid-'40s, from the country club, from her music club, from the quintet she played piano with. It was a fairly well-to-do crowd, though some were more wealthy in education and culture than in filthy lucre.

I always enjoyed talking with Paul Smith. He'd been sacked from the State Department during the McCarthy purges of the '50s. He brought his blind sister Frances who'd worked on mainstreaming blind and otherwise impaired kids into the school system. I used to read to her after school and she'd reward me with Scotch in a tumbler.

I talked to old family friends Dolly and Morton Ware. Morton carried on the Gause-Ware Funeral Home business, the longest continually running business in Fort Worth. He was quiet, said hi, and went off to get another drink. Dolly always had plenty to say. She was a member of Yogananda's SRF, Self-Realization Fellowship, and had once met the famed guru. It was her son-in-law Bob Howe who turned me on to Fred Kimball. In her home she had a large poster on the wall inspired by psychic Kimball which identified the meanings of itches on different parts of the body.

Dolly was a sponsor of bringing Dr. Tony Agpaoa to the U.S. to perform psychic surgery. That ended with him being charged with fraud and skipping out on bail to fly back to Manila. Dolly was a student of Max Freedom Long, who had created a quasi New Age religion out of what he called Huna, claiming that he was unveiling ancient Hawaiian magic and spirituality. He'd died and now she had the Max Freedom Long library and archives in her home. She was an advocate of eating organically grown fruits and vegetables. I knew they owned some large tracts of farmland and asked if they were using organic methods. "Of course not," she said. "That would be impractical."

"So when are you going to stop playing your little Zen game," she asked, "and come home and take over the family real estate business?"

"Of all people, you should be more understanding," I said. It was so weird. Mother's other friends were positive and curious about what I had been involved with.

"You should follow in the footsteps of your father," she said. "You know it was he who taught me about the pineal gland and the nature of mind. He saved my life. And when he died, he was perfectly enlightened. Now you come back and continue the business he started, or it will shrivel up. He would be so disappointed."

"You're beautiful and I love you," I said, and gave her a hug and a kiss which pleased her. She was pretty sexy for a woman in her late fifties.

She was completely off about what my father, who died when I was eleven, had in mind for me. In his will he left my sister and me a percentage of his estate to be available when we were older—at Mother's discretion—and he stipulated that he hoped it would help us to pursue spiritual studies without being overburdened by having to make ends meet. He also stipulated that mother should feel free to remarry. Mother told me she had friends whose children, even after becoming adults, had strenuously opposed their mother being with any other man.

The large crystal bowl had been brought out to hold Mother's intoxicatingly delicious eggnog. Appetizers and drinks were served by staff she hired for the evening. More help doing prep in the kitchen. John arrived late and played the piano. Tawny read from a play he'd just completed. I sang a raunchy song that went over well.

No one else in my family had a tendency to drink too much booze. Mother told me she could get sick if she had more than two drinks. She thought of that as a blessing. Over half of her guests drank a lot, some so much they'd be stumbling out the door when they left. No one got loud or angry or acted bad though, something I'd seen plenty of in other circles. The last guest left at about two hours into the new year.

Ward, who had been like a brother, spent the night in the other of my twin beds as he had so many times. But we didn't go to bed right away. We helped Mother do some cleanup and then sat on the front porch steps talking about when we were younger.

We missed the swimming hole with its rope swing and water moccasins in the Edwards Ranch walking distance from home. Edwards held out as long as he could, but now it was being subdivided.

We recalled the pungent odor of pig and cow fat mixed with warm blood wafting in from the Armour and Swift slaughterhouses when there was what we called a Northerner—wind from the north. Often, I'd wake to the thrilling sounds of lions roaring and elephants trumpeting from the nearby zoo. Then around 7 a.m., there'd be a rumbling hum as they warmed up the fleet of six engine B-36 Peacemakers eight miles away at Carswell Air Force Base.

And the train sounds. Always the wonderful train sounds. We paused to listen to the whistle of a distant freight train. Till I was twelve, we lived in a home closer to the zoo and the tracks. I grew up with the whistles, horns, the music of trains, percussion from train cars coupling and uncoupling. I'd go to sleep to those penetrating yet soothing sounds. As teenagers, Ward and I would go sit right by the tracks at night waiting for the power of an approaching then passing locomotive followed by an uncountable number of boxcars rushing by a few feet from our noses. I told him I was sorry I never wrote, and he said, "That's alright, David. I always know how you are." As a teenager I'd get a feeling, go to a couch in the den and sit by the phone no more than a minute for it to ring with a call from Ward.

Mother still had a drawing I made in 1962 in high school art class displayed on a counter in the kitchen next to her well-worn cookbooks. I drew it in reddish-brown chalk on thick art paper. It had a minimal sketch of a person looking out a window—the window I was sitting at when I drew it. A poem written with the same chalk took most of the space up.

> *I don't want to draw*
> *Anything including*
> *A woman in the raw*
> *Or a pretty many hued thing*
> *Or a brown budding tree*
> *Or the posture of some boy*
> *Or the choppy churning sea*
> *Or the shadows of a toy*
> *Or surrealistic rot*
> *With colors cold and hot*
>
> *I just want to sit and stare*
> *Blankly at the blowing air*

Dawning of 1968

On New Year's Day, I picked up the phone, dialed zero for the operator, and said, "I'd like to speak to a toll station operator in California please." Once connected, I said, "I'd like to make a ringdown to a toll station—Tassajara Springs number one. Mark other plus 408 plus 181." That was the Tassajara phone number. No wonder most reservations were made through the San Francisco office. I wanted to wish happy new year to all my dharma pals, to whomever answered the phone—if anyone was in or around the office.

The operator said no one answered. I asked her to keep trying. It could be heard ringing from the kitchen. A minute later Jane Runk answered, and we wished each other happy new year. She said they'd had a New Year's Eve party orchestrated by Kobun Chino who introduced them to the Japanese custom of making mochi from gluten rice on New Year's eve. Paul Discoe hollowed out an oak stump and made two large pestles. Earlier the rice had been soaked and steamed. For hours those few who'd stayed for the winter interim pounded sticky white rice in the large, rounded wooden mortar while another turned the wet dough and folded it over. There was zazen till midnight. Those present took turns hitting the large densho 108 times to welcome in 1968.

New Year's morning for breakfast was chewy mochi—filled with reddish brown splinters. The mortar and pestles were too soft—needed to cure for a year or more. Jane said she'd pass on my new year wishes to the others.

It was great to be home with family and friends—checking in on the past and present of where I'd grown up and whom I'd grown up with. But the silent song of the triple treasure—buddha, dharma, sangha—was calling me back to California—to Suzuki, Katagiri, Kobun, Richard, Bob, Niels—all my fellow students—and to Tassajara.

To be continued…

NOTES

This book tries to stick to the vernacular of the day. For instance, Indians, as Native Americans was not used much including by Native Americans at that time. Also, we didn't use the words vegan or gay back then. The term Negro was still widely in use and black wasn't commonly capitalized.

In the piece called *Landmarks on the Road*—I remembered what Fred Tuttle told me about the spring catchments and some places along the road, but I used the names, description, and details about the road given by David Rogers, the ultimate authority on pre-Zen Center history and everything else related to the area Tassajara is in. See listings for his books on Tassajara history and flora at cuke.com/ts.

Building Walls relied on the Tassajara section of *Zen Architecture* by Paul Discoe and dirtcheapbuilder.com/Articles/Good_Life_Center.htm.

The material about Ed Brown and Tim Burkett came almost entirely from interviews, emails, and podcasts, but both have written extensively about their Zen practice. See cuke.com/ts for lists of their books and other related publications.

Also found at cuke.com/ts: A bibliography, many more notes, photos/images, maps, an index for this book, errata, corrections, reviews, and comments such as extensive ones I expect to get from Richard Baker when he finds the time.

Apologies to those whose photos appear herein without credit. We were careless back then and didn't think to write the photographer's name on the back of most of them. We have access to few photos from the Shunryu Suzuki days other than those with Suzuki as they were systematically digitized. We'd love to add to our collection of photos from back then. Please contact us about this and anything else at info@cuke.com.

Cuke Archives—Doing our bit to help preserve the legacy of Shunryu Suzuki and those whose path cross his—and anything else that comes to mind.

Cuke.com—door to all Cuke and DC material.

ABOUT THE COVER PHOTO

Fall 1967, after the first practice period.

Names of those mentioned in the book in bold.

L to R top row: **Gossip Oak,** Jim Morton, __, __, **Niels Holm,** __, __, E.L. Hazelwood, **Liz Wolf, Tim Buckley, Kobun Chino Otogawa,** Chris Flynn, **Mike Daft,** __, __, **Noah (dog),** Doug Anderson, **Nancy Lay.**

Middle row: **Bob Halpern,** John Palmer, **Paul Discoe,** Helen Knox, __, **Loring Palmer,** Jack Elias, **David Chadwick, Ed Brown, Louise Pryor, Dan Welch, Shunryu Suzuki, Clarke Mason, Bob Watkins, Sandy Watkins,** Stan White, Fran Keller, Dot (Luce) Kostriken.

Front row: __ **Ruthie Discoe, Peter Schneider, Jane Runk (Schneider),** __.

Photo by Minoru Aoki

ACKNOWLEDGMENTS

Nine bows to my Cuke Archives colleagues Peter Ford and Wendy Pirsig for all the time and effort spent in meticulously going over the text of *Tassajara* Stories with me for I forget how many months. Bows to Peter Ford for managing Cuke Archives so industriously which has freed me up to concentrate on getting *Tassajara Stories* out the door and for assisting tirelessly in various tasks that had to be done to bring the book to completion. Bows to my retired agent and co-conspirator Michael Katz for his on-going advice, support, and encouragement without which there would likely never have been any books or websites, audiobooks, or podcasts. Endless gratitude to my wife Katrinka McKay for her constant support and feedback and for the more than twenty years of love, stability, and sobriety she has brought into my life. Many thanks to my sister Susan Chadwick and Linda Hess for their helpful input.

Tassajara Stories reflects material and memories derived from my own experience, and countless interviews, podcasts, conversations, letters, emails, and social media exchanges. I didn't note every time that, while working on this project, I wrote or called someone who was there back then to see what they recall about something so thanks a lot to them all. A few whom I communicated with multiple times concerning this volume are Richard Baker, Ed Brown, Paul Discoe, Bob Halpern, Richard Levine, Elizabeth and Ken Sawyer, Peter and Jane Schneider, Bill Shurtleff, Alan Winter, and Liz Wolf.

The *Wind Bell* publications of the San Francisco Zen Center going back to 1961 were a great help (they're all on cuke.com).

A special thanks to Paul Cohen and Jon Sweeney of Monkfish for publishing *Tassajara Stories* and to Jon Sweeney, the book's editor, for his excellent suggestions and guidance. Thanks to Arnie Kotler for sending me their way. And thanks, Jon, for coming up with the "Sort of" in the book's subtitle. When I read that, I thought, *These are people I can work with*.

A deep bow to all those who have hit the donate button on cuke.com and shunryusuzuki.com and supported Cuke Archives of which *Tassajara Stories* is a major project. Great thanks to the Pacific Zen Institute and The Institute for Historical Study for being our fiscal sponsors. Without our generous contributors, this book would still be just an idea.

First use of Shunryu Suzuki's sumi circle as described in chapter 1, *The Site*, page 30.